Auden's Games of Knowledge

POETRY AND THE MEANINGS OF HOMOSEXUALITY

Richard R. Bozorth

COLUMBIA UNIVERSITY PRESS   NEW YORK

Columbia University Press
Publishers Since 1893
New York   Chichester, West Sussex

Copyright © 2001 Columbia University Press

Library of Congress Cataloging-in-Publication Data
    Bozorth, Richard R.
    Auden's games of knowledge : poetry and the meanings of homosexuality /
    Richard R. Bozorth.
    (Between men—between women)
    Includes bibliographical references and index.
    ISBN 0–231–11352–8 (cloth)
    ISBN 0–231–11353–6 (paper)
    1. Auden, W. H. (Wystan Hugh), 1907–1973—Political and social views.
    2. Homosexuality and literature—England—History–20th century. 3. Homo-
    sexuality, Male, in literature.   4. Gay men in literature.   I. Bozorth, Richard R.
    II. Title.
    PR6001.U4 Z615   2001

Casebound editions of Columbia University Press books are printed on permanent
and durable acid-free paper.
Printed in the United States of America

3 2 1

3 2 1

for Kevin Gustafson

CONTENTS

ABBREVIATIONS

CP   Auden, *Collected Poems* (1991)
DH   Auden, *The Dyer's Hand*
EA   Auden, *The English Auden*
FA   Auden, *Forewords and Afterwords*
J   Auden, *Juvenilia*
P   Auden, *Prose*
PDW   Auden and Isherwood, *Plays*
SE   Freud, *Standard Edition*
SP   Auden, *Selected Poems*

ACKNOWLEDGMENTS

Few poets offer as many expressions of gratitude in their work as Auden, and it is a pleasure to emulate him here by naming names.

The staff at Columbia University Press has made publication of this book a good experience from the very beginning. I especially thank Ann Miller for her encouragement and advice, and Robert Hemenway for his meticulous editorial assistance and good sense. I am grateful to the Henry W. and Albert A. Berg Collection of English and American Literature at the New York Public Library and the Astor, Lenox, and Tilden Foundations, for allowing me to examine Auden's 1929 Berlin notebook and for granting me permission to quote from it.

At Southern Methodist University, the Dedman College Research Council has been exceptionally generous in supporting the completion of this book, and its publication has been aided by financial assistance from the Duwain E. Hughes Fund. In addition to reading my work, my colleagues have listened, questioned, and encouraged me in ways that have made me think harder and more happily. I particularly thank Dennis Foster, Bruce Levy, Beth Newman, Nina Schwartz, Willard Spiegelman, and Trysh Travis for making Dallas such a good place to teach, write, and live. Out of all the students who have taught me things about Auden, Wendy Pickett has been the most important.

Any work on Auden relies on that of Edward Mendelson, and I am grateful for his knowledge, his interest in this project, and his generous assistance as Literary Executor of the Estate of W. H. Auden.

Among others whose scholarly attentions have been invaluable, the outside reviewers deserve my particular thanks. At crucial moments, Robert Caserio and Jahan Ramazani have helped me to refine my thinking and rekindled my sense that these ideas matter. My longest-standing intellectual debt is to Samuel Hynes, not only for first intro-ducing me to Auden's poetry in the classroom, but also for serving as a model of the humane teacher and critic. My single greatest intellectual debt is to Jerome McGann, whose mind, conversation, and energy I have long felt lucky to know.

Of those who, in their different ways, have sustained me while working on this book, I am especially grateful to Donald Eby, Mary Esteve, Tom Heacox, Jack Martin, Max Nuñez, Steve Powell, Will Reay, Alan Shepard, David Stone, and Rajani Sudan.

Above all, and in the most important sense, before all, I thank the one to whom this book is dedicated: for what—and how much—he knows.

Auden's Games of Knowledge

INTRODUCTION

In May 1951, Guy Burgess and Donald Maclean—soon to be revealed as two of the infamous "Cambridge Spies"—defected to the Soviet Union after years of passing secrets from their posts in the British foreign service. In his last days before fleeing London, Burgess telephoned Stephen Spender several times, trying to reach W. H. Auden, whom he had known since the 1930s. By this time, Auden had left London for Ischia, where he and his partner, Chester Kallman, spent their summers. After his arrival there, Auden found himself confronted with reporters and police: it was now widely assumed that Burgess had defected, and he was rumored to be seeking sanctuary with Auden. In fact, Burgess never went to Ischia at all, traveling instead to Moscow via Prague. But before the episode was over, Peter Roger, a friend on his way to visit Auden, was arrested in Naples by the police, who mistook him for Burgess.[1]

Why was Burgess trying to contact Auden? Was he seeking advice? Did he (as rumor had it) hope to find some sort of sanctuary with Auden? It is hard to imagine what Auden could or would have done to protect him, since they were not close friends, and there is no evidence that Auden knew Burgess was a Soviet agent. As Robert Cecil has suggested, Burgess was probably just trying to distract pursuers while he fled to Moscow (138).

Nevertheless, the episode resonates intensely for anyone familiar with Auden's career in the 1930s. For as Richard Davenport-Hines observes, here are all the elements of secrecy, border crossings, missed connections, mistaken identity, and political betrayal that defined "the Audenesque" as a period style and atmosphere (275). Moreover, in the way our curiosity is provoked—we want to know what Burgess was up to, what Auden knew, and so on—the episode leaves us as Auden's early poems often do: fascinated but unsure what it all means. The incident exists in a limbo of historical indeterminacy—a striking moment that falls somewhere between the significant and the trivial. But precisely because of such uncertainties, this makes an exemplary story with which to begin a book about Auden as a homosexual poet.

Communist subversion and sexual perversion have long been bound together in the cultural imagination of the Cold War, and this linkage has, of course, served forces of homophobia and red-baiting. But it has also served less reactionary agendas, as in Julian Mitchell's *Another Country,* the play (1981) and film (1984) modeled on Burgess's life, and in John Banville's novel *The Untouchable* (1997), based on the life of Anthony Blunt, who was exposed in 1979 as "the fourth man" of the Cambridge Spies. Banville's protagonist, Victor Maskell, recalls Marxism's allure in a way that makes the linkage of espionage and homosexuality seem inevitable:

> We were latter-day Gnostics, keepers of a secret knowledge, for whom the world of appearances was only a gross manifestation of an infinitely subtler, more real reality known only to the chosen few, but the iron, ineluctable laws of which were everywhere at work. This gnosis was, on the material level, the equivalent of the Freudian conception of the unconscious, that unacknowledged and irresistible legislator, that spy in the heart. Thus, for us, *everything was itself and at the same time something else.*
>
> (45; emphasis in original)

For Maskell, politics and psychology become aspects of a single mystery cult, founded on the hermeneutics of suspicion. Read in this light, Auden's 1951 encounter with Burgess seems an irresistible emblem of occult conjunctions in a homosexual poet famously absorbed with Marx and Freud. Here would be a key to Auden's own "more real reality," initiating us into a poetic and cultural gnosis. But to step back is to realize that this is a tale of *non*-encounter—more a gap in history than a moment of truth. By 1951, Auden had long ago turned away from the left, and since it is not clear that Burgess ever intended to visit him, to read anything into the episode is to risk becoming Burgess's dupe. Beyond the few bare facts, it proves little or nothing about Auden, and if we take his non-meeting with Burgess too seriously, we are merely embracing the hermeneutical circle to practice criticism by conspiracy theory.

This, then, is the exemplary value of the Auden-Burgess story: not that it contains the truth about Auden, but that to entertain our suspicions about it can reveal something about our desires as his readers. Throughout his career—from his concept of parable in the 1930s to his comments in the 1960s on the poem as dialogue of poet and reader— Auden theorized poetry as a mode of knowledge, and this book explores how his work provokes a dynamic of knowledge bound up with homosexual desire and identity. In many poems considered here, homosexuality is itself the object of knowledge: that which Auden seeks to explain psychologically, politically, ethically, theologically. In this, his work belongs to an era shaped by the Victorians' "invention of homosexuality" as a categorical identity (see Foucault, *History* 1, 36–49). But Auden's is also a self-directed inquiry, with a personal investment that gay and lesbian readers will be quite familiar with. His importance as a homosexual *poet,* I argue, consists in his lifelong practice of poetry not as the bearer of compelling certainties—what he calls "rhetoric" or "magic"—but as an open-ended engagement with his own desires and with those of his readers as real lovers or virtual intimates: poetry as "joking," "parable," "analogy," or "game of knowledge."

As an exercise in literary history, this book argues that Auden's work embodies a process of homosexual self-interrogation with few parallels in modernist literature: he should be seen not just as a major figure in twentieth-century poetry in English, but as a crucial one in gay/lesbian literary history. Auden is, I suggest, the modernist heir of Byron and Wilde, for his career constitutes a staging of public and private selves through a range of codings of queer desire. That Auden was preoccupied with the relation between public and private, the personal and the political, is hardly news. But I argue that his ongoing grapplings with these fraught binaries reflect in large measure his negotiation of the constraints on speakability traditionally faced by gay, lesbian, and queer writers.

As an object of readerly knowledge, Auden's homosexuality has historically had a peculiar status: obvious to some, invisible to others, and with some notable exceptions, consciously or unconsciously treated by critics as a matter of little or no importance. Apart from Walt Whitman, Oscar Wilde, and E. M. Forster, no male homosexual writer in English has achieved Auden's stature or influence. Yet he has been almost entirely ignored in academic lesbian/gay literary studies, despite his influence on English and American poets since the 1930s.[2] One reason for this neglect may be that he can be credibly cast neither as martyr, like Oscar Wilde, nor as victim, like Hart Crane. His stature has almost certainly been a barrier as well, for unlike, say, Gertrude Stein, he can hardly be recruited to show the blindness of canon-formation to lesbian and gay writers. Auden is, after all, often taken as a later T. S. Eliot. He may have crossed the Atlantic in the opposite direction, but he too (the tale would run) evolved from a figure of the avant-garde to a conservative Christian apologist squarely in the high modernist, Symbolist line. As Eliot's stock in the academy has fallen, so, one suspects, has Auden's. But he is far less Eliot's heir—politically, aesthetically, or theologically—than such a view implies. Indeed, one implication of this book is that, rather than simply the Symbolist inheritor of Yeats and Eliot, Auden should be seen as central to a tradition of gay poetics of indeterminacy, linking Rimbaud, whom Auden liked to imagine as a kind of poetic queer uncle, to John Ashbery and Frank O'Hara.[3]

Whatever his neglect says about academic culture wars, it is also true that Auden has rarely been seen as a "gay poet" because he made it so easy not to do so. Unlike Christopher Isherwood, he did not identify publicly—or, it seems, privately—with gay liberation, even though he lived until 1973 and in New York until 1971, two years after the Stonewall Riots. Unlike Forster, he did not arrange a posthumous literary coming out. When Robert Duncan wrote him in 1945 to propose an essay on homoeroticism in his poetry, Auden asked him to refrain.[4] When his most explicitly homosexual text, the pornographic poem "The Platonic Blow" ("A Day For a Lay"), was pirated in 1965 by the Fuck You Press, he disowned it (though privately he was quite proud; see Carpenter, *Auden* 359–60).

So too, in his published work, homosexuality only rarely becomes something the reader *must* acknowledge, and Auden's own homosexuality would be, according to his oft-asserted view, irrelevant to the meaning of his poetry. Thus, in his important 1964 essay on Shakespeare's sonnets, Auden declared that "most genuine artists would prefer that no biography be written" (*FA* 90), and he sought to enforce this in his own case by asking in his will that recipients of letters destroy them.[5] His later prose, moreover, can easily be harnessed to New Critical tenets about the self-sufficiency of the poetic artifact and the biographical fallacy. Consider, for example, a passage from "The Virgin & The Dynamo" that refines Archibald MacLeish's aphorism:

> It has been said that a poem should not mean but be. This is not quite accurate. In a poem, as distinct from many other kinds of verbal societies, meaning and being are identical. A poem might be called a pseudo-person. Like a person, it is unique and addresses the reader personally. On the other hand, like a natural being and unlike a historical person, it cannot lie.
>
> (*DH* 68)

With his nod to I. A. Richards's theory of "pseudo-statement," Auden portrays the poem as a structure of meaning and being detached from biography, culture, and history.[6] In "Writing" (1962), he comments that in a poem, "all facts and all beliefs cease to be true or false and become interesting possibilities" (*DH* 19). This sounds like very much the New Critical line, whereby referentiality and the "sources" of a poem in the poet are irrelevant to its meaning and truth-value. To read Auden's own work thus would be to bracket out the facts of his life, including the sexual ones.

But there is a deviousness to Auden's formulations on such matters, emblematic of a broader pattern in his theories of poetry and in his own readerly habits. Robert K. Martin has commented that Auden "insisted . . . that his poems must not be seen as homosexual, that they were universal" (xix). This book follows, therefore, Thomas Yingling's lead in asking, "From what vantage point is the universal constructed, why did Auden find it the 'proper' one for poetry, what subjects did it make illegitimate?" (16). But Auden's aspirations to universality should be questioned even more radically, for "insistence" in the realm of sexual politics can be a rhetorically intricate gesture, equal parts truth and lie, as in Wilde's famous assertion during his trial that Greek Love was a matter not of the body but of the soul. When we read Auden on the ahistorical being/meaning of poetry or on the irrelevance of biography to art, Eliot's dictates on impersonality ought to echo no louder than the voice of Wilde: "Even things that are true can be proved" (236); "Art never expresses anything but itself. It has an independent life, just as Thought has, and develops purely on its own lines" (319). We are by now used to seeing the sexual politics at work in the discourse of Wilde's aestheticism, and so we should with Auden: "poetry makes nothing happen" (*EA* 242), after all, may be read as another way of saying, "All art is quite useless" (Wilde 236). Such an argument requires more than anecdote, of course, and this book aims, among other things, to justify the comparison with Wilde. But to keep Wilde in mind is to suspect that Auden was often acting out the truth of lying, wearing a mask of the modernist poetic sage when he attacked the biographical fallacy, begging the question when he wrote that "love, or truth in any serious sense, / Like orthodoxy, is a reticence" (*CP* 621). He was, in fact, an inveterate reader of literary biography and editions of writers' letters, and his pronouncements on the subject routinely came in the context of reviewing such works. By the end of his life, one cannot but feel that Auden enjoyed "dropping his pearls" in print, as when he carefully explained the psychoanalytic meanings of oral sex, anal sex, and mutual masturbation among gay men in the course of reviewing J. R. Ackerley's *My Father and Myself* for *The New York Review of Books* in 1969.[7]

Such moments make a social game out of the open secret of Auden's own sexuality, and by and large, those who have argued for his canonical importance have ignored the game, for it cuts against the criteria by which his work can be judged a cultural touchstone. Until his death, one of few critics to discuss Auden explicitly as a homosexual poet was James Southworth. In *Sowing the Spring* (1940), he argued

that Auden's two major concerns were politics and his own sexuality—
a claim exceptional in its own openness and in its perception of Auden's:

> With an honesty akin to that of Gide's in *Si le grain ne meurt,* Mr. Au-
> den has recorded the history of his attempt at reaching a satisfactory
> emotional adjustment. . . . Aware of the anomalous position of the
> Urning in modern society he has sought by his frankness of utterance
> to rid himself of any guilt or inferiority.[8]

As quaint and clinical as this sounds, Southworth was decades ahead
of many Auden critics, who saw or claimed to see a very different
writer—certainly nothing like Gide. Thus Edward Callan was unusual
only in stating openly in 1983 what so many had long assumed tacitly:
"Most of Auden's published work may be read for its artistic, psychological, or philosophical interest as one might read E. M. Forster's
masterpiece, *A Passage to India,* without any awareness of its author's
homosexuality" (36). This is a description of readerly behavior disguised as an observation about Auden's work, and as a defense of critical practice, it relies on assumptions no longer sustainable, if they ever
were. First, a reader's passive ignorance automatically licenses a critic's
active silence. Second, homosexuality is irrelevant to a writer's "artistic,
psychological, or philosophical" concerns so long as it has no claim on
the reader's "interest." Such views have historically aided Auden's construction as a poet of universal human values, for which homosexuality
would mark him as a problematic advocate. Thus it is hardly surprising that studies dating from the height of his academic reputation, like
John Blair's *The Poetic Art of W. H. Auden* (1965) and Richard Johnson's *Man's Place: An Essay on Auden* (1971), never mention his sexuality. Blair argues that Auden offers "profound insights into the nature
of man" (9), while Johnson's thesis is that Auden's work is fundamen-
tally about "becoming fully human" (246).

But just as Auden himself was adept at encoding homosexuality in
his work, so too are those who form what may be termed the "pathologizing" school of Auden criticism.[9] The significance of this line of
criticism is that it makes fairly explicit the sexual politics operative in

critical evaluations of his work. Rather than directly attacking his homosexuality, this approach encodes it in terms of his lack of "maturity," "seriousness," or "wholeness." For Joseph Warren Beach, writing in 1957, Auden's best poems are "earnest, direct, and manly in their rendering of the poet's sentiments" (247), but his ideological shifts and revisions of his earlier work raise "a question of identity" (254). We might hesitate to infer that Auden is too often insincere (urnist?), indirect, and unmanly, were it not that others had said so for years. The notorious hostility of F. R. Leavis and *Scrutiny,* for instance, reflects sexual as well as cultural and literary politics, whereby Auden was a case of homosexual failure. In Auden's first commercial book, the 1930 *Poems,* Leavis saw "extreme examples of . . . withdrawal from the objective into the subjective world" (Haffenden 90). Discussing *Paid on Both Sides,* he began a line of attack whose sexual subtext he returned to regularly: "in its combination of seriousness and flippancy," he wrote, Auden's play reflects "the stultifying division in his own consciousness." In *The Orators,* Leavis wrote in 1932, Auden "does not know just how serious he is," relying on "undergraduate cleverness" and boyish "romantic habit" (101). A 1934 review charged Auden with a "profound inner disturbance" (141) and "uncertainty of purpose and of self" (142). By 1950, Leavis seems almost to have given up on Auden as incurable:

> [*Paid on Both Sides*] might have represented the very green immaturity of a notable creative talent. . . . [But] the childlike vividness of imagination was accompanied by . . . an obscurity of the wrong kind . . . a surprising radical adolescence that should have been already well outgrown. It seems to me that Auden has hardly come nearer to essential maturity since, though he made a rapid advance in sophistication.
>
> (140)

This innuendo-laden vocabulary encodes class prejudice, stereotypes about English public schools, and Freudian clichés of arrested development.[10] With his emphasis on incoherence of self, Leavis seems almost to imply that the closet ruined Auden's work (though one doubts he thought Auden should have come out). Such claims have a history of application to homosexual writers; Leavis's views bear an uncanny likeness to the critical topos of Hart Crane's "failure" from the debilitating effects of homosexuality (see Yingling 59–60).

Auden is linked to Crane, in fact, by Randall Jarrell as an example of how "the feelings of isolation and the guilt feelings associated with sex are enormously intensified" when the family, "our culture's normal complex of togetherness (Sex-Children-Authority) is broken up" (167). Jarrell's "Changes of Attitude and Rhetoric in Auden's Poetry" is invaluable, not least for its brilliant parsing of the syntactic and figurative components of Auden's early style. And while, like Leavis, he treats Auden as a case study, he is the most astute early commentator on homosexuality in Auden's work. Suspicious, Jarrell writes, of "the general world-picture of the late-capitalist society," the young Auden "is conscious of a profound alienation, intellectual, moral, and aesthetic—financial and sexual, even" (115–16). In response, Auden "synthesizes . . . his own new order from a number of sources," including Marx, Freud, folklore, and "Homosexuality"—"a source of positive revolutionary values." But Jarrell sees that homosexuality has contradictory valences for the embattled early Auden: "in Us [Auden and his group] it is a quite natural relationship shading off into comradeship," but "in Them [the Enemy] it is just another decadent perversion" (127). Jarrell made these comments in 1941, but by 1945, his tone had darkened: in "Freud to Paul: The Stages of Auden's Ideology," he saw Auden as having failed to outgrow his earlier "sexual isolation." In embracing existentialism Auden had narcissistically rationalized his own anxieties by projecting them onto everything: "In the end he submits to the universe without a question; but it turns out that the universe is his own shadow on the wall beside his bed" (186). For all its conceptual sophistication, Auden's work of the 1940s, it seems, was a lonely invert's metaphysical pillow talk.

Boiled down, Jarrell's argument might be said to be that Auden was self-absorbed and narcissistic. The power of such a view might account at least partly for the rather overdetermined quality of attacks on Auden's political disloyalty or cowardice, whether for leaving Britain in 1939 or for abandoning the left. It might also explain something about the paradoxical view critics sometimes offered in later years that Auden's technical virtuosity showed his decline into superficiality. My own argument stands in oblique relation to pathologizing readings of

Auden in general. From one point of view, these are merely the ob-
verse of universalizing readings: where some see Auden articulating
the human condition or the spirit of an age, others see him failing to
do so because of his own condition. These two alternatives imply a
false dichotomy grounded in normalizing assumptions about sexuality
and literary value. But critics like Leavis and Jarrell do perceive that
homosexuality engenders and exemplifies fundamental, persistent contradictions for Auden: contradictions that I argue energize his work
rather than debilitate it. Much of his early writing is obsessed with
whether homosexuality can engender a progressive political identity
based on difference, conferring an empowering distance on England
and its ills, or whether this is a childish and dangerous, even fascistic
illusion. Phrased less abstractly: Auden struggled with whether and
how he could be a public poet with a leftist voice if he was a homosexual poet. So while this book rejects both universalizing and pathologizing vocabularies, it finds Auden himself preoccupied by questions
of his relation to his readers and culture. As for so many in Britain in
the 1930s, these issues took an explicitly political cast for Auden. But
even after he had left the 1930s (and Britain) behind, homosexuality
continued to engender questions of sameness and difference, marginality and commonality. It shaped his concerns with emotional coercion
in love and with erotic freedom, and it informed his frequent assertions in later years that poetry has its meaning and its value as a site of
sacred encounter between singular persons.

Along with Auden's death, the waning force of universalizing and
pathologizing approaches to his writing has allowed scholars to address his homosexuality more directly than before. This book makes
use of work by Robert Caserio, John Fuller, Anthony Hecht, Alan Jacobs, and Gregory Woods, among others. Woods's and Caserio's studies, however, are more limited in scope than mine, while Hecht, Fuller,
and Jacobs take up many aspects of Auden's work besides sexuality. In
addition, the work of John Boly and Stan Smith has shown how poststructuralist and new historicist approaches clarify Auden's "contradictions" and "incoherence." As readers will quickly see, Edward Mendelson's *Early Auden* and *Later Auden* are frequently cited here, for these
studies are candid and thoughtful about Auden's homosexuality. But

while Mendelson is concerned to establish Auden's place in both the civic and the visionary traditions of English poetry, this book focuses on Auden's historical position as a self-consciously homosexual writer and on his significance for gay/lesbian/queer studies. I stress, therefore, the degree to which his efforts to become a public poet were conditioned by a sense of his own eccentricity in such a role—an attitude with important predecessors in Byron and Wilde. Indeed, it is precisely Auden's perception of homosexuality *as a difference* that energizes his concerns with how poetry addresses others collectively and individually.

Since Auden's work predates the rise of gay liberation in the 1970s, "the closet" is an inevitable concern here. This book owes much to Eve Kosofsky Sedgwick's theorizations of sexuality and critical practice in *Epistemology of the Closet,* in particular her analyses of universalizing and minoritizing theories of sexuality and her explications of the binaries of secrecy and revelation, speakability and unspeakability. I trace the workings of such binaries in Auden's work by situating it in a series of overlapping contexts—intellectual, social, ideological, literary, and material—that help to lay bare his historically occluded engagements with sexual politics. The organization of this book is basically chronological, but not because I wish to recapitulate simplistic distinctions between "early" (political, psychoanalytic) and "later" (apolitical, Anglican) Auden. Rather, such a structure best illustrates how his poetic engagements with sexuality reflect both the changing personal, social, and historical conditions of his career, and an ongoing process of thinking about poetry and about homosexuality whose internal logic is dialectically related to these conditions.

In arguing, therefore, that Auden's earliest poems (roughly from 1927 to 1931) explore unspeakability and the closet, chapter 1 considers them in the context of the Auden group's interest in sexual liberation and censorship. Methodologically, this chapter entails reading his poems in their textual embodiments: their initial private printing by Spender in Auden's 1928 *Poems,* and their commercial publication by Faber in 1930.[11] Seen thus, they show him assimilating Mortmere, the coterie mythology invented by Christopher Isherwood and Edward Upward as Cambridge undergraduates. In Mortmere (to use Victor

Maskell's words in *The Untouchable*) "everything [is] itself and at the same time something else," and Auden adapted its discursive obliquities for a coded poetic about homosexual desire and identity. The readers of the 1928 *Poems* were largely friends with whom Auden was playing a game of knowledge about his romantic and erotic infatuations. Transposed into the 1930 Faber *Poems,* these same texts capitalize on the closet, eroticizing secrecy in order, as it were, to cruise the general reader.

By attending to the sociology of his early work, in other words, we can see Auden learning to practice sexual politics as the manipulation of signs, so that homosexuality becomes something that both *is* and *is not* there in his poetry. Chapter 2 introduces a second context for his work as a homosexual poet—one that is also very much a matter of signs: psychoanalytic theory. Using the largely unpublished journal Auden kept while living in Berlin in 1929, I explore how his theoretical responses to Freud, D. H. Lawrence, and others reflect an effort to interpret homosexual desire as a psychological disorder and homosexual identity as a cultural signifier. Auden's journal and his poetry of this period exemplify what Foucault terms the modern "medicalization of homosexuality." At the core of Auden's effort are two contradictory views: that homosexuality signifies diseased self-consciousness, arrested development, and cultural degeneracy; and that the self-acknowledged homosexual can embody liberation from repressive bourgeois norms.

Auden's inability to resolve these views theoretically, I argue, led him to reconsider the logic of psychoanalysis and the aims of poetry as a quasi-analytic endeavor. Chapter 3 examines how *Paid on Both Sides* (1928–29) and *The Orators* (1932)[12] show him beginning to think through the political implications of same-sex desire in contemporary England. These works also merit attention as signal moments in queer literary history, for here Auden deploys literature as a distinct mode of psychosexual and sexual-political inquiry. In the feuding tribes of his play *Paid on Both Sides,* he performs a semiserious diagnosis of the homoerotic group bonds supporting the male power structure of modern England. At the same time, the play's dream sequence— dramatizing a cryptic ritual of trial, punishment, and rebirth—portrays the hero's ideological awakening as a sexual awakening. Lending itself to quite incompatible readings in terms of sexual liberation and sexual cure, the play reflects Auden's theory of "ritual drama" as a therapeutic mode of joking contradiction.

In *The Orators: An English Study*—easily the most avant-garde work Auden ever wrote—contradiction develops into what can rightly be called a queer aesthetic. Analyzing rhetoric as a public, linguistic analogue to sublimated homoerotic group bonds, *The Orators* implies that the discursive and psychosexual underpinnings of English culture are protofascistic. But in Book II, "Journal of an Airman," Auden adopts the persona of the homosexual poet as cultural trickster; the journal outlines a pseudoscience to explain the Airman's deviant ancestry and narrates his war of practical jokes against "the enemy." In the Airman, I argue, Auden personifies an oppositional queer aesthetic grounded in logical and discursive contradiction.

For all its militant energy, *The Orators* also testifies to Auden's doubts about avant-garde form: the madcap paranoia of the Airman's efforts and the futility of his war against the enemy imply the ultimate impotence of politics-as-discursive-subversion. Chapter 4 examines how Auden sought a more accessible and politically effective voice as homosexual poet in the 1930s. Examining a number of shorter poems in detail, including the notorious "A Communist to Others," I suggest that his inability finally to commit to communism involved uncertainty about how homosexual identity might coincide with a political identification with the working class. As the 1930s went on, both the right and left launched homophobic attacks on Auden and his group, and this chapter considers "Letter to Lord Byron" (1936) as his defense. Abjuring the demand that a political poet adopt a polemical voice, Auden presents himself as Byron's modern heir. Through imitation of *Don Juan*, he attacks the tendency toward ideological cant in "serious" political art, indulging privacy, effeminacy, and eccentricity (both poetic and sexual) as alternatives to conformist politics of masculinity on the right *and* the left.

By concluding with an analysis of Auden's 1935 comments on what he calls "parable," chapter 4 serves as a linchpin for this book's overall argument. For in parable, Auden first theorizes poetry as a noncoercive way of making the poet's experience useful for the reader. Auden's concern to do so reflects not just another way to explain what it meant to be a public poet, but an evolving effort to mediate his own particularities as a homosexual poet and those of readers. Dovetailing with his habitual coding of homosexuality as crookedness, "parable" implies the obliquity and indirectness with which such a mediation takes place.

Auden's anxieties about coercion and particularity inform not only his politics but his love poetry, which is the subject of chapter 5. From one point of view, his conscious imitations of Shakespeare's sonnets in the 1930s suggest an abandonment of modernist modes for safer, more traditional ways of expressing homosexual love. But Auden's Shakespearean obsession with truth and lies also reflects his sense of the peculiar ethical cruces of homosexual love. The lover, in Auden's poems, is forever in danger of effacing the difference of the beloved by absorbing him into narcissistic erotic fantasy. Similar issues of freedom and difference govern the love poetry Auden wrote after 1939, when he emigrated to the United States and met Chester Kallman. In three decades of poems, Auden produced what amounts to a biography of this relationship, from his initial "Vision of Eros," through the collapse of their "marriage," to long-term love and companionship without sexual fidelity. Together, his concerns with the "I-Thou" relation in love and in lyric, and with the infidelity of poetic language to fact, suggest that by the 1950s and 60s Auden saw *all* poetry as a kind of virtual lovers' discourse. Addressed—often ambiguously—to Kallman and to others, his later love poems interpellate every reader as the beloved, seeking to honor the multiple, conflicting responsibilities of erotic experience.

In devoting chapter 6 to Auden's religious poetry and thought, I examine how questions of unspeakability and particularity inform his existentialist Protestantism. For while Auden professed the traditional belief that homosexuality was sinful, his religious poetry typically transposes secrecy into a metaphysical condition, in which the divine is the unknowable object of desire—the unspeaking, unspeakable *deus absconditus*. This chapter explores how Auden's games of theological knowledge use sexually coded tropes of angularity and crookedness to render the relation between the human and the divine. Auden's own sexual particularity, that is, serves as a consciously tendentious paradigm of human contingency. The chapter concludes with two 1948 poems that best illustrate the nexus of eros and agape in Auden's "queer theology." "Pleasure Island" renders an insider's critique of a homosexual male vision of free love as paradise, exposing the deathly impli-cation of this fantasy in envy and humiliation. But in his most famous religious poem, "In Praise of Limestone," unashamed homoerotic fan-tasy becomes Auden's analogy for what it would be to exist in the presence of God, where "the blessed" have "nothing to hide" (*SP* 187).

As will be obvious to some readers, the argument of this book im-plies that some of the most urgent issues in queer studies today have a longer history then we tend to realize. Not least among these are ques-tions about sexual identity and about identity politics that have be-come acute since the rise of queer theory in the 1990s. In its critique of essentialist models of identity and in its rejection of conceptual depen-dence on the grounding power of norms, queer theory has manifested itself as a by-now-familiar reaction against "gay" and "gay and lesbian" studies.[13] Analogously, Auden's poetry is obsessed from early on in his career with an array of contradictions that fracture homosexual iden-tity. As we shall see in chapter 1, the figure of the secret agent is the emblem in Auden's early poetry of these contradictions at the level of the subject: wary of opponents, victimized by his own side, he disinte-grates into enemy forces of desire and prohibition, implying that the closet does not mask an essential homosexual self so much as show it for a delusion.

Further, in his effort to harness psychoanalysis to explicate homo-sexual desire and identity, Auden certainly manifests the duality that Foucault associates with the medicalization of homosexuality: Auden is clearly anxious for cure, but Freud, Lawrence, and other theorists also provoke him into positing homosexual self-consciousness as the seed for new, even revolutionary identity.[14] Such a hope, explored in "1929," *Paid on Both Sides,* and *The Orators,* is never unproblematic, since it is clearly at odds with Auden's sense that the closet implies the dissolution of the subject. From another angle, the weird homosocial, homoerotic world of Auden's early work—interpreted so variously by critics—illustrates the tensions between what Sedgwick identifies as universalizing and minoritizing models of same-sex desire (*Episte-mology* 82–90), correlating for Auden with quite contradictory politi-cal overtones. Thus, when he posits the revolutionary possibilities of homosexuality in works like *Paid on Both Sides* and *The Orators,* he also worries about political complicity: same-sex desire, here, is both subversive and normatively fascistic. These works, in turn, strikingly anticipate Leo Bersani's arguments about the questionable political valences of gay male desire—gravitating as it so often does to an idealized masculine strength—and about the limits of discursive opposition, especially when based on the subversive ambitions of parody.[15]

Inevitably, my own views of Auden have been shaped by work in lesbian/gay literary studies and queer theory, and while parallels between Auden's writing and concerns of contemporary queer studies are sometimes addressed directly in the body of this book, they are more often left at the level of implicit suggestion or minimal reference. I have sought, for historicist reasons, to allow Auden's writing to generate its own forms of knowledge about sexuality, on the principle that this approach shows most compellingly how, in the decades before gay liberation and academic queer studies, literary modes served homosexual writers as vital ways of exploring and contesting issues of sexual politics: for Auden, poetry was queer theory *avant la lettre*. Such a proposition raises several inescapable questions—questions taken up at greater length in the "Afterword," which explores the value of historical study and literary criticism for queer studies, as well as the attendant epistemological risks. There are dangers in treating pre-Stonewall gay and lesbian writing as an object for illumination by historicist contextualization and "theory"—not least, dangers of logical circularity. Auden's work, I argue, speaks importantly to queer readers about such concerns, but it also offers a lens through which to consider centrality and marginality, essentialism and constructionism, fruitfully complicating another binary of vexed status in the academy today: that of canonical and minority literature. By provoking a game of knowledge about the poet's desires and meanings, Auden's poetry invites readers to engage in an exemplary process of fluid identifications of themselves and their own desires.

This introduction would be incomplete without comment on the terminology and the limits of what follows. By now, discussions of terminology may seem a tedious ritual in queer studies, but they are also unavoidable, since they get to foundational issues about identity and desire. While mindful of their origins in the pseudoscience of sexology, I have opted typically to use words like "homosexual" and "homosexuality" as the least question-begging. Although something may be

lost by not adhering to the younger Auden's usage of "bugger,"
"crook," and "invert," he seems not to have been systematic, and in any
case, "homosexual" and "homosexuality" are often his words of choice,
routinely so in later years. It has become harder in academic discourse
to avoid the implications of essentialism that lurk in "gay," so I have
largely avoided it, but as is already clear, "queer" is immensely useful
for describing Auden's own critiques of essentialist identity and normative regimes of thought.

The boundaries of this study are foremost a matter of the volume
and variety of Auden's writing. With the exception of *Paid on Both
Sides,* which Auden routinely reprinted with his poetry, this book does
not examine his drama in any detail. Apart from reasons of space, my
justification is that his influence and position in literary history (like
Yeats's or Eliot's) come from his poetry, not his plays. Similarly, a
treatment of his libretti and his writings on opera would have made
this study unwieldy, although their absence may be less defensible.[16]
Even within the demarcated limits of Auden's "poetry," this book concentrates, with the exception of chapters 3 and 4, on shorter poems
and lyrics. Again, reasons of space come into play, but this is also a
matter of an argument that Auden's significance as a homosexual poet
lies in his deployment of the individual poem, particularly the lyric, as
a site of epistemological and erotic encounter. To be convincing, such
an argument requires detailed reading procedures that cannot be extended to every possible shorter poem, much less to the longer works
of the 1940s neglected here: "For the Time Being" (1941–42), published together with "The Sea and the Mirror" (1942–44) in *For the
Time Being* (1944), and *The Age of Anxiety* (1947).[17] Finally, this book
concentrates on Auden's earlier work because it was in the 1920s and
'30s that he was most acutely preoccupied with making theoretical
sense of homosexuality. I have tried whenever possible to draw attention to other poems that exemplify or complicate matters at hand, but
readers will doubtless think of poems I do not address. If such responses indicate the limits of this study, I hope that they also point to
its suggestiveness and utility.

Chapter 1

"BUT WHO WOULD GET IT?":
SEXUAL POLITICS AND COTERIE POETRY

Near the start of John Hollander's *Reflections on Espionage* (1976), agent
Cupcake, whose coded dispatches comprise the book, informs his con-
trol of the death of agent Steampump, who has "died quietly in his /
Hotel room and his sleep":

> He taught me, as you surely
> Know, all that I know; yet I had to pass him
> By in the Square at evening . . .
> Without even our eyes having touched, without
> Acknowledgment. And thereby, of course, we were
> Working together. (3)

In September 1973, W. H. Auden had died in his sleep in a Vienna hotel, and *Reflections on Espionage* acknowledges him not only here, with
a code name that alludes to the mining machinery of his early work,
but in its structuring conceit of poetry as espionage. What Hollander
"knows" from Auden is that poetry is an activity of coding where reticences are giveaways. The two agents pass "without / Acknowledgment," but their silence says it all: "thereby, of course, we were / Working together."

The figure of the secret agent resonates provocatively in Auden's
early work, and it is central to this chapter's concern with the unspoken and the unspeakable, with obscure meanings and meaningful obscurities. In literary-historical terms, the cryptic quality of his poems of

the late 1920s has typically and rightly been understood to reflect a precocious absorption of high modernist technique. Auden's embrace of modernism, however, also embodies an intricate response to a problem many other writers have faced: how to write public poetry out of the closet. In the work of poets as varied as Byron, Whitman, Dickinson, Hopkins, H. D., Stein, and Lorde, critics have traced complex encodings of same-sex desire.[1] Like Byron and Wilde, Auden grew adept not only at literary "passing" but at devious, deviant wieldings of secrecy and privacy as public gestures.[2] If he never achieved celebrity on their scale, neither did he pay their price for testing England's tolerance for open secrets. But at the start of his career in the late 1920s, Auden developed and put into practice a poetic of self-conscious coding to negotiate the closet as a structure both psychic and social. The result was a body of poetry unparalleled in its exploration of modern homosexual subjectivity and, in Sedgwick's apt phrase, the "epistemology of the closet."[3]

Such an argument does risk reductiveness: as D. A. Miller has noted, outing the lesbian or gay writer can seem but another form of "police entrapment," and it would be wrong to reify Auden's intentions by seeking a latent, unitary "homosexual meaning" below the surface of his poems.[4] The distinctive topoi and terrain of these poems—where mysterious forays are made on guarded frontiers, and loyalty is always suspect—have been read quite plausibly in terms of modernist alienation, radical politics, psychic schism, and adolescent angst. We need not reject such readings of his work, as if these things did not impinge on sexual politics. In fact, we *must* not reject them, for it is crucial to the signifying operations of Auden's early poems that we be able to read them "innocently," as having nothing to do with homosexuality.

"Plausible deniability," in other words, is as crucial in the closet as it is in espionage. But to observe this is also to realize that at the level of individual readings, this argument fails the test of falsifiability.[5] The first part of this chapter responds to this problem by seeking to recover a crucial, largely neglected aspect of the social and discursive context of Auden's early poetry: the Auden group's collective concern with sexual liberation and censorship in the late 1920s. These two issues are intertwined: homosexuality registers in their writing through

distinct codes and is thematized as a matter of coding in the group discourse of "Mortmere." Turning then to Auden's poetry itself, I offer an
exemplary reading of the poem "Control of the passes" against the social and material backdrop of its private printing in Auden's 1928 *Poems*. This poem crystallizes my major points: that his figurations of desire invite reading specifically in terms of homosexual desire; that the
spy serves as a figure for the closeted homosexual and the homosexual
poet; and that his tropes of espionage conjoin the psychic dynamics of
closeted desire and the social dynamics of writing for readers knowing
and unknowing, known and unknown.

Auden's coded poetry, I shall argue, offers a proto-Barthesian textual erotics—a sign system for exploring and representing homosexual
desire. But while the secret agent embodies the seductive powers of
semiotic instability, Auden also portrays the secret agent as victim of
the duplicity in which he traffics. The last part of this chapter pursues
this tension through several of Auden's most characteristic early poems, arguing that their peculiar topography and style serve to revise
the so-called Greater Romantic Lyric by way of Mortmere. Rather
than ratifying a relation of sameness between the lyric "I" and the
reader through a sincere invocation of Nature, his landscape poems
employ a rhetoric of overt duplicity, making the text a site for a revelation of tantalizing difference and opacity. In seeking to transform unspeakability from a condition of repression into a weapon against the
uninitiated reader, these poems not only exemplify the Auden group's
fight against censorship, but dramatize it and critique it.

I

In 1988 Stephen Spender published *The Temple,* a novel first drafted in
1929 and based on his travels in Germany. *The Temple* recounts how
Paul Schoner, a young Englishman, discovers in late-Weimar Germany
the cult of youth and the male body, and its disturbing overlap with
the rise of the Nazis. In its blend of fiction and fact, its depictions
of Auden as Simon Wilmot, Isherwood as William Bradshaw, and
Spender himself as Paul Schoner, *The Temple* stands in contradictory
relation to the past. Like Isherwood's *Lions and Shadows* (1938) and

Goodbye to Berlin (1939), it is fiction. But in disclosing once-unprintable aspects of Spender's youth, *The Temple* makes a gesture of belated truth-telling akin to *Christopher and His Kind*, Isherwood's 1976 outing of his life in the 1930s. In his introduction, Spender recalls circulating typescripts of the novel among friends, much as E. M. Forster showed *Maurice* to his friends in the 1930s to test out different endings.[6] Spender also showed it to his publisher, Geoffrey Faber, who "pointed out that there could be no question of publishing a novel which . . . was pornographic according to the law at that time" (*Temple* x). Recent years, Spender notes, had seen the infamous cases of *Ulysses* and *The Well of Loneliness,* the censorship of which forms a crucial social context for the self-construction of the Auden group:

> In the late Twenties young English writers were more concerned with censorship than with politics. . . . 1929 was the last year of that strange Indian Summer—the Weimar Republic. For many of my friends and for myself, Germany seemed a paradise where there was no censorship and young Germans enjoyed extraordinary freedom in their lives. . . .
>
> Another result of censorship was to make us wish to write precisely about those subjects which were most likely to result in our books being banned. . . .
>
> All this explains, I think, a good deal about *The Temple*. This is an autobiographical novel in which the author tries to report truthfully on his experiences in the summer of 1929. In writing it I had the sense of sending home to friends and colleagues dispatches from a front line in our joint war against censorship.
>
> (x-xi)

It is not news, of course, that the Auden group had a sense of common purpose. Spender's 1951 *World Within World* fleshed out the coterie's origins at Oxford in the 1920s, but the legend was well underway in the 1930s. After Michael Roberts and John Lehmann's formative 1932 anthology *New Signatures,* critics began to treat these writers as a movement, and the Auden group reinforced this sense with dedications to each other and allusions to each other's work. What is striking about Spender's comments is his stress on a common agenda that was not a matter of leftist politics but one of sexual politics: "Writing

The Temple, I felt that I was very much one of my generation, exploring new territory of living identified with a new literature" (xi). Poetry and fiction of the 1930s abound in topographical language and tropes, but that this "new territory" was not just literary is clear from a letter Spender sent to Lehmann from Berlin around 1929: "Whatever one of us does in writing or travelling or taking jobs, is a kind of exploration which may be taken up by the others" (xi).

Spender's novel begins with an "English Prelude" in which Paul's comically pathetic inhibition ruins any chance for romance with a friend during a walking tour along the Wye.[7] Only in Germany—which Simon Wilmot (Auden) declares "the Only Place for Sex"—does Paul's sexual repression dissolve (7). From one angle, Germany seems to have represented for Auden and his friends what France did for Wilde and the decadents of the 1890s, and southern Europe for writers like Pater and Forster. More relaxed attitudes about sex were clearly much of the attraction: "Is Berlin very wicked?" Auden asked David Ayerst in a 1927 letter (Carpenter, *Auden* 84). Auden later elaborated on his motives for choosing Germany: "I felt out of sympathy with French culture, partly by temperament and partly in revolt against the generation of intellectuals immediately preceding mine, which was strongly Francophile" (*FA* 521). Auden refers here to the legendary 1920s coterie centered on Harold Acton and Brian Howard, who had revived aestheticism and made homosexuality fashionable at Oxford a few years earlier. His own Oxford aesthetic had a decidedly modernist inflection—instead of Wilde's espousal of style over sincerity, he emulated the cool impersonality of Eliot. Accordingly, while Acton and Howard looked back to France, Auden and his friends were drawn to Germany not only as the land of England's recent enemy (thus giving homosexuality a frisson of criminality) but as the culture that produced the pioneering scientific and legal work of Freud, Richard von Krafft-Ebing, and Magnus Hirschfeld.[8] Moreover, unlike Wilde, Symonds, and Forster, the Auden group was relatively uninterested in seeking authority for their sexuality in the literature or landscape of the ancient Mediterranean; to turn instead to Germany was to seek a forward-looking sexual utopia in another northern culture.[9] And in idealizing Weimar culture, Auden and his friends also reflected a more self-consciously political attitude toward sex, in keeping with the increasing political consciousness of undergraduates during and after the General Strike of 1927.[10]

Still, Germany made a peculiar "front line in our joint war on censorship" since—no less than, say, Capri—it was attractive precisely as a retreat (in every sense) from English constraints. Outside of safely unpublished fiction, censorship was harder to challenge. It took sixty years, after all, for *The Temple* to reach print. For that matter, as the source for the militantly uninhibited Simon Wilmot, the young Auden wrote his most sexually explicit poems in German, and they were shown only to a few friends, remaining unpublished until 1990.[11] They are quite unlike his English poems at the time—and not just because in German Auden felt free to write frankly about sex with men. Syntactically and semantically straightforward, they wholly lack the distinct landscape and tone of his early work in English. If German was for Auden, as for Isherwood, a language "irradiated with sex," it was also safely foreign (*Christopher* 21).

But while self-censorship is one result of constraints on expression, the Auden group's resistance against censorship left traces in their published work, both as an encoded subject and as the impetus for certain discursive practices. Sedgwick has argued that "ignorances, far from being pieces of the originary dark, are produced by and correspond to particular knowledges and circulate as part of particular regimes of truth" (*Epistemology* 8). Silences under a regime of censorship are not simply hollow: they are silences about something and invite interpretation. Thus, while it went unpublished in the 1930s, *The Temple* did become public as an allusion in the first ode of *The Orators* (1932), where Auden has "Stephen" crying out, " 'Destroy this temple' " (*EA* 95). Beyond the biblical reference, the line would mean little to readers ignorant that "the temple" is Spender's image for the eroticized male body. But such ignorance is to the point: the allusion classifies readers according to what they know (or suspect) about the Auden group and homosexuality. The next stanza finds "Christopher . . . wincing / In front of *ignorance*—'Tell the English,' he shivered, / 'Man is a spirit' " (my emphasis). These lines are not just cryptic but encrypted—and even more blatantly in later printings, where Auden substitutes the names "Maverick" and "Pretzel." If these are obvious code names, so are "Christopher" and "Stephen," whose identity could be known for certain only by the favored few. Such codes not only divide the poem's audience but do so candidly, with the reader's knowledge: they tell the uninitiated that they are just that.

These are hardly the only coded allusions in the work of the Auden group; *The Orators* is full of them, and a list of coded allusions to members of the group, other friends and boyfriends, would be a long one.[12] To be sure, not all codes in their work call such attention to themselves. Many would be recognized only by the initiated. Very few, for example, would know that Auden's 1929 lyric "Before this loved one" (*EA* 31), a lament that "This gratitude for gifts is less / Than the old loss," analyzes Isherwood's infatuation with a beautiful, impoverished boy he met in a gay bar in Berlin (Isherwood, *Christopher* 5). Mendelson offers a compelling reading of the poem in terms of the weight of history that makes love difficult, a theme he traces through much of Auden's early writing (*Early* 6–7). Indeed, the obscurity of the poem's referents invites this kind of generalizing reading. At the same time, this obscurity veils the poem's significance in the homosexual subculture of late-Weimar Berlin. In the context of that subculture, the poem analyzes the power relations between patrons of the bars and boys like "this loved one," who get food and gifts in exchange for sex. Such relations, Auden implies, do not embody what the patron likes to feel he is buying—love. "Touching is shaking hands / On mortgaged lands": the boy's "gift" of his body is not a gift at all but a sign of "mortgage" to material poverty.

If Auden's intentions for poems like this one included camouflaging their specificity, it is also true that he often emphasized the personal occasions for his work by inscribing in friends' copies of his books the names or initials of those about or to whom poems were written (see Carpenter, *Auden* 76). Such private inscriptions imply that in offering readings of Auden's poems abstracted from the social conditions of their production, we are—knowingly or not—reading under a regime of censorship. Censorship is, in fact, part of the meaning of "Before this loved one," for its public form underscores both his suppression of private relations for a public audience, and the network of personal relationships in which the poem had a private meaning. To read such a poem with a consciousness of censorship is to be reminded that what is true for all writing is acutely so for lesbian and gay writers—that meaning is initiated and elaborated in social networks and institutions where truth is very much a matter of what is speakable.

The social forces of censorship and the closet come together in the characteristic topography of Auden's early work. Its sources lay partly in the northern English landscape Auden knew as a child, and in later years he read his ideal landscape in more or less psychological and erotic terms.[13] From the standpoint of sexual politics and social history, however, it is revealing that the landscape of "Auden Country" gained its famous atmosphere of danger and intrigue only after he went to Oxford. For the genealogy of this discursive terrain owes much to Auden's being drawn into the circle of Isherwood and Edward Upward, who as Cambridge undergraduates had created the fantasy world critics usually refer to as Mortmere.[14] Isherwood describes it in a well-known section of *Lions and Shadows:*

> Everywhere, we recognized enemy agents. . . . I was buying some clothes at a draper's. "This tie's rather nicer," I said. And the shopman, with what we later described as a "reptilian sneer," answered smilingly: "Yes—they're *all* rather nicer. . . ." There was a college waiter who murmured into one's ear, as he took the order: "Most *certainly* sir." This man seemed positively fiend-like: he must surely be an important spy.
>
> (49)

Mortmere, here, deploys the hermeneutics of suspicion in a semiserious game of intergenerational warfare, where the Enemy is institutional adult authority disguised as the servant class. As the Auden group's "myth about themselves," it reflects, as Samuel Hynes has argued, a generational sense of having missed the most dramatic fight of recent history, The Great War (*Auden* 19–24). But like so many conspiracy theories, Mortmere also implies nostalgia for an era of innocence when one could trust those in charge. "They" are the ones who practice massive deception, pretending benevolence. To recognize their duplicity is to be forced to play the counterspy, attuned to the fluidity and permeability of signs. Mortmere is both an imaginary world and a game about the real world, played in the coded, underground discourse of those who have seen through its appearances.

Mortmere's most obvious traces in the published work of the Auden group are the obscure, unexplained names that appear there, and such instances serve to cement the coterie through privileged knowledge. But Mortmere's concern with secrecy also involves sexual politics, and most clearly in Isherwood's prose of the 1930s. To say this is to question what is perhaps his famous claim—that he effaces his narratorial identity in order to bear witness to history like a "camera." But this pretense of objectivity requires us to delimit Isherwood's writing as fiction, without exploring his narrative techniques as rhetorical gestures with social, historical meanings. For his reticence is also a pose— his markedly colorless narrators, who bear his name or some variant thereof, are rhetorical tools in games of knowledge with the reader.[15]

One such game occurs at the very start of Isherwood's third novel, *The Last of Mr. Norris* (1935). The narrator, William Bradshaw, is sharing a compartment on a train headed for the frontier of that new territory, Germany:

> My first impression was that the stranger's eyes were of an unusually light blue. They met mine for several blank seconds, vacant, unmistakably scared. Startled and innocently naughty, they half reminded me of an incident I couldn't quite place; something which had happened a long time ago, to do with the upper fourth form classroom. They were the eyes of a schoolboy surprised in the act of breaking one of the rules.
>
> (1)

The stranger is Arthur Norris, a shady character with a toupé who is engaged in vague, illicit business in Germany. Norris's disquiet results from a question from Bradshaw: " 'I wonder, sir, if you could let me have a match?' " Norris fumbles for his lighter, and Bradshaw then comments on the procedure:

> The tiny flame of the lighter flickered between us, as perishable as the atmosphere which our exaggerated politeness had created. The merest

breath would have extinguished the one, the least incautious gesture
or word would have destroyed the other.

(2)

The whole bizarre episode—the speculative, anxious eye contact and
Bradshaw's sense that Norris resembles "a schoolboy surprised in the
act"—is initiated by what is, of course, a classic pickup line. The ritual
with the lighter resonates with the tension of sexual encounter—both
men apparently pretending that they are really only talking about
smoking. But although Norris uses makeup and perfume, his sexual
tastes run to schoolgirls. The scene on the train reads like a pickup, but
in fact, Norris is being furtive for other reasons—the two men really
are talking about smoking. And while he is a perceptive, camera-like
observer, Bradshaw betrays no sense of the suggestiveness of the exchange; we learn far more about Norris than about our narrator, who
is as asexual as the "Chris" of *Goodbye to Berlin*.

In purely narrative terms, the homosexual overtones of this scene
are gratuitous—its queerness foreshadows nothing definite in the story
about Norris or Bradshaw. These overtones serve largely as gestures
Isherwood directs at his readers, and at this level, not that of the narrative itself, the resonances in the text are sexual signs. The general
reader could not know—though Auden, the book's dedicatee, surely
did—that Arthur Norris was based on Gerald Hamilton, an equally
shady character the Auden group knew in Berlin (see Isherwood,
Christopher 72–78; Page 183–90). Unlike Norris, Hamilton *was* homosexual, and readers like Auden could "recognize" him and Isherwood
and read in the scene an allusion to their homosexuality. The scene
both evades censorship and exploits it to cement the insider's status by
way of private knowledge. But the encounter in the train compartment
is also a closet drama in which the outsider might turn out to be a
player as well as a spectator: it is an epistemological cruising, a solicitation to see if the anonymous reader will pick up on the sexual implications at play.

Auden's early poetry often makes such gestures, but by means of
techniques unavailable in Isherwood's relatively conventional prose
style. A closer analogue to Auden's methods is Edward Upward's story

"The Railway Accident" (1928), for many years the only "pure" Mortmere text in print. In his foreword to the first publication of the story in 1946, Isherwood described Mortmere:

> Life in Mortmere is like a poker-game between telepathists, in which everybody is bluffing and nobody is fooled. We too, in the everyday world, have our social pretences. For us, too, there are fantastic realities which we conspire to ignore.
>
> (Upward 34)

One of the jokes here is that, in Mortmerean fashion, Isherwood is being both honest and misleading. As of 1946, recent events offered many once-secret "fantastic realities" for readers to imagine, and the story's climax—the mysterious crash of an ultramodern stainless-steel train—might be read as figure for European history's recent turn. But in the surreal world of the story, it is hard to know just what the characters "conspire to ignore." Isherwood does not say, and for all the hints at conspiracy, Upward never explains the train crash or its relation to the rector's treasure hunt to which the characters are traveling. The simile of a poker game, in other words, describes both social relations within the story and the relation between writer and reader. But the deck is stacked—the general reader will not know that in the unpublished version, the train crash parallels the rape of a male character by three choirboys. Insiders would know this—readers like Isherwood and Auden, and Upward himself.[16] Isherwood's foreword plays a game in which homosexuality is one open secret we "conspire to ignore," and his game is possible because different readers will bring different degrees of knowledge to the text. He responds to the dynamic of the open secret not by revelation but by conflating revelation with concealment in a text of "secret openness" quite in keeping with Upward's story. For a sense of unspoken realities pervades even the censored version of "The Railway Accident," both in its obscure plot and in its style, which is so eccentric that we can never feel certain about the semantic range of any word. The result is a kind of readerly paranoia in which we finally suspect everything—including, as Isherwood says, the sanity of the narrator (Upward 34).

The story's intricacies of plot and implication defy easy summary; suffice it to say that as in *The Last of Mr. Norris,* our narrator— Hearn—is on a train with a stranger. Their destination is the village of Mortmere, and in the course of the ride, this stranger—Shreeve, a local headmaster—gives us reason to be suspicious. Hearn repeatedly catches him lying about minor things, and he claims to be privy to various secrets. Shreeve acts more and more oddly during the trip, and he seems to know that their train is doomed, as indeed it is. They barely escape before being struck from behind by the sleek Mortmere Express, and the story ends with their arrival in Mortmere, where an arrest is announced for train wrecking.

As superficial as this summary is, none would be truly adequate, for the story leaves much unexplained, and what answers it gives are quite unsatisfying. The man arrested for sabotaging the trains—Wrygrave— is a master under Shreeve, who recalls during the ride having once " 'surprised him in the act' " in a dormitory inspection (53). While he never specifies this "act," his phrasing recalls Bradshaw's comment that Mr. Norris reminded him of "a schoolboy surprised in the act of breaking one of the rules." Implications of homosexuality do come to the surface when Shreeve recalls the comment of another person that Wrygrave's " 'vice is branded on his face,' " so that we are invited to link sexual deviance with crime (57). But since we never meet Wry- grave, all indications of his guilt come to us from the questionable Shreeve. Moreover, as the story proceeds, our narrator's reliability be- comes more and more questionable, so that in the end, we cannot even be sure the train was sabotaged. We are left with a mystery not so much about the culprit as about whether we should see the story as a mystery at all, and if so, whether it has a solution. Shreeve's comment to Hearn at one point is perfect advice for the reader: " 'Mind you,' he seriously, theatrically commented, 'I'm not guaranteeing you'll see any- thing. And if by any wild chance you do, it will be something so inde- finable that afterwards you won't be sure that you haven't imagined it' " (52).

"The Railway Accident" might be seen as proto-Dada, except that the *way* it leaves questions unanswered, its epistemological disrup- tiveness, is not adequately accounted for by ascribing to it primarily metaphysical implications. Characters speak so elliptically at times, in a parody of upper-middle-class public school slang, that they seem almost to be employing a strange dialect. The effect is such that, while Hearn's narration periodically turns to quasi-impressionist internal monologue, one always feels that its semantic weirdness may serve social rather than metaphysical ends—that the words may encode meanings for specific readers. It is tempting to suspect that the unexpurgated version, with its homosexual rape, solves the mysteries of the published version. But we cannot assume so, and Upward may be mainly interested in promoting the suspicion of secret solutions where none exist.

Like Isherwood and Upward's game of Mortmere at Cambridge, "The Railway Accident" exemplifies an insider discourse about the interpretation of signs, a discourse grounded in the sense that social reality is not as it seems and that all signs are first and foremost social gestures, and therefore suspect. For the insider, it is perhaps less necessary to know what these signs mean than to deploy them as an insider—that is, to imply the secret knowledge of the initiate. Ambiguity of sexual signifiers in "The Railway Accident" is therefore more than just one of the ways the story foregrounds interpretation of codes. Upward's story deploys all signifiers in the manner of Isherwood's homosexual codes in *The Last of Mr. Norris,* so that every word or gesture of the characters, every event (or pseudo-event) in the story, resonates for the reader with the ambiguity of William Bradshaw's request to Mr. Norris for a match.

Auden was a latecomer to the coterie discourse of Mortmere, but it is this kind of uncertainty that his early verse incites in the reader. Mortmere provided him with discursive resources to resist censorship and write about the unspeakable. But it also worked to unsettle the reader's assumptions about meaning through semantic and syntactic instabilities that link the duplicity of signs not to abstract or ontological conditions so much as to social ones. In grafting Mortmere onto his own private landscape, Auden created a textual arena where the reader is forced to think like a spy because the poet is one himself.

II

The remainder of this chapter considers how Auden's early poems adapt the techniques of Mortmere for a game of knowledge with the reader as potential lover. This argument would ideally bring to bear as much historical detail as possible about the coterie readership of these poems. But while informed speculation about particular readers is possible in some cases, it is often hard to speak with confidence: little evidence exists that Isherwood, Spender, or others in Auden's circle read specific coded meanings into his poems beyond allusions of the sort we have seen already. Such uncertainties are less critical for this argument than it might appear, however. First, "proof" of intentionality for a coded poetic cannot be of the sort that satisfies, for instance, an argument for literary allusion. Furthermore, it is clear that secrecy and deception interest Auden at least as much on a psychological as on a social level: with such intricately self-referential poems, it would be foolish to argue for exclusive, unitary meanings encoded for specific readers. Thus while Auden circulated many of these poems among a coterie readership, he seems to have been at least as interested in experimenting with lyric as an erotic game of knowledge about what the poet and reader might *not* already know. And in this regard we see him experimenting with ways of engaging the uninitiated general reader.

To introduce these issues with as much historical precision as possible, this section considers the relations between sexual politics, coterie sociology, and Auden's poetic techniques in a single, exemplary poem titled "The Secret Agent" in the 1945 *Collected Poetry* and thereafter:

> Control of the passes was, he saw, the key
> To this new district, but who would get it?
> He, the trained spy, had walked into the trap
> For a bogus guide, seduced with the old tricks.
>
> At Greenhearth was a fine site for a dam
> And easy power, had they pushed the rail
> Some stations nearer. They ignored his wires.
> The bridges were unbuilt and trouble coming.

The street music seemed gracious now to one
For weeks up in the desert. Woken by water
Running away in the dark, he often had
Reproached the night for a companion
Dreamed of already. They would shoot, of course,
Parting easily who were never joined.[17]

In 1930 this sonnet appeared in Auden's "first book" as we conventionally use the term—*Poems*, published in London by Faber & Faber. But like much of this book, it had been printed two years earlier in a volume, also called *Poems*, that Auden assembled in the summer after finishing at Oxford. The 1928 *Poems* came about when Spender was printing his *Nine Experiments* on a handpress. He offered to print a book for Auden, and in addition to setting up type and working on the actual printing, he helped decide what to include. Of the twenty numbered poems, "Control of the passes" was among the most recent, apart from a few later incorporated into *Paid on Both Sides*. Dedicated to Isherwood, the book claims an impression of "About 45 copies," and among its recipients were friends like Spender and Isherwood, A. L. Rowse, E. R. Dodds, Sidney Newman, C. Day Lewis, Gabriel Carritt, David Ayerst, and later Cyril Connolly and John Layard.[18]

This information offers material evidence that Auden's early work was first produced within and received by a limited, coterie readership, rather than within a commercial publishing framework for a mostly anonymous public. Few of Auden's academic critics refer to the 1928 *Poems*, and those who do have not pursued the implications of its sociology for his work.[19] For while the 1930 text of "Control of the passes" is virtually identical to the 1928, the two are in crucial ways very different because they were produced in different social networks. It is far easier to read the 1930 and later printings of the poem in universalizing terms, and many have done so. Humphrey Carpenter, for instance, sees it as one of many Auden poems that "entirely transcend the personal circumstances behind them" (*Auden* 77). Such readings, however, unconsciously replicate the occlusion of the poem's origins as a coterie text through its mediation by institutions of commercial publication.

We can begin to recover the meanings of the 1928 "Control of the passes" by noting that Auden wrote it in January 1928. In the chronological ordering of *The English Auden,* it is bracketed by two love poems—"From the very first coming down" (December 1927) and "Taller to-day, we remember similar evenings" (March 1928). Auden later glossed the first of these with initials in Chester Kallman's copy of the 1934 Random House *Poems*—"W. M."—indicating it referred to William McElwee, a fellow undergraduate. While the exact nature of their relationship is uncertain, Auden was apparently in love with him. During this same period Auden seems to have been in an emotionally fraught relationship with another student, Gabriel Carritt, who had been at McElwee's public school (alluded to in "Taller to-day").[20] As for "Control of the passes," Mendelson notes that Auden seems never to have recorded any initials next to it in friends' copies, and he argues, "The division it concerns is not only sexual: it is *any* separation from unity or satisfaction."[21] We cannot know that Auden wrote "Control of the passes" with either Carritt or McElwee in mind, but he did write it in a time of acute frustration with both relationships. Carpenter states: "It is impossible to be certain what sort of relationship Auden had with McElwee. Most of Auden's friends had the impression that McElwee was not prepared to respond to Auden's love, and would not go to bed with him, though he was flattered by the attention" (*Auden* 69). As we shall see later, such a scenario does fit "From the very first coming down," in which the speaker deals with a disappointing, distancing letter. As for Auden and Carritt, who were introduced by McElwee in the fall of 1927, "The two of them then had what Spender described as a 'mildly tormenting and tormented relationship,' which was painful to Auden because Carritt would not respond to his sexual advances" (76).

Even if we cannot reconstruct fully the circumstances in which Auden wrote "Control of the passes," we can now see clearly what only his circle could know then: that he wrote it in a time not of undefined sexual or romantic frustration, but of frustrated homosexual desire. As others have noticed, the poem can be read as an allegory of both romantic rejection and the psychic tension between desire and repression.[22] But we can focus such readings more precisely by interpreting "this new district" as the body, which illicit desire seeks to "control."

Desire is then discovered by will (the "bogus guide"), its collapse figured as a failure to procure reinforcements ("They ignored his wires"). Or the second quatrain may be read in terms of the lover's failure to follow through once his intentions are exposed—he is foiled by discovery, and then his own will fails. Either way, frustration has both "internal" and "external" sources, and in an allegory of spying, the potential for these two readings does not point simply to its "universality" or to an abstract concern with self-schism. For this conjunction of psychic and social borders defines the closet, where social prohibition reinforces psychic inhibition, and vice versa. Against prohibition and inhibition (two aspects of one force), neither desire nor the desiring subject can proceed except as "secret agent," for discovery can lead all too easily to disaster—"They would shoot, of course." Are "they" the spy's enemy, who have trapped him with a "bogus guide," or his own side, who have "ignored his wires" to leave him out in the cold? In the end we cannot say: the two readings offered here collapse into each other in the closet's sustaining conjunction of social and psychic prohibitions.

Neither McElwee nor Carritt seems to have considered himself homosexual or reciprocated Auden's sexual interest. But if we cannot know that the poem refers to either one, its figurings of frustration and deception convey neatly one problem of desire in the closet, where "Is he/she or isn't he/she?" is an inevitable question when there are no obvious clues. The spy is "trained" to pick up signs, and he knows that "Control of the passes" is "the key"—"passes" having obvious sexual undertones. He must be able both to interpret such signs and to "control" them, yet he seems to have been fooled, having "walked into the trap / For a bogus guide, seduced with the old tricks." With nice irony, "seduced" implies his own deception, his mistaken trust in the "bogus guide." (Or one may read the trained spy as the bogus guide who has been trapped.) The poem, that is, allegorizes cruising as espionage: disguise is crucial but fallible (since one must risk exposure), and interpretation of verbal and bodily signs is always tentative and often risky. As Auden puts it in "Upon this line between adventure" (1929), later titled "Do Be Careful": "But should the walk do more than this / Out of bravado or drunkenness / Forward or back are menaces" (*EA* 33).

This kind of reading can be extended quite far, for the potential duplicities of imagery and semantics in the text are manifold. "Power," for instance, often has erotic connotations for Auden (see Mendelson, *Early* 9, 87). So building a "dam" at "Greenhearth" for "easy power" might suggest how one may exploit friendly affection if the object in question is new at this game, i.e. has a "green heart."[23] But something goes wrong, apparently on both sides. The spy never gets reinforcements, and his counterpart turns out to be no novice at all. By the sestet, the spy's plan is foiled, and all he can do is to "reproach the night" for the lover he never had, the "companion / Dreamed of already." This last phrase has its own bitter undertones too, suggesting that he has been merely fantasizing a lover "all ready" for him—who evidently *was* "all ready" to fend him off. Multiple readings inflect the closing lines as well. "They would shoot, of course," could refer to the spy and his "companion"—his would-be lover (i.e. they would shoot each other). But "they" could also be the allies who have abandoned him, making this last gunfight merely his projection of *self*-destruction onto the "companion" he never had. If "Control of the passes" is a commentary on Auden's failed desire for McElwee and/or Carritt, with Auden cast as "the trained spy," he is unable to locate the source of failure precisely, for he leaves unresolved whether that failure proceeds from inhibition or rejection, and he seems uncertain whether rejection is avoidable. Perhaps the most chilling touch is how the final, stoic acceptance of failure parodies sexual consummation: "They would shoot, of course, / Parting easily who were never joined."

One can, of course, read "Control of the passes" in terms of generic romantic frustration, and viewed in literary-historical terms, it marks a brilliant adaptation of overtly modern conceits to the concerns with desire and secrecy that have energized sonnets from Petrarch onward. Or one can read it as a modernist allegory of alienation or fragmentation of self: with the trained spy unidentified, the reader is free to construct him as Everyman. But while the poem permits such responses, they alone are inadequate to its suggestiveness. For it also makes a fascinating allegory about knowledge, secrecy, and reading, and from this angle, its capacity for readings that have nothing to do with homosexuality and the closet implies not its transcendence of personal sources, but its implication in the charged dynamics of sexual revelation and concealment. In the context of a coterie readership, "Control of the passes" suggests a kind of test for the reader.

Most of the recipients of the 1928 *Poems* were connected with Oxford, and the book's coterie quality registers in references to names and places that would have been meaningless to outsiders. Such references occur in poems more or less explicitly concerned with desire. Auden's embarrassingly clumsy phrase "a snub-nosed winner," which he later used in an unpublished poem addressed to Gabriel Carritt, appears in "Because sap fell away" (see Carpenter, *Auden* 76). Dated November 1927, this poem reads almost like a dry run for "Control of the passes," but instead of allegorizing sexual desire in the mission of a spy, Auden invokes the proverbial homoeroticism of the locker room, where the players "sniff with distaste / At a mouldy passion" (*EA* 441). This poem's imagery also prefigures "Control of the passes": "Love, is this love, that notable forked-one, / Riding away from the farm, the ill word said, / Fought at the frozen dam?" In both poems, the unbuilt or unworking dam suggests unachieved erotic potential. Since Carritt received a copy of *Poems,* he could have picked up on Auden's reference to him in "Because sap fell away," as well as the allusion to his school in "Taller to-day, we remember similar evenings."[24]

Whether Carritt, for instance, read "Control of the passes" in terms of his "tormented" relations with Auden we cannot know. But in the context of a book with a small, close readership, its peculiar susceptibility to multiple interpretation is intriguing. Like many of Auden's poems from the period, it projects the reader as an insider able to set this poem within some larger scheme. "Control of the passes was, he saw, the key / To this new district"—the definite articles, personal pronoun, and demonstrative adjective all put this poem *in medias res,* but do not specify the *res.* The question "But who would get it?" can then be read self-referentially: "Who would understand it?" "It" may stand not only for the "new district" of a potential lover's body but for the text itself—"*this* new district." If the poem allegorizes homosexual desire and its frustration, it is also a test in which the (desiring) poet and (desiring?) reader vie for interpretive power—control of the passes of meaning.[25] This power, for which cruising would be an ideal analogy, involves the ability to signify duplicitously and to interpret with an eye to duplicity. If so, the spy's failure itself may be deceptive. Read in the context of Auden's relations with Carritt and McElwee, the poem seems less an epitaph to desire than an ongoing seduction, for whether Auden is the "trained spy" who is caught out, or the "bogus guide" setting his "trap" for the reader, the poem exposes *some*one's desire.

Does Auden want the reader to "get it"? And if so, what? Some readers, it seems safe to say, were meant to get nothing. One recipient of the 1928 *Poems,* E. R. Dodds, later confessed, "I found many of [the poems] maddeningly obscure (as I still do); the connections of thought often baffled me; but I recognized the tones of a new, completely individual voice and the presence of some highly compressed message which was trying to force its way into expression" (Carpenter, *Auden* 83). Such responses, which are common in early reviews of Auden's work, are the germ of universalizing academic readings of his poetry; in the absence of privileged knowledge, the reader assumes that it is the abstruseness or compression of what is being said that makes it obscure. But it is worth asking what is being "compressed." My reading of "Control of the passes" suggests that its obscurity points not simply to Auden's "individuality" or "originality" but to his encoding of the unspeakable and his concern with unspeakability. Even with regard to insiders, however, it is not so easy to be certain of Auden's intentions. As a poem about closeted desire, "Control of the passes" portrays a scenario illuminated by biographical data. But however thoroughly we may recover the sociology of the closet in which Auden was living and writing, we cannot fix his intentions for this poem. As a solicitation of interpretive attention and a game of textual erotics, it hardly implies revelation as a more desired end than concealment. If Auden is "cruising the reader," it is not very hopefully—the fate he imagines is a double bind of disastrous discovery and self-induced failure. Spender later recalled that as an undergraduate, Auden sometimes "gave the impression of playing an intellectual game with himself and with others"—a quality he connects with Auden's early poems (*World* 49). His comment that "in the long run [Auden] was rather isolated" implicitly reads such detachment as self-destructive. Still, if coding bears witness to the constraints of the closet, the spy is also an empowering mask for the closeted poet precisely because he stays so overtly undercover. Perhaps frustration serves Auden's purposes—after all, part of the aim of a coded poetic is that some *not* "get it." To "get it" has another slang meaning as well, and as an erotic game, "Control of the passes" seems aimed more at ongoing play with sexual secrecy than with anyone "getting it." As a poetic game, it offers an open-ended exercise that does not expose the poet's intentions so much as test the reader's interpretive and erotic orientations.

This poem has implications for the Auden group's "joint war against censorship," for if it testifies to discursive and erotic repression, its resistance is compromised by the very coding with which it contests the closet. One might say that it forswears victory for opposition, accepting the closet in order to exploit it for an erotics of textual obscurity. And as an allegory about closeted subjectivity, it undermines the expressionist assumptions about identity implied by a simple war to liberate speech and desire. The persona of the spy would seem to intimate a stable, secret self beneath the cover, but that stability dissolves in the second quatrain, where the spy's own side betrays him: the enemy is within as well as without, so that any demarcation between friend and foe, public and private, is uncertain. The very secrecy necessary under a regime of censorship dissolves the subject into contending forces of desire and prohibition. Paradoxically, then, this *is* a poem of impersonality, for it witnesses to a dissolution of subjectivity and personal agency into impersonal forces. It is, however, not the impersonality of a poem like *The Waste Land*, the young Auden's esteem for Eliot notwithstanding. The psychic dissolution it portrays does not reflect spiritual or metaphysical crisis; it proceeds from the social forces defining the closet, about which Auden is ambivalent. Toward the unknowing reader, he stands poised between motives of revelation and concealment: the desire to preserve and exploit privileged knowledge for poetic power, and the desire to overcome the gulf between poet and reader in the hope that the fractures of the closeted subject can be healed.

III

As an adolescent, Auden began writing very much in the Romantic vein that continued to define "poetry" for middle-class readers in the early twentieth century. The 1928 *Poems* bears traces of later influences, like Eliot and Hopkins, but it is haunted by Wordsworthian Nature, even if only in the attenuated manner of Edward Thomas.[26] As an indicator of Auden's poetic "growth," this book shows him very much in stylistic transition. But this stylistic uncertainty indicates something more—a breaking away from Wordsworthian subjectivity, with its normative assumptions about the relation between poet and reader in a lyric of sincerity. The 1928 *Poems* is therefore also a crucial document in Auden's development of a lyric mode capable of engaging, under the constraints of the closet, not only a coterie readership but a wider one.

The remainder of this chapter considers how a number of Auden's best-known works in the 1928 *Poems* transmute the Greater Romantic Lyric, with its conventions of sincerity and self-revelation, into a kind of lyric of the closet, mapping the duplicity of signs in and through landscape.[27] In place of a redemptive drama of the recovery of psychic coherence and common humanity in Nature, Auden's landscape poems offer a revelation of alienation and social difference. For instead of adopting a voice of sincerity and openness, they hover equivocally between revelation and concealment, exploiting this tension for a self-conscious poetic masquerade where the unknown may—or may not—be the unspeakable. Auden's masquerade as secret agent conjures an erotics of reading and writing without consummation—an ongoing solicitation of the reader but a refusal to throw off disguise.

Auden's characteristic landscape first appears in juvenilia describing limestone quarries, cliffs and valleys, lead mines and mills. At this stage of his work, such elements comprise a private, vaguely numinous (though not obviously erotic) realm into which the speaker ventures—even if only, as in "Lead's the Best," to dismiss these images as merely "Themes for a poet's pretty sunset thoughts."[28] Auden begins to transform the Greater Romantic Lyric when this landscape becomes a medium for exploring homosexual desire, leading the reader into a terrain in which the healing power of Nature is deconstructed, rather than sentimentally played out.

Thus, in "From the very first coming down," which Auden later revealed was occasioned by his feelings for McElwee, romantic rejection challenges the speaker's assumption of the benignity of Nature.

> From the very first coming down
> Into a new valley with a frown
> Because of the sun and a lost way,
> You certainly remain. . . .   (*EA* 25)

Two kinds of literary settings, Jacob Stockinger notes, figure promi-
nently as redeemed spaces for same-sex desire: the open country and
the enclosed room (143). The latter, of course, can signify the imprisonment of the closet as well as the safety of secrecy. The best examples
of the open country as redeemed same-sex space are in Whitman's poetry and the greenwood of Forster's *Maurice*. Similarly here: we may
see Auden's lyric exploration of a "new valley" as enacting a conventional retreat to Nature as an escape from social constraints. But the
opening lines are unsettling in ways their relaxed rhythm makes it easy
to miss. The "frown" may come from "the sun and a lost way," or not:
the addressee may be finding himself "lost" in more than a spatial
sense. As it happens, the speaker's assertion that "You certainly remain" turns out to be mistaken. He receives a letter "Speaking of
much but not to come"—canceling any illusion that Nature erases the
closet, not just by conveying rejection or inhibition, but by proving
the writer's physical distance.

   Conventionally enough, the speaker responds to loss by trying to
recover some relation between Nature and Self:

> I, decent with the seasons, move
> Different or with a different love,
> Nor question overmuch the nod,
> The stone smile of this country god
> That never was more reticent,
> Always afraid to say more than it meant.

In seeking consolation in natural cycles, these lines assume a composure rather more studied than it first seems. The speaker—so "decent
with the seasons" in the face of loss—is not unlike Nature, "this country god" who, like the beloved, gives nothing away with a smile. The
handling of sound and rhythm in the last four lines is beautiful, and
the analogy between Nature and the beloved is itself subtle and "reti-

cent" in the skeptical, latter-day Romantic manner of Hardy or Edward Thomas. But the lines' implications are quite at odds with their controlled tone and form. As an inscrutable male deity "Always afraid to say more than it meant," Nature is very much in the closet, and its sinister "stone smile" recalls Mortmerean duplicity more than the "presence that disturbs" but comforts Wordsworth. Auden's country god may not betray the heart that loves him either, but only in the most ironic sense. For Nature turns out to be but an extension of the social world of censorship and constraint, where equivocal signs suggest a lot but give nothing away. Nor does this text: the lyric subject is as reticent about his feelings as the writer of the letter, who is neither named nor gendered in the poem.

In spite of these tensions, however, the relatively poised syntax and idiom of this lyric have more in common with Auden's juvenilia than with the other landscape poems in the 1928 *Poems*. By imbuing the Greater Romantic Lyric with Mortmere's semantic and syntactic complexity, Auden radically upped the interpretive ante for the reader. A striking way to see this process, and its relations to sexual politics, is to set a characteristically difficult poem first printed in the 1930 *Poems*, "From scars where kestrels hover," against an earlier version printed only in 1928.

The earlier poem enacts Romantic retreat from the social into the natural realm:

> I chose this lean country
> For seven-day content,
> To satisfy the want
> Of eye and ear, to see
> The slow fastidious line
> That disciplines the fell,
> A curlew's creaking call
> From angles unforeseen,
> The drumming of a snipe,
> Surprise where driven sleet
> Had scalded to the bone
> And streams were acrid yet
> To an unaccustomed lip.   (*EA* 439)

The first line evokes the meditative mode of Greater Romantic Lyric, but what follows connects "this lean country" as much with bodily sensation as with emotional crisis. The "acrid streams" recall the un-dammed waters in "Control of the passes," so it seems likely that, as in several other poems in the 1928 book and in *Paid on Both Sides,* freezing connotes (conventionally enough) frustrated desire. But if so, the speaker is ambivalent about what this terrain offers—"satisfaction," but also erotic "discipline," relief from the "driven sleet" that "scalded to the bone." Perhaps developing out of the reference to "angles unforeseen," the next stanza presents more precisely coded symbol-ism: the speaker "climb[s] a crooked valley," and "crooked," like "left-handed," is a key Auden code word for "homosexual" (see Mendelson, *Early* 225–26).

This "crooked valley" offers a scene reminiscent of Auden's juve-nilia—"Sheds crumbling stone by stone, / The awkward waterwheel / Of a deserted mine." ("Awkward" may also exploit sexual overtones in its obsolete usages: "turned the wrong way, averted, back-handed; not straightforward, oblique" [*OED* B.1].) In the third stanza, this terrain dissolves into fairly explicit sexual vision, implying that the speaker's retreat from the world has been a failed effort at repression:

> Last night, sucked giddy down
> The funnel of my dream,
> I saw myself within
> A buried engine-room.
> Dynamos, boilers, lay
> In tickling silence, I
> Gripping an oily rail,
> Talked feverishly to one
> Who puckered mouth and brow
> In ecstasy of pain,
> "I know, I know, I know"
> And reached his hand for mine.[29]

This stanza seems to portray a wish-fulfillment replete with both oral and anal overtones. The setting of an abandoned engine room at a mine combines both kinds of redeemed space mentioned by Stockinger, and here Auden depicts a moment of sexualized union and reciprocated self-revelation: "I know, I know, I know." The stanza transfigures the sexually innocent, though numinous, terrain of Auden's juvenilia into a distinctly homoerotic analogue to the male body, a "lean country" with secret openings to an empowering interiority. But with its strange suggestions of sadism, this is hardly a benign vision.

The rest of the poem enacts the conventional return to the social, but without any renewal of the speaker. The psychic implications of the dream find no resolution or explanation. Whatever erotic or imaginative consummation it hints at is taken away in the last stanza, where the speaker admits that the quarry he gazes on is "water-logged." The poem closes with a Romantic return that means the death of bodily desire:

> A blackbird's sudden scurry
> Lets broken treetwigs fall
> To shake the torpid pool;
> And breaking from the copse,
> I climb the hill, my corpse
> Already wept, and pass
> Alive into the house.

Where the Wordsworthian subject discovers a healing coalescence of Nature and Mind, Auden exposes visionary imagination as merely the projection of fantasy onto landscape—fantasy born in loss: the "torpid pool" is the pool of Narcissus and a pool of tears. The return to the social—"pass[ing] / Alive into the house"—is not the return of a self healed of schism, but a return to the closet, where the body is a "corpse," the subject only nominally "Alive."

Compared to "From the very first coming down," this is a much less polished poem, for Auden employs undiluted both the structure of Greater Romantic Lyric and its rhetoric of sincerity. The directly sexual third stanza feels dropped into the poem, and while this may be the earliest instance of Auden's standard critique of the narcissism of Romantic epistemology, the speaker's self-pity never becomes particularly interesting. Even so, this poem marks a crucial transition in Auden's move away from a Romantic epistemology and landscape to his own.

The revised version, from the 1930 *Poems*, is much more original and impressive. For rather than portraying the absence of Nature's sanction for desire as a personal crisis, it exploits this situation to confront the reader with a landscape and style of unsettlement:

> From scars where kestrels hover,
> The leader looking over
> Into the happy valley,
> Orchard and curving river,
> May turn away to see
> The slow fastidious line
> That disciplines the fell.
>
> . . . .
>
> The tall unwounded leader
> Of doomed companions, all
> Whose voices in the rock
> Are now perpetual,
> Fighters for no one's sake,
> Who died beyond the border.[30]

Auden's most obvious revision is also his most radical one: he has replaced the lyric "I" with a "leader." This change yields what feels like a more "impersonal," modernist poem, but also because, in Mortmerean fashion, the added lines lend a strong but indeterminate resonance: "The tall, unwounded leader," "voices in the rock," "fighters for no one's sake," "the border." The lines retained from "I chose this lean country" (the "curlew's creaking call," etc.) have in themselves a precision that seems to locate them in perception of a material world. But displaced from a first-person lyric into a context of obscurely portentous language, they no longer ground us in the conventions of Romantic landscape poetry. Is this an erotic terrain, as in "I chose this lean country," an allegorical terrain where the politics of desire are acted out, as in "Control of the passes," or an actual place described in code?

The next stanza only adds to the confusion, asserting (but *who* is

doing the asserting?) that "bravery" means "resisting the temptations /
To skyline operations." "Yet," we are told,

> glory is not new;
> The summer visitors
> Still come from far and wide,
> Choosing their spots to view
> The prize competitors,
> Each thinking that he will
> Find heroes in the wood. . . .

Like the rest of the poem, these clauses have grammatical links that
ought to express logical connection, but since the nouns have no clear
reference or signification, the function of a conjunction like "Yet" is
unclear. It is rather like trying to read a language in which one can
identify parts of speech but cannot define the words. Rather than dramatizing a lyric speaker's retreat to Nature to heal the heart, and then
undercutting the imaginative vision of sexual union, Auden erases any
subject position with which to identify and forces the reader into a position of extreme hermeneutic uncertainty. Auden replaces lyric as moment of communion between poet and reader, with lyric as mode of
alienation: the poet is no longer the guarantor of a unified point of
view. We are left in an epistemological flux where categories like "the
psychic" and "the social" are no longer helpful, where our only guide
is Shreeve's comment to Hearn in "The Railway Accident": " 'I'm not
guaranteeing you'll see anything. And if by any wild chance you do, it
will be something so indefinable that afterwards you won't be sure
that you haven't imagined it' " (Upward 52).

Viewed as a tactic in the Auden group's "joint war against censorship," the poem begins to make social sense. For its peculiar obscurity
implies that someone somewhere knows what it all means. Isherwood
once claimed that Auden's famous obscurity was achieved by salvaging
verses Isherwood liked and inserting them into other poems "regard-
less of grammar or sense": "In this way, whole poems were constructed which were simply anthologies of my favourite lines" ("Some
Notes" 19). Apocryphal as this sounds, this poem really does read as
though it was constructed this way, with the joke on the serious

reader. But the joke also has a sociological meaning. Writing about lesbian poetry, Diana Collecott invokes Michael Riffaterre's concept of the *ungrammatical,* by which "any ungrammaticality within the poem is a sign of grammaticality elsewhere."[31] To make sense of apparent meaninglessness in the work of Audre Lorde and H. D., argues Collecott, one must seek grammaticality in intertextual relations when the text is manifestly ungrammatical. Auden's poem does not present ungrammaticality, exactly, for it hardly lacks syntactic pointers; instead, the ones it has do not help much. But its grammaticality might be meaningfully construed in relation to the work of the Auden group collectively. Its imagery and vocabulary recall not only Mortmere texts like "The Railway Accident" but the fiction of Rex Warner and the poetry of Day-Lewis and Spender. (Spender's 1934 *Poems,* for instance, opens with "He will watch the hawk with an indifferent eye"). This topography, in other words, is textual and intertextual: it exists on the page where the poem is printed, as well as in other texts where Auden or other members of the group conjure it up. Rather than offering a site in which a lyric "I" finds himself psychically whole and affirms his commonality with every reader, Auden's poem dissolves the subject into multiple figures (leader, heroes, fighters, prize competitors, host) that remain opaque in isolation from other texts of the Auden group that imagine a war of liberation.

Such a sociology suggests, further, that this poem may be partly a commentary on a war of sexual and discursive liberation. In a war against constraints on sexuality and expression, heroic endeavor is futile, for

> Heroes are buried who
> Did not believe in death
> And bravery is now
> Not in the dying breath
> But resisting the temptations
> To skyline operations.
> . . . .
> But leaders must migrate:
> "Leave for Cape Wrath to-night,"
> And the host after waiting

> Must quench the lamps and pass
> Alive into the house.

One might say that Auden is offering the group the advice to "lie low" in every sense of "lie." This poem does just that—not making grand statements (like "heroes" who think themselves invincible) but employing a covert discourse that "must migrate" to escape capture. At the same time, secrecy seems to compromise a war against repression, leaving no "leader," just an abandoned "host" who can only leave the field and slip back into the closet ("pass / Alive into the house"). Auden's later title for the poem is apt: "Missing." It describes the fate of heroes who are out in front, but it also captures the sense of loss that pervades his poetry about homosexual desire. It suggests the absence of a governing ego, a "leader" of the psyche. And if it implies that this poem misses the target in a war against repression, it also suggests that the reader may miss the point.

These issues are played out in one of Auden's finest early lyrics from the 1928 *Poems,* later titled "The Watershed." Written two months after "I chose this lean country," it renders the same landscape but very differently. Rather than having a lyric "I" articulate its own disjunction through an external scene, Auden sets us on the border of a private landscape to which entrance is denied. The composition history of this poem shows him drawing on elements from two different kinds of poems: those of a sort he had been writing since adolescence about the lead-mining industry and landscape of the Pennines; and the more recent lyrics motivated by his erotically fraught relationships with friends like McElwee and Carritt (see *J* 219). The result is not, however, an elucidation of the nexus of associations that constitute his private psychosexual reality. Instead, Auden effectively inverts the conventions of Greater Romantic Lyric, replacing first-person, meditative description, with hortatory address, making the reader survey a terrain that bespeaks not imaginative community but difference.

The notorious obscurity of the opening comes from a relentlessly destabilizing syntax that never settles into a governing point of view:

> Who stands, the crux left of the watershed,
> On the wet road between the chafing grass

> Below him sees dismantled washing-floors,
> Snatches of tramline running to the wood,
> An industry already comatose,
> Yet sparsely living. A ramshackle engine
> At Cashwell raises water; for ten years
> It lay in flooded workings until this,
> Its latter office, grudgingly performed. . . .   (*EA* 22)

Like allusions to "this new district" or "the happy valley," these lines specify without explaining; the difficulty is to know whether these words have referents or merely signifieds. The diction seems archaic and stilted, like a beginner's translation from another language: "Who" seems to mean "whoever," but we are apt to read it first as an interrogative pronoun ("Who stands?"). To "stand" implies a stability promptly subverted by "the crux left of the watershed," a phrase with no grammatical connection to the clause in which it appears. As several critics note, "left of" can mean "to the left of" or "left behind by," so the phrase could denote a relation in space or in time.[32] "Crux" and "watershed" could refer to a physical place, but they also have abstract meanings. The movement of the poem extends this very ambiguity—we are "shown" the detritus of a decayed mining district, "[a]n industry already comatose," but while it is offered as significant, one cannot be sure whether it is an abstract or concrete topography, a physical or mental world. Such ambiguity serves sublime ends in Greater Romantic Lyric, indicating a revelatory coalescence of subject and object, but here it is the source of hermeneutical uncertainty at the start.

In the context of the 1930 *Poems* this landscape can be read as a politically charged terrain, the face of Depression-era England that Auden describes in a poem like "Get there if you can," his 1930 rewrite of "Locksley Hall." But in the 1928 *Poems,* these lines resonate with Auden's imagery of erotic frustration. We "stand" (whatever that means) not at the source of power or climax—"the watershed"—but at a site of obscure conjunction: "the crux." A "ramshackle engine" has been revived to pump water, "Its latter office, grudgingly performed"—an activity analogous to building dams. Then, in notably passive constructions, more details appear, not of this landscape itself but of a history buried there:

> And further here and there, though many dead
> Lie under the poor soil, some acts are chosen
> Taken from recent winters; two there were
> Cleaned out a damaged shaft by hand, clutching
> The winch a gale would tear them from; one died
> During a storm, the fells impassable. . . .

Why are these "acts . . . chosen / Taken from recent winters"? By whom? The lineation provokes further questions, separating two participles that are not quite synonyms: "taken" arrives with the abruptness of a dropped stitch or a skip in a record, suggesting something lost in the telling, but perhaps suppressed. We may want to read the winch and shaft in sexual terms, but we also notice that their significance is both rhetorically emphasized and withheld. This heroic pair (such a reading might run) are trying to regain the empowering depths dreamed of in "I chose this lean country"; they emblematize a group fight for sexual liberation. But if so, they fail, and their inaccessibility is also a figure for this poem's secretiveness. They remain codes whose meaning is "buried," like those "Heroes . . . who / Did not believe in death."

The second stanza warns away the reader: "Go home, now, stranger, proud of your young stock, / Stranger, turn back again, frustrate and vexed: / This land, cut off, will not communicate." The division between private and public openly turns against the reader here, reinforcing earlier concealments, making it impossible to feel sure of what we are being warned away from. What is striking, however, is Auden's infusion of the language of perception with tropes of erotic power and pain:

> you may hear the wind
> Arriving driven from the ignorant sea
> To hurt itself on pane, on bark of elm
> Where sap unbaffled rises, being Spring. . . .

Auden took these lines from "Quique Amavit" (March 1927), an obscure lament for erotic frustration and self-consciousness he dedicated (in an allusion to Shakespeare's *Sonnets*) "To the onlie begetter Mr

W.L."—William McElwee (see *J* 181–82). As in "From scars where
kestrels hover," the sensations expressed by a lyric "I" in an earlier
poem are here displaced outward, in this case projected onto a "you."
The poem ends, however, by refusing any consummation of understanding: "But seldom this. Near you, taller than grass, / Ears poise
before decision, scenting danger." The obscurity of this threat is also its
power, for its defiant gestures of concealment only excite curiosity,
teasing rather than defusing interpretive desire: we want to know what
is so dangerous.

Accordingly, we might speculate that the poem masks Auden's uncertainty or fear about the relation between sexual frustration and a
private terrain in which he had long felt a deep but quite mysterious
psychic investment. From this angle, the poem would testify to the
power of the closet to forestall self-knowledge. But to psychoanalyze
Auden thus is to embark on a journey in which we never can be sure
we have arrived anywhere. In the words of "Control of the passes," we
would be walking into a trap for a bogus guide who has, after all,
warned us, "Don't go there." Auden declines to use a numinous, private topography so as to unfold a Wordsworthian gesture toward our
common humanity. Instead, he preserves this topography in the closet
but flaunts its closetedness, using its cruces to make the reader feel repression at least as much as the poet. The poem becomes, in other
words, an anti-closet that exploits self-enclosure, turning silence enforced from without into a refusal to let the outsider in. In his seductive refusals of understanding, Auden puts all readers of this poem in
the closet: members of the group—whose losing fight against repression is figured here—but even more, the uninitiated reader who stands
uncertainly in a closet of interpretive repression.

IV

Notwithstanding the influence of *The Waste Land,* Auden's landscape
poems reject both Romantic subjectivity as conceived by Wordsworth
and Eliotic high modernist impersonality. Instead, they revive a perfor-
mative mode favored by writers like Byron and Wilde, who exploited
the tensions between public and private, normal and deviant, finding

truth neither in sincere self-revelation nor in transcendent objectivity. Years later Auden would gloss this aesthetic by writing that "love, or truth in any serious sense . . . is a reticence" (*CP* 621). But he recognized early on that a poetry of reticence also makes an effective tool for literary self-promotion and the promotion of the group, and his adaptation of the discourse of Mortmere was crucial to such ends. This poetry has its risks—taken to an extreme, it verges on total concealment, a nonsense poetry that defeats its own efforts at seduction:

> Having abdicated with comparative ease
> And dismissed the greater part of your friends;
> Escaped in a submarine
> With a false beard, hoping the ports were watched.
> How shall we greet your arrival;
> For it isn't snowing
> And no one will take you for a spy.   (*EA* 45)

The poem goes on like this for another twenty-three lines, amassing absurd details in a knowing, insider's tone. But neither the syntax nor the language is interesting enough to make us slow down and care about what possible dramatic context might make sense of the poem's details. Our inability to do so may well be the point—so that the only dramatic situation here is the scene of our own reading. If so, the poem may form a test of coterie membership—a performance where signs are deployed solely to create an atmosphere and tone manifestly and comically secretive. In this regard, to search for a precise meaning implied for the inside reader would be to fail the test, revealing oneself an outsider.[33]

By contrast, poems like "Control of the passes" and "Who stands, the crux left of the watershed" are really *more* challenging, for they place us in an odd realm that threatens distinctions between revelation and concealment: what we know, what we don't know, and what we suspect. And in conflating sexual desire with an ongoing desire to *know*, Auden's poems suggest both the ancient biblical sense of "knowledge" and Roland Barthes's postmodern meditations on textual pleasure:

Is not the most erotic portion of a body *where the garment gapes?* In perversion (which is the realm of textual pleasure) there are no "erogenous zones" . . . it is intermittence, as psychoanalysis has so rightly stated, which is erotic: the intermittence of skin flashing between two articles of clothing . . . it is this flash itself which seduces, or rather: the staging of an appearance-as-disappearance.

(Barthes 9–10)

To be sure, Auden's coded poems of the closet might seem to revel much less than Barthes in the tension between revelation and concealment. Typically, after all, Auden conveys some degree of nostalgia for revelatory expression: "This land, cut off, will not communicate." One is tempted, therefore, to say that for Auden, textual pleasure masks a yearning for sincerity, for removal of all garments. But in poetry that treats subjectivity as itself a masquerade, all desires are by definition suspect, even—maybe especially—an implied desire for openness between reader and writer: love, like truth, *is* a reticence here—"the staging of an appearance-as-disappearance"—and there is no resolving the contradiction into a comforting certainty about what Auden really wants.

But the political and psychic contradictions of this poetic strategy are impossible to ignore. We recall Spender's comment on *The Temple:* "In writing it I had the sense of sending home to friends and colleagues dispatches from a front line in our joint war against censorship" (xi). In Auden's early poetry, the self-referential imagery of warfare is often imagery of doom; this battle to liberate expression and desire is a losing one, the brotherhood of heroes dying or dead. In "Look there! the sunk road winding" (1931), Auden announces the imminent End Time, "The sound behind our back / Of glaciers calving," but "we" are not really up to the fight:

In legend all were simple,
And held the straitened spot;
But we in legend not,
Are not simple.

> In weakness how much further;
> Along what crooked route
> By hedgehog's gradual foot,
> Or fish's fathom.   (*EA* 56–57)

As a poem in code, this constitutes another volley in the war against censorship. But it also distinguishes the heroism possible in poetic "legend" from the motives of those who write it: "But we in legend not, / Are not simple." "We" are following a "crooked route," our furtiveness ironically linking us to lower forms of life, for like this very poem, "we" are not going straight to the point. The way to overcome sexual and discursive repression, after all, is not to fool the censors. In this war, the "crooked route" is as much the disease as the cure, and the last line in each stanza, unrhymed and metrically awkward, bespeaks constriction and collapse: "But we in legend not, / Are not simple." Auden foresees a final battle, but the apocalypse he pictures will consume the would-be heroes:

> Bitter the blue smoke rises
> From garden bonfires lit,
> To where we burning sit:
> Good, if it's thorough.
>
> It won't be us who eavesdrop
> In days of luck and heat,
> Timing the double beat
> At last together.

The crooked prophets of desire, "burning" in the hills, will get their revolution. But real consummation—"the double beat / At last together," both metrical and sexual—will belong to others. The contradictions of the closet that were poetically empowering for Auden, in other words, seemed another matter when he thought about them politically and psychologically. And in the late 1920s, he was thinking about them a great deal, and with impressive theoretical sophistication.

Chapter 2

"THE QUESTION IS WHAT DO WE MEAN BY SEX": DIAGNOSIS AND DISORDER

The word "diagnosis" has long been invoked to describe one mode of Auden's early writing, and justly so. He was fond of quasi-scientific idioms and a prognostic pose, and some of his best-known early poems portray the Condition of England with a pathologist's eye for symptomatic detail. His work reflects a wider sense in the 1920s that Freud's ideas not only authorized aesthetic innovation but might, in tandem with Marx, help reanimate poetry as a social force. But it is clear that Auden's interest in the curative promise of psychoanalysis was at least as much personal as it was political: it was "a change of heart" that he famously petitioned for, not a change of government (*EA* 36). It is also clear, especially in his private prose writings, that the disorders that preoccupied him implicate some major schemas for theorizing sexuality in the 1920s. This decade, after all, saw the growing stature not only of Freud, but also of thinkers concerned less with applying science to the erotic life than with recovering sexuality's moral and spiritual energy. For Auden, the most important of these were D. H. Lawrence and John Layard, the intellectual guru he met in Berlin in 1928.

Few writers, in fact, evince as clearly as Auden the intellectual and cultural effects of the "medicalization" of sexual deviance. Advanced by Foucault, this term denotes the Victorian shift from the traditional religious censure of deviant sexual acts to medical discourses that invented the homosexual as a distinct identity (*History* 1, 36–49). Along with renewed efforts at legal prosecution of "the pervert," such discourses underwrote new institutions and mechanisms of control. But as Foucault also observes, the new discourses of sexuality were not just agents of repression: in making sexuality speakable, they also enabled the affirmation of new self-understandings and sexual identities.

Auden's life in the late 1920s reflects this duality. In 1928 he traveled to see a psychoanalyst in Spa, Belgium, apparently hoping to be cured of homosexuality (see Carpenter, *Auden* 82–84). He wasn't cured, but he continued to concentrate his energies on trying to make theoretical sense of his sexuality. The most compelling evidence of this attempt can be seen in the journal he kept in early 1929, when he was living in Berlin. The right-hand pages of this notebook, written in diary form, are devoted largely to his sex life, recording names of boys he picked up, when and where, and what he did with them. The tone of one entry typifies the Auden group's response to Weimar Germany: "The sense of bare flesh, the blue sky through the glass and the general sexy atmosphere made me feel like a participant in a fertility rite."[1] The left side, by contrast, offers an engrossing, chaotic record of Auden's abstract and abstruse theories about psychology, poetry, and—quite often—sexuality. His journal makes clear, first, that however busy his sex life, Auden viewed his homosexuality as a psychological and intellectual crux. His musings also show that far from being tangential to his other theoretical concerns—the relation of mind to body, the course of psychic and political progress and decay, what modern poetry should be like—Auden's worries about his own sexuality were deeply entangled in such matters. And notwithstanding his evident anxiety about and wish to cure his homosexuality, the journal testifies to the real value that psychology—Freudian, Lawrentian, and otherwise—had for his efforts at self-understanding.

Auden's 1929 Berlin journal constitutes crucial evidence for this chapter, which studies the connections of his early poetry to various theories about sexuality. Like the secret agent, the diagnostician specializes in reading signs, and consummately so in Auden, with his interest in Freud and Layard: the theoretical gaze is only a step away from the erotic gaze. Auden's theories about desire and identity, therefore, are much concerned with what he calls, after Lawrence, "self-consciousness"—a disorder in the relation between mind and body. Like Lawrence and Layard (and Blake), Auden often sees health in the release of desire from the prison of mind. But just as his poetry of the closet stages a tension between revelation and concealment, his theories about self-consciousness are contradictory. Not only does his poetry of diagnosis depend on rationalist detachment to map the convolutions of self-consciousness, his coded poetry implicitly valorizes the power of mind. Accordingly, Auden also theorizes the self-conscious mind as an evolutionary advance, rather than a disease, thus raising the other major theme in his poetry of diagnosis, and the focus of the second part of this chapter: growth. Like Lawrence, he tends to see disease in the light of developmental models of culture and self. But again, Auden contradicts himself on what sexual deviance means. He often treats homosexuality as symptomatic of a stifling past—psychic, familial, cultural, and even biological. He thus reflects a broad but hardly uniform theoretical heritage: Lawrence and Freud, but also the ongoing influence of Victorian degeneration theory. At the same time, Weimar Germany points for Auden to a future of sexual freedom, so he is also apt to see the release of bodily desire from mind as crucial to the liberation of self and culture from a repressive past.

In following these contradictions through Auden's poems, we see him struggling with problems he never resolves at a theoretical level. But this work embodies a remarkable moment in lesbian and gay literary history. Auden is surely one of the earliest poets to engage extensively with recognizably modern conceptualizations of sexual identity. At the same time, his very effort to use poetry as a deliberate mode of both cultural diagnosis and self-diagnosis testifies to the historical importance of the aesthetic as a mode of homosexual self-contemplation.

I

Shortly after arriving in Berlin in the fall of 1928, Auden met John Layard, an English anthropologist with whom he lived for a time and had a relationship occasionally the stuff of melodrama.[2] Layard was a disciple of Homer Lane, an unconventional American educator who taught the basic goodness of impulse, the suppression of which leads to neurosis. One of Auden's journal entries puts Lane's ethic (as con-

strued by Layard) thus: " 'Be good and you will be happy' is a danger-
ous inversion. 'Be happy and you will be good' is the truth" (*EA* 300).
Much of Auden's journal is taken up with analysis of his relations with
Layard, whose intellectual influence on him has been described by
many, starting with Isherwood.[3] But in "Letter to Lord Byron" (1936),
Auden himself best explained the attraction of these ideas:

> Part came from Lane, and part from D. H. Lawrence;
>   Gide, though I didn't know it then, gave part.
> They taught me to express my deep abhorrence
>   If I caught anyone preferring Art
>   To Life and Love and being Pure-in-Heart.
> I lived with crooks but seldom was molested;
> The Pure-in-Heart can never be arrested.
>
> He's gay; no bludgeonings of chance can spoil it,
>   The Pure-in-Heart loves all men on a par,
> And has no trouble with his private toilet. . . . (*P* 333–34)

More than any detached summary of the ideas in question, these lines
suggest that Auden was attracted to Layard's theories largely because
they justified an ethic of sexual liberation—being "gay" and loving "all
men on a par." To enjoy what Berlin had to offer was to embrace
goodness, to be "Pure-in-Heart." Code words and double entendres
notwithstanding, Auden is far less coy on this score than his critics,
who have little to say about this aspect of Layard's influence.[4] The
diary on the right-hand pages of his journal shows how much he
sought to put Layard's ideas into practice.

Nevertheless, Layard's ideas are somewhat more complex than Auden suggests in "Letter to Lord Byron," and their complications did affect Auden's thinking. First, "God" equals "our desires," but in our
fallen state, He "appears unreasonable because He has been put in
prison and driven wild" by the "Devil" of "conscious control," which is
"reasonable and sane" (Isherwood, *Lions* 239). Second, bodily diseases
are symptoms of psychic disorder, and to treat them as simply physical
is to follow the Devil. Thus cancer reflects a refusal of creativity, while

deafness and nearsightedness seek "to shut out the exterior world" (241). While this symptomatology reflects the work of Georg Grod-deck,[5] it is basically a psychologized form of physiognomy that recalls elements of degeneration theory. As for the worship of impulse, the conflict between God and the Devil reads like a simplification of *The Marriage of Heaven and Hell*, with the meanings of Blake's "God" and "Satan" reversed. But as Auden and others have noted, the main sources are more recent—Gide and D. H. Lawrence. Taken as a whole, Layard's theories offered Auden contradictory ways of evaluating self-consciousness. The worship of desire over reason reflected a Law-rentian denigration of self-consciousness, but Auden's application of the theory of psychosomatic illness predicated cure on a highly self-conscious hermeneutics of body and mind.

Perhaps it should not be surprising that Auden was more intellectu-ally engaged by Layard's hermeneutics of disease than by his worship of impulse. Out of all of Auden's poems in this period extolling desire, only one is relatively uninterested in self-consciousness—the 1930 song "What's in your mind, my dove, my coney" (*EA* 56). It is an advice poem in the voice of a lover, and this is rhetorically fitting, given the prescriptive elements in Layard's ideas. The speaker asks, "Do thoughts grow like feathers, the dead end of life. . . ?" His answer to this Lawrentian question—to sex-in-the-head—is to shift briskly into carpe diem mode:

> Rise with the wind, my great big serpent;
> Silence the birds and darken the air;
> Change me with terror, alive in a moment;
> Strike for the heart and have me there.

Implicitly these lines are an argument against thought—their imagery designed to do little more than connote (and promote) emotional and sexual arousal—and they hardly demand much interpretation. Not sur-prisingly, Auden more frequently writes about the condition of self-consciousness affecting the silent addressee of this poem. In the 1929 song "It's no use raising a shout" (*EA* 42–43), the problem is the same, but the solution less clear:

> In my spine there was a base,
> And I knew the general's face:
> But they've severed all the wires,
> And I can't tell what the general desires.

The Lawrentian anatomy, with its great sources of life in the nether regions, has been sundered, leaving mind with the same refrain, stanza after stanza: "Here am I, here are you: / But what does it mean? What are we going to do?"

The contest between desiring body and self-conscious mind is the subject of another, more complex poem adapting Mortmerean tropes of warfare. In mode, it is rather like a blazon, but rhetorically it too is a kind of advice poem. Auden's annoyed 1945 title is helpful here: "Shut Your Eyes and Open Your Mouth." Like many of his later titles, it makes fun of his youthful work, in this case telling the reader, in effect, to skip the printed text and to seek wisdom elsewhere. But his title also distills the poem's message quite wittily:

> Sentries against inner and outer,
> At stated interval is feature;
> And how shall enemy on these
> Make sudden raid or lasting peace?
> For bribery were vain to try
> Against the incorruptible eye
> Too amply paid with tears, the chin
> Has hairs to hide its weakness in,
> And proud bridge and indignant nostril
> Nothing to do but to look noble. (*EA* 33)

Their figurative workings fairly plain, these lines might serve as a key to Auden's poems about the closet. The Mortmerean sentries are obviously the facial "features" that solicit erotic attention but stand guard against the potential "enemy," who threatens through "bribery" and exploits "weakness." At the same time, the poem suggests the price of self-consciousness, the sentries guarding a wealth of tears amassed in frustration. The remainder of the poem, in fact, reads self-protection entirely in terms of repression, focussing on another less reliable facial "feature": "But in between these lies the mouth; / Watch that, that you may parley with: / There strategy comes easiest. . . ." The mouth is ever willing to become a double agent:

> It will do murder or betray
> For either party equally,
> Yielding at last to a close kiss
> It will admit tongue's soft advance,
> So longed for, given in abandon,
> Given long since, had it but known.

If the kiss symbolizes the mouth's disloyalty, its refusal to be faithful to the charge of guarding frontiers, these lines are also about speech—the way the mouth wields language beyond the mind's control. Looking back, we see that the words of the poem began to be double-edged once we got to the mouth, which "lies" on the face "in between" chin and brow, which will "admit" the tongue, and with which "you" can "parley." The "you" here is also ambiguous. It can refer to the defensive self or to a "you" seeking entrance. What starts as an analysis of the self-conscious mind in control of the body ends up offering the enemy a map of invasion routes. By the last line, any distinction between inner and outer enemies is moot: from the perspective of the beginning, the poem's point is the enemy's—that the self-conscious mind is fighting what it really wants, which is to abdicate to the body. As Auden's later title so aptly suggests, the poem is a symptom of the problem just by being so witty and mental: the only cure is to "Shut Your Eyes and Open Your Mouth."

"When man became self-conscious," one entry in Auden's journal asserts, "he created his most important detachable organ, the intellect, and since it was itself living, the most dangerous. Intellect alone can co-ordinate desires. It alone can set them at each other's throats" (*EA* 297). This passage suggests as well as any how much Auden is influenced—and troubled—by Lawrence's ideas about self-consciousness. Like Lawrence he is at pains to theorize the moral meaning and value of desire as a problem of the relation between mind and body. Auden sees the birth of self-consciousness as the Fall—a formulation that in itself ascribes no moral value to desires or their rational control. His is a discourse of health, not morality, and it therefore implies no moral judgment about desire. On the other hand, the healthy ideal of desires "co-ordinated by Intellect" recalls the thoroughly orthodox belief that Reason should govern Passion. It also brings to mind Freud, who saw a scientific imperative in bringing reason to bear on the erotic life, and linked culture to the rational taming of the unconscious.

Auden's uncertainty in his journal about the value of self-consciousness reflects a vacillation between Freud and Lawrence, but this uncertainty is charged with a linkage between self-consciousness and homosexuality. The key text for this linkage in Auden's thought was Lawrence's *Fantasia of the Unconscious* (1922). Lawrence, of course, attacked what he saw as Freud's scientism, and *Fantasia* makes this clear at the start. But however different their idioms and aims, Lawrence's views often parallel Freud's, as is especially clear in his discussion of homosexuality, which recalls Freud on narcissism.[6] To be sure, Lawrence uses neither the word "narcissism" nor the word "homosexuality" in *Fantasia,* and his system of "upper" and "lower" planes of the self is homegrown. But the similarity to Freud is obvious as Lawrence describes the dangers facing the child (i.e. son) in puberty if his parents (i.e. mother) have wrongly been treating him as an adult, in the modern fashion:

> Child and parent intensely linked in adult love-sympathy and love-will, on the upper plane, and in the child, the deeper centers aroused, but finding no correspondent, no objective, no polarized connection with another person. . . .
>
> This is how introversion begins. . . . There *must* be some reaction. And so you get, first and foremost, self-consciousness, an intense consciousness in the upper self of the lower self. This is the first disaster. Then you get the upper body exploiting the lower body.
>
> . . . The mind becomes full of sex: and always, in an introvert, of his *own* sex.
>
> (172–73)

Instead of bodily directed sexual desire, Lawrence says, the result is sex-in-the-head: "The child does not so much want to *act* as to *know*. The thought of actual sex connection is usually repulsive. . . . This is the secret of our introversion and perversion to-day" (173–74). While it is easy to wonder why "perversion" results from self-consciousness, and not the other way around, Auden's ideas on self-consciousness owe much to Lawrence. For Auden too, homosexuality is a problem of self-consciousness, an awareness of body as separate from mind. The poem "Sentries against inner and outer" exemplifies this linkage quite clearly, particularly in its implication that desire must be released from a sterile, purely internal economy.

But one assumption of Auden's poetry about self-consciousness and desire is radically at odds with Lawrence—the idea that same-sex desire can ever have a healthy, outward object, rather than being the paradigm of incurably self-directed desire. More importantly, Auden expends a good deal of space in his journal theorizing the positive value of self-consciousness—not as the inhibition of the closet, but as the evolving subject's realization of the liberation of mind from body. Auden's interest in such a view is understandable. We recall that Lawrence infers "the secret of our introversion and perversion to-day" from the fact that "The child does not so much want to *act* as to *know*." By contrast, Auden's poetry of the closet portrays bodily desire as kindled by epistemological desire.

Two important entries in his Berlin journal seek to theorize and justify a poetry of self-consciousness:

> The progress of man seems to be in a direction away from nature. The development of consciousness may be compared with the breaking away of the child from the Oedipus relation. Just as one must be weaned from one's mother, one must be weaned from the Earth Mother (Unconscious?). Along with the growing self-consciousness of man during the last 150 years, as illustrated for example by Dostoevsky, has developed Wordsworthian nature-worship, the nostalgia for the womb of Nature which cannot be reentered by a consciousness increasingly independent but afraid. Rousseau is a nice example of the two tendencies. The motor-car and other improvements in quick transport are altering this and I am glad. The first sign of

change is an impoverishment in feeling, noticed and criticised by many. This is [the] necessary accompaniment to weaning; every adolescent feels it.

Mind has been evolved from body, i.e. from the Not-self, whose thinking is community-thinking, and therefore symbolic. While Yeats is right that great poetry in the past has been symbolic, I think we are reaching a point in the development of the mind where symbols are becoming obsolete in poetry, as the mind, or non-communistic self, does not think in this way. This does not invalidate its use in past poetry, but it does invalidate it in modern poetry, just as an attempt to write in Chaucerian English would be academic.

(*EA* 298)

Together, these passages present a brief literary history, a critique of Romanticism, a theory of modernism (and of modernity), a self-analysis, and a theory of identity. The critique of Wordsworth, in fact, masks a theory of Auden's own poetic growth away from the Romanticism of his juvenilia. Transposing Schiller's concept of the sentimental into Freudian terms, Auden implies that his own early, neo-Georgian lyrics, like Wordsworthian Romanticism, exemplified an inability to outgrow consoling but false myths about the symbiosis of self and nature. Modern poetry must accept, as Dostoevsky did but Yeats did not, the parallel divisions between mind and body, Self and Not-Self, consciousness and nature. What Lawrence describes in *Fantasia of the Unconscious* as a diseased condition of modernity, Auden posits in his journal as an evolutionary advance away from the "Earth Mother."

While Auden casts these ideas in universalizing terms, his statements illuminate his poetry of the closet in important ways. We have seen how his alienating inversions of Greater Romantic Lyric solicit but thwart the Wordsworthian desire of "independent consciousness" to return to Nature. The truth such poems tell—which Auden suggests here is the *only* one they can—is an anticommunal truth of the modern disjunction of mind and body, the death of unity of being.[7] The figures these poems manipulate are not "symbols," for they do not invoke any transcendent realm. Instead, these poems offer signs whose numinous aura is the effect not of immanent meaning but of meaning rhetorically withheld. They are textual analogues to a sexuality that is both self-conscious and—the age-old reproach—"unnatural."

Nevertheless, it is easy to suspect Auden's journal passages of a fair amount of wishful thinking. While his poetic games of knowledge exploit the split between mind and body for textual play, these are not poems of mind totally freed of the body. Rather, these are poems that cannot let go of the split, for they also portray this split as loss.[8] For that matter, Auden's own theory rests on the Oedipal paradigm, according to which male homosexuality is not a rejection of maternal love but its reaffirmation. These problems will be taken up later, however. Here we need to see how Auden actually writes poetry extolling homosexual self-consciousness.

In a 1930 poem later titled "The Question" (*EA* 54–55), Auden adopted the riddling manner of Laura Riding's poetry to write his most subtle early poem about homosexual desire and self-consciousness:

> To ask the hard question is simple;
> Asking at meeting
> With the simple glance of acquaintance
> To what these go
> And how these do:
> To ask the hard question is simple,
> The simple act of the confused will.

This stanza places the reader in a very strange position. The vocabulary is not challenging—far from it; apart from lines four and five, the syntax is quite easy. Yet this is one of the most difficult poems Auden wrote. We are apt to wonder, almost immediately, "What *is* the question?" But the simplicity of idiom suggests that we should not have to, that this should all be transparent. Our readerly uncertainty is not Mortmerean, for there is little implication that meaning is being deliberately withheld, that ignorance comes from being an outsider. Rather, the poem is difficult because it functions at a level of extreme abstraction. It is as close as Auden ever comes to the nonsymbolic, anticommunal poetry of pure mind that his journal proposes as the only viable modern poetry.

But if this idea of poetry involves for Auden a link between self-consciousness and homosexuality, it seems likely that the abstractions of this poem are abstractions from something. The "simple glance of acquaintance" (though not really simple at all) is, I suggest, Auden's archetypal figure for sexual encounter—the self-aware, erotic gaze at "meeting"—and its textual analogue in reading. It is here that questions arise of "To what these go / And how these do." Fuller observes that these clauses recall those polite, empty questions we ask upon meeting someone—"Where are you going? How are you doing?"—and he suggests that the poem is posing them as truly profound ones to which there are no easy answers (83). If so, it is an error to abstract too promptly, or we risk missing why such existential questions are mediated by particular social experience. First, in the context of a "glance of acquaintance" at this particular type of "meeting," these are questions to ask about what is being intended in a glance, where pursuing the glance will lead, how well things would work out, and so on. They can also be read as coded questions asked out loud: posed at the "simple glance of acquaintance," such questions as "Where are you going?" and "How are you doing" (like William Bradshaw's "I wonder, sir, if you could let me have a match?") can be pickup lines.

Still, Auden is doing more than just rehearsing the secret agent scenario in order to make a philosophical point about the opacity of people's motives. He is making such a point, to be sure, and quite effectively: the reader's bewildered encounter with this text has its analogue in the social encounter the poem evokes. But he is also talking about the inscrutability of the *fact* of homosexual desire. And the *way* these questions are posed, with all their semantic oddness, is crucial. The phrasing—"To what these go / And how these do"—is awkward but also precisely literal, lending the lines a kind of pornographic clinicality, as if they are asking what goes where and how to do what. It is, as it were, the very concreteness of homosexual desire that is conceptually opaque: these are figuratively hard questions—difficult, troubling—precisely because they are about something literally hard in the crudest, most physical sense. The "hard question" is, in sum, "What does homosexual desire mean?" and it is "simple to ask" as soon as one thinks about it, just as it is so simple not to ask it about heterosexual desire, which is so laden with (apparently transparent) meanings that the mere fact of it need not invite explanation.[9]

But "to ask the hard question" is, Auden says, "The simple act of the confused will," and "simple" can mean "foolish" or "naïve" as well as "easy." It is foolish or naïve to ask the hard question because as the "act of the confused will" it shows that desire has taken on the characteristics of mind. (Auden may be echoing Shakespeare's usage of "will" to connote sexual desire or genitals.) In the next stanza we see desire confused with mind—self-conscious desire whose "acts" seek an epistemological objective in a physical object. The mind presses the senses into active service—"ears listening / To words at meeting" and "eyes looking / At the hands helping." But the senses "Are never sure / Of what they learn / From how these things are done." The price of thus recruiting the senses is that they can perceive sexual acts only as "methods," ways of acting that signify meaning neither as original motive nor as objective. Nor does refusing to think solve anything:

> And forgetting to listen or see
> Makes forgetting easy;
> Only remembering the method of remembering,
> Remembering only in another way,
> Only the strangely exciting lie,
> Afraid
> To remember what the fish ignored,
> How the bird escaped, or if the sheep obeyed.

If self-conscious attention to sex does not yield meaning, neither does "forgetting" to attend, as if unconscious immersion in desire could recover—"remember"—desire's meaning. Sex pursued this way is only "the method of remembering"—a way of putting members together with no point. It is only a "lie" (Auden's favorite Shakespearean pun), a statement and an act with no truth content. It seems to mean something, but it is a self-deception and an evasion.

By now it should be clear why asking "the hard question" is the "simple act of the confused will." The meaning of homosexual desire reveals itself neither in detached, self-conscious attention to sexual acts nor in an equally self-conscious, deliberate "forgetting" to attend to desire. In both tactics the mind is fending off the truth that animals illustrate without knowing it. Fish, bird, and sheep act unconsciously: swimming, flying, obeying are the actions that define them, and they neither ponder nor will behavior. The self-conscious mind in search of the meaning of desire is "Afraid / To remember" this "answer" because it is a "hard" one. For the answer is *not*—simply—that homosexual desire is instinctual in the animal way and that in it we find our unity of being; *that* is merely "the strangely exciting lie." Rather, the hard answer is the truth of self-contradiction, that our nature is to be self-conscious about desire ("What the fish ignored"), just as the nature of animals is not to be. To seek the meaning of desire through analytic detachment will fail. So will trying to "forget" the question by immersing ourselves in desire. It may seem to work for a while, but eventually,

> losing memory,
> Bird, fish, and sheep are ghostly,
> And ghosts must do again
> What gives them pain.

The cost of forfeiting the insight of self-contradiction is to be doomed to animal instinct without escaping consciousness—to become the ghosts of our evolutionary ancestors, not haunting but haunted by our derivativeness and inauthenticity:

> Cowardice cries
> For windy skies,
> Coldness for water,
> Obedience for a master.

Although there is one more stanza, this is as far as the argument of the poem goes, and as far as Auden goes in theorizing homosexual self-consciousness until he begins in the 1930s to consider desire ethically. "To ask the hard question" explores the two views of closeted subjectivity we have been considering—the idea that alienation of mind from body is epistemologically empowering, and the idea that it is debilitating. Auden's conclusion is that it is neither. The mind cannot answer the question of what desire means, for in posing it the mind sets itself outside desire. But while the question can be ignored, it cannot be disposed of. Self-consciousness is neither an epistemological asset nor a curable disease. That such a conclusion is not really an "answer" is true, as the last stanza implicitly testifies by asking new questions:

> Shall memory restore
> The steps and the shore,
> The face and the meeting place;
> Shall the bird live,
> Shall the fish dive,
> And sheep obey
> In a sheep's way;
> Can love remember
> The question and the answer,
> For love recover
> What has been dark and rich and warm all over?

While the hard truths of this poem are that homosexual desire must remain opaque, that self-consciousness is inescapable, these lines amount to no more (or less) than a prayer for cure. The cure would be "love," in which reason and desire, "face" and "meeting place," question and answer, would be "remembered"—recovered and reunited in a condition where self-consciousness about categories like will and environment would no more debilitate.

Auden imagined this resolution some twenty years later as a landscape whose enfolding maternal warmth—"What could be more like Mother" (*SP* 185)—is prefigured here as "What has been dark and rich and warm all over." But "In Praise of Limestone" also concedes that "this land is not the sweet home that it looks" but "A backward / And dilapidated province" (186). So too here: Auden's questions at the end look backward to "restore," "remember," and "recover" loss. This poem is an extraordinary example of modern homosexual self-contemplation, and it reflects the sophistication with which Auden appropriated the

Lawrentian linkage of deviance and self-consciousness. But it is finally haunted by the psychic past—in the terms of Auden's journal, "the nostalgia for the womb of nature which cannot be re-entered by a consciousness increasingly independent but afraid." And in evoking psychic nostalgia, Auden's ideal of recovery suggests a related, much more troubled idea he was exploring in this period: the theory that homosexuality is a sickness of psychic regression. For alongside—and within—his theoretical concern with self-consciousness run various models of homosexuality as growth and as degeneration.

II

The best way to begin is with a 1929 poem we have looked at already as a coterie text: "Before this loved one" (*EA* 31). As a coded insiders' poem, its strength comes from a tantalizing opacity to readers ignorant that it refers to Isherwood's relationship with a German boy nicknamed "Bubi" ("Baby"). For the initiated, I argued, it analyzes the pathetic economics of sexual exchange in Weimar Berlin. Rather than real love, Isherwood's relationship with "Bubi" implies only an "instinctive look / A backward love," for the boy is trading sex for money in Berlin only because he flees poverty: "This gratitude for gifts is less / Than the old loss. . . ."

But the poem diagnoses homosexual subjectivity, as well as the material conditions of desire, and to see how, we need to start at the beginning:

> Before this loved one
> Was that one and that one
> A family
> And history
> And ghost's adversity.
> . . . .
> Frontiers to cross
> As clothes grew worse
> And coins to pass
> In a cheaper house

Before this last one
Before this loved one.

"This loved one" may be Isherwood's boyfriend, but the subject of the poem can be read either as this boy or as Isherwood himself, who has crossed the "frontier" from bourgeois English gentility to an uncloseted life in Berlin. The poem then refutes Isherwood's wish that this love signify a "new year," a break with the past, and it does so by recalling previous lovers: "that one and that one." The lack of punctuation at this point obscures the connection of these words to what follows—"A family / And history / And ghost's adversity." The easiest reading is that all these things are further in the past than previous lovers. But the lines suggest a more complex, disturbing idea: behind "that one and that one"—i.e. not just prior to but *within* these lovers— lie all the family bonds that the homosexual subject seeks to escape. The current relationship is not a new one at all—"no real meeting" but a "backward love," and this loaded closing verse is both code and critique. As a code, it combines homoerotic suggestion (like Wilde's "Bunburying") with implications of left-handedness. With its suggestion of mirroring, this trope also diagnoses the lover as narcissistic.[10] The love in question is "backward" because it is concerned not with the beloved but with the baggage of the lover's own psychic past.

So while "Before this loved one" excludes outsiders, this exclusion is not an occasion for textual play at their expense. Instead, the text offers the *in*sider a psychic etiology for homosexuality, denying his purported liberation by way of a hermeneutics that exposes the backward-looking, reactive element in his desire. The absence of a lyric "I" places Auden outside the object of analysis, a diagnostician safely apart from the patient. Such detachment is quite problematic, of course: if the unnamed subject can be Isherwood or his boyfriend, it can also be Auden, who came to Berlin for the same thing Isherwood did—boys. And as "To ask the hard question" shows, Auden is skeptical of the liberating power of diagnostic impersonality. This poem would seem to avoid such problems by focusing on the psyche of another, but it still implicitly seeks health—in this case, meaning liberation from the past—through an exertion of rational detachment on desire. It epitomizes Sander Gilman's claim that depictions of disease objectify it so as to fend off the "loss of control" and "missing fixity for our understanding of the world which the reality of disease denies" (2). We need to explore further why diagnosis is bound up with the idea of liberation for Auden, and we need also to fill out the theoretical context for his view of homosexual desire as a disease of the past. We can do both by seeing how his journal reformulates Freud's opposition between Eros and Thanatos in *Beyond the Pleasure Principle* (1920).

In positing a death instinct, Freud rejects the notion that instinct serves "change and development," arguing that *"an instinct is an urge inherent in organic life to restore an earlier state of things"* (*SE* 18, 36; emphasis in original). External forces once brought about the birth of organic life and "the development of consciousness" (38). The death instinct, Freud says, began as the effort of life "to cancel itself out" and "return to the inanimate state," and he concludes that *"the aim of all life is death"* (emphasis in original). By contrast, the sexual instincts— which Freud calls "the true life instincts"—arose with the capacity of certain "germ-cells" to detach from their host organisms and combine with other germ-cells, forming the unity of a new organism and delaying death (40). This theory of organic life, Freud notes, parallels his view of mental life as dominated by "the effort to reduce, to keep constant or to remove internal tension":

> The life process of the individual leads for internal reasons to an abolition of chemical tensions, that is to say, to death, whereas union with the living substance of a different individual increases those tensions, introducing what may be described as fresh "vital differences" which must then be lived off.
>
> (55)

In his journal, Auden appropriates Freud's opposition of Life and Death instincts but theorizes quite differently the meaning of sexual desire in relation to these instincts:

> The question is what do we mean by sex. The union or the fission of sex cells, i.e. love or hate. Freud makes sex the first and places it in op-

position to the death wish. It seems to me jolly similar. Death [is] that which precedes life. The real "life-wish" is the desire for separation, from family, from one's literary predecessors.[11]

Several points need to be made here. First, since Auden went to Berlin in large part to escape bourgeois constraints, his collapse of sex into the death instinct seems to contradict his definition of the "life-wish" as in part "the desire for separation" from "family." It seems likely, then, that he is reevaluating, not the "life-wish" in his desire to separate from England and family, but the hope that his freer sex life reflects this desire: it is "a backward love." He therefore echoes Freud's view of the death instinct as a desire to resolve tensions and return to the past. In aligning sex with death, Auden is extrapolating from one aspect of Freud's theory: the view of Eros as an instinct directed at combination ("union," Auden calls it). By this logic, sex is not at odds with the death instinct at all, for it involves a loss of separateness or individuation, and this loss satisfies the desire for self-cancellation basic to organic life. But he rejects the priority Freud gives to the death instinct (e.g., "the aim of all life is death") by affirming a "real 'life-wish' " in "the desire for separation" from the past. One corollary of Auden's remarks is unstated here, but implicit in his poetry about the death instinct: if the body is fatally implicated in the death instinct, the "real 'life-wish' " would involve detachment of mind from body—a notion that accords with Auden's theory of a postsymbolic poetry of the mind.

As a diagnosis of homosexual desire, "Before this loved one" rests on Freud's Eros and Thanatos but, like Auden's journal entry, revises their meaning. It diagnoses the homosexual's effort to separate himself from the past through sexual love as not just a failure but a fallacy. His sexuality represents (as he puts it in "Before this loved one") an "instinctive look" in the precise Freudian sense of "an urge . . . to restore an earlier state of things." For the very loves he chooses express the power of the past: "A family / And history / And ghost's adversity."[12] In poem after poem, "family ghosts" haunt desire: "Fathers in sons may track / Their voices' trick" (*EA* 29); "Father by son / Lives on and on" (34); "It is your face I see, and morning's praise / Of you is ghost's approval of the choice" (32). The note of futility—the sense that desire is *always* enslaved to the past—is nicely glossed in Auden's journal: "The Tyranny of the Dead. One cannot react against them" (*EA* 299). But he is interested in fatalism as more than a literary or existential attitude, for he theorizes the power of the past as in effect a disease. Habit, he says in his journal, is "the inheritance of thoughts and emotions. Parental authority"; death results from a kind of psychic self-poisoning, the "failure to get rid of metabolic products, i.e. interest in the past" (Mendelson, *Early* 50). Far from a liberating violation of the authority of the past, homosexual desire merely signals its continuing sway: to seek the satisfaction of such desire is ultimately to seek one's death.

That the past for Auden is above all familial points to another element in Freud's work—his developmental model of psychosexual organization, in which homosexuality signifies a form of psychic immaturity.[13] Freud explicates male homosexuality by way of a teleological, normative view of heterosexual object-choice as the outcome of a successful resolution of the Oedipal complex and as the culmination of psychosexual growth. This model, as Jonathan Dollimore notes, shows Freud as secular heir to the belief in reproduction as the divinely ordained end of sexual desire, with perversion as a turning away from that end; for St. Augustine, perversion is the definition of evil (Dollimore 131–44, 196–97). Since, in Freud's view, homosexual object-choice is normal at earlier stages of erotogenic organization, the adult male homosexual evinces arrest at such a stage and an inability either to relinquish the mother as love object or to violate the father's sexual privilege. These ideas are basic to popular conceptions of Freud's work, but they are worth rehearsing here. For commentators all too often point out the influence of Freud in the powerful maternal figures in Auden's work, without noting the implications for male sexual orientation. Dominant mothers appear throughout his writing, in guises both benevolent and monstrous, and while it is often unclear how seriously he takes the Oedipal model, he seems unable to do without it. In his 1929 journal, for instance, Auden uses it in quite different ways to explain homosexuality. In one entry he describes a current sex partner as his "son," calling the relation "substitute and incestuous": he is identifying with his mother. Another entry wonders whether homosexual interest in the penis is explained by "lack of breast feeding." In still another, he says that like compulsive heterosexual desire, homosexuality is a "criticism of the mother as a love-object. Whores [to the heterosexual] a more conscious rejection against [*sic*] her sexual teaching. The bugger presumably though finds his mother more satisfying . . . i.e. the bugger got too much mother love, so sheers off women altogether, the whorer too little, so must always have another."[14]

As if by definition for Auden, the homosexual lives in his own psychic past, in bondage to parental figures.[15] But except for the mother of the Shaw clan in *Paid on Both Sides,* parents figure in Auden's poems more as "ghosts"—as absent ancestors—than as people. They do so partly in order to stress the psychic force of Oedipal relations, but also because Auden's Freudianism is inflected by the hereditary focus of Victorian degeneration theory. That such ideas should color his thinking in the late 1920s is not so odd when we recall the cultural apocalypticism to which some strands of high modernism are given, as well as the role of degeneration theories of race in fascism. Indeed, *The Orators* draws this latter connection in the mock-eugenics of "Address for a Prize-Day." Since that speech parodies English public-school rhetoric, one suspects that Victorian theories of degeneration had a more than residual force in the culture of Auden's childhood.[16] Moreover, as many have noted, Freud's model of psychosexual development stands in complex tension with degeneration theory: he both revises and reflects earlier biological models that located determining power in heredity.[17] In *Beyond the Pleasure Principle,* he draws a connection between the death instinct and the embryo's passage through earlier stages in the evolution of the species (*SE* 18, 37). The principle invoked here—that ontogeny recapitulates phylogeny—grounds not just Freud's displacement of sexual development onto the psychic realm of the infant, but also a host of earlier theories that saw sexual perversion as a deviation from the normal or a decay of the type, manifest in the hereditary constitution of the individual pervert. Unlike Freud, of course, degeneration theory was not concerned with the therapeutic adjustment or cure of the individual, since a hereditary degenerate is incurable. Rather, it was interested in the health of the state, whose potential decline was symbolized in the condition of the individual.[18]

The symptomatic significance of the individual seems to have fascinated Auden as much as it did degeneration theorists. In practice, his poetry of diagnosis is linked to both Freudian psychoanalysis and degeneration theory by its explicitly interpretive stance. In some ways, in fact, Auden's diagnoses recall degeneration theory more than Freud, for the target of attention is the physical body, rather than the psyche. The assumption behind this poetry is that manifest health must be read through, like the cover of a spy:

> Watch any day his nonchalant pauses, see
> His dextrous handling of a wrap as he
> Steps after into cars, the beggar's envy.

> "There is a free one," many say, but err.
> He is not that returning conqueror,
> Nor ever the poles' circumnavigator.

> But poised between shocking falls, on razor-edge
> Has taught himself this balancing subterfuge
> Of the accosting profile, the erect carriage.   (*EA* 31)

The diagnostic poet operates here as counterspy, applying hermeneutics of suspicion to decode this representative member of the moneyed set. His "nonchalant pauses" and "dextrous" (ostensibly right-handed?) gestures are a self-conscious, "balancing subterfuge." His very composure is the symptom of inner malady: the strength and heroism that a man of his bearing should embody are only signs of the decay of aristocratic strength, like ancient coats-of-arms sported in the absence of old warrior virtues. Still, the poem is not simply satirical— or, to be more precise, not satirical in any simple way. In contrast with a poem like "Get there if you can and see the land you were once proud to own," this is not vitriolic condemnation of ruling-class hypocrisy. The tone of the first two stanzas can be taken satirically, but they almost suggest empathy, or even admiration for such suavity, thus complicating Auden's posture of clinical detachment. While the second stanza refutes the social pretenses of greatness, the third suggests a lesser kind of heroism in straddling the "razor-edge" of psychic schism. The imagery recalls the Mortmerean world of dangerous borders and

"skyline operations," as well as the end of "Upon this line between adventure," one of Auden's less gamey advice poems about closeted desire: "On neither side let foot slip over," he says; "On narrowness
stand, for sunlight is / Brightest only on surfaces; / No anger, no trai-
tor, but peace" (*EA* 33). But in "Watch any day his nonchalant pauses,"
closeted self-consciousness signifies degenerated bloodlines. One may
try to "cancel the inertia of the buried," as Auden puts it in the final
stanza, but this is merely "Travelling by daylight on from house to
house / The longest way to the intrinsic peace, / With love's fidelity
and with love's weakness."

That the death instinct will win is the theoretical point of this diagnosis, but these last lines sound much less cool and detached. This
shift in tone is not surprising, for his journal worries about whether
being a "bugger" is a sign of degenerate manhood. "It is not always
realised by half that the attraction of buggery is partly its difficulty and
torments," he writes in one entry. In another: "All buggers hate each
other's bodies as they hate their own, since they all suffer under the reproach, real or imaginary[,] of 'Call yourself a man' " (Mendelson,
Early 59). A later entry, in a long section titled "Buggery," includes the
comments on the "Mental" roots of homosexuality in an "Inferiority
Complex": "Lack of skill in games at school, or anything that tends to
make him feel 'I'm not a he-man' makes him fall in love with hookers.
If not hookers, small boys[.] Sex relation an act of sympathetic
magic."[19]

Along similar lines, Isherwood recalls in *Lions and Shadows* how as
an adolescent he had developed the idea of "The Test" to prove one's
manhood. His Test took the form of a fantasy about being an embattled school prefect who eventually succeeds in taking control of an un-
ruly house. Behind the daydream, Isherwood says, lay the War—a Test
which his generation missed but which killed his father—and "homosexual romanticism."[20] For Isherwood, passing The Test would be the
sign of genetic authenticity—the proof that he has lived up to his father.

Like Isherwood, Auden came to see such notions as false hopes of
the Truly Weak Man, as against the Truly Strong Man, who has no
need to prove his masculinity.[21] Both *Paid on Both Sides* and *The Orators* critique normative English constructions of masculinity. But linked

to a diagnosis of sexual degeneracy, anxieties about living up to the father serve Auden quite handily for social satire:

> On Sunday walks
> Past the shut gates of works
> The conquerors come
> And are handsome.   (*EA* 33)

These beautiful Bright Young People of the 1920s all "Say what they say" and "Know what to know." They are the next generation of the governing class, in whom the absent father "Lives on and on," since "father's son / Knows what they said / And what they did" (34). But the sons are also neurotic, troubled at night by "waking fright." Mothers perpetuate their sons' neuroses by repeating the myths of paternal greatness: "Not meaning to deceive, / Wish to give suck / Enforces make-believe. . . ." The point here is not simply that mothers delay their sons' emotional weaning. It is also that the sons' psychic sickness is itself a "wish to give suck" (both breast-feeding and oral sex as sympathetic magic): a wish bound up, like Isherwood's Test, in "make-believe" masculinity. What the fathers were, the sons can only emulate in distended, artificial form:

> what was livelihood
> Is tallness, strongness
> Words and longness,
> All glory and all story
> Solemn and not so good.

Paternal "livelihood" has become "tallness"; "strongness" has degenerated into elegiac "Words and longness," "glory" and "story."

Such sons epitomize what Guy Hocquenghem calls "homosexual neurosis"—the culturally enforced "backlash to the threat which homosexual desire poses for Oedipal reproduction":

> The homosexual is possible socially only if he has a neurotic "fixation"
> to his mother or father; he is the by-product of a line which is finished
> and which turns his guilt at existing only in relation to the past into

the very meaning of his perversion. The homosexual can only be a degenerate, for he does not generate—he is only the artistic end to a
species.

(107)

Auden's degenerate sons "exist only in relation to the past," for they
are very much "the artistic end to the species": "Words and longness, /
All glory and all story." And it is a short step to perceiving an analogous diagnosis of the Auden group's textual games in their war for
sexual liberation. One thinks of the buried heroes beneath the terrain
of those poems, and the implication that today's fighters cannot live
up to stories of the past:

> In legend all were simple,
> And held the straitened spot;
> But we in legend not,
> Are not simple.   (EA 56)

If Auden's poems of the closet allegorize the war for sexual liberation,
their fatalism may not only suggest the dim prospects for that fight. It
may also reflect the theoretical view that homosexuality is irremediably
implicated in the psychic past, that the backward boy is the harbinger
of the end of the species.

This theory would dovetail with one cultural prejudice that seems
to drive Auden's more openly political poems: that sexual depravity
implies the decadence of the governing classes—in late-1920s Britain
not the aristocracy so much as the professional and business classes.[22]
Auden's poems diagnosing social crisis encode both bourgeois fears of
degeneration and antibourgeois, leftist attitudes. "Consider this, and
in our time" (EA 46–47) discovers a veritable handbook of degen-
erates masquerading as upright citizens—"handsome and diseased
youngsters," a financier who keeps a boy and a typist, those "Who are
born nurses, who live in shorts, / Sleeping with people and playing
fives." "It is later than you think," he tells them all: "You cannot be
away . . ." (47). In "Since you are going to begin to-day" (EA 44–45),
the speaker is Evolution herself ("Lizards my best once"), explaining
the current crisis to a puzzled species:

> Think—Romans had a language in their day
> And ordered roads with it, but it had to die:
> Your culture can but leave—forgot as sure
> As place-name origins in favourite shire—
> Jottings for stories, some often-mentioned Jack,
> And references in letters to a private joke
>
> . . . .
>
> And your conviction shall help none to fly,
> Cause rather a perversion on next floor.

All the schoolroom platitudes about cultural greatness give way before the evidence of decay—including, we note, the obscure, unidentified "Jack" and the "private joke." Even "your conviction"—the effort to confront guilt—cannot save the children upstairs: it only makes them queer. The poem's final judgment is that this is a culture of arrested development, its people "Holders of one position, wrong for years."[23]

There is something of the Hyde Park orator to Auden's apocalypticism, and his precision of analysis in exposing cultural degeneracy is often quite comic. But given his intense interest in theories of sexual deviance, it is hard to believe these poems are wholly burlesque. How, then, should we take their comic quality? Frederick Buell has argued that their tone is that of the knowingly guilty rebel—the *"enfant terrible"* who does not seek "to seriously unseat an authority-figure or a social order" but "plays with ideas that 'responsible' people . . . would like to take seriously."[24] Auden's target, then, would be not degeneracy but the serious attempt to apply such theories to social analysis. If so, of course, his own private writings are perfect examples of such attempts, so that his diagnostic poems would also reflect self-critique. By implication, his complicity with those he observes would undermine his rhetorical posture of detachment.

Such a view of the burlesque element in these poems gains credence from two provocative journal entries. For the aerial perspective these poems assume—"As the hawk sees it or the helmeted airman"—is one that Auden precisely identifies with the death instinct: "Security. Habit. Deeper in the mine, or higher in the air" (Mendelson, *Early* 50). The elevated posture of the diagnostician is the inverse of the regression embodied in the degenerate, but it too reflects the desire to recover inanimation. To predicate cure on analytical detachment is, first, to objectify disorder, and second, to seek health in what Freud sees as the instinct to reduce "tensions": both motives inform diagnosis, which depends on a rational subsumption of symptoms to an ordering scheme. To recall Gilman's terms, "depictions of disease" respond to the "loss of control" and "missing fixity for our understanding of the world which the reality of disease denies" (Gilman 2).

Immediately after his entry on "Security" and "Habit," Auden offers a complementary theorem: "Satiety. Mutation. Persisting in folly brings wisdom" (Mendelson, *Early* 50). He is directly attacking the scientific—and especially Freudian—valorization of reason: analytic detachment cannot lead to real change, for it denies the complicity of observer with observed.[25] "Mutation" rests on a Blakean illogic, by which change comes not in rationalist detachment on disorder but in immersion. In Layard's theories, this is the doctrine that "Every disease . . . is in itself a cure—if we know how to take it. There is only one sin: disobedience to the inner law of our own nature" (Isherwood, *Lions* 239). Living in Berlin, Auden certainly sought physical "satiety," and he posits in his journal an analogous idea of psychic "Mutation" born in "Satiety." As a gloss on his poetic attacks on cultural degeneracy, this theory suggests that their burlesque quality may be read as the "folly" of the poet who knows himself "sated" with the disorders he attacks. The "wisdom" they imply is that the only way to diagnose degeneracy is through firsthand experience. The old cliché is as useful for the theorist as for the secret agent of the closet: "It takes one to know one." Such "wisdom" springs not from logic and detachment but from their death by contradiction—or more precisely, "Mutation." And in the last part of this chapter we shall see how Auden accepts the conjunction of homosexual desire with death, but tries to transvalue it from the end of degeneracy to the basis of psychic and intellectual change.

III

Between April and October of 1929, the very period of his Berlin journal, Auden wrote a four-poem sequence he considered important enough to place sixteenth out of the thirty in his 1930 *Poems*, reprinting it thereafter as a unit titled "1929." It is a useful work for rounding out this chapter, first, because it reflects many of the theories about self-consciousness and development considered in his journal. But it is useful also because, as Mendelson observes, it is an extremely problematic work. In spite of Auden's obvious effort to give it symbolic unity, the theories it offers—of mind and body and change—are by no means in accordance. My aim is not to argue the basic coherence of "1929" but to explicate its tensions within the sexual-political and theoretical frameworks set out already. For doing so enables us to see how Auden seeks a formal rather than theoretical resolution of these tensions—a resolution that does not quite work in "1929" but foreshadows his turn toward an aesthetic that indulges contradiction in *Paid on Both Sides* and *The Orators*.

"1929" is stylistically unusual for Auden's writing at the time in its conspicuous echoes of Yeats: its meditative tone and idiom are clearly indebted to the great long poems published a year before in *The Tower*. Such a style implies a different kind of diagnostic poem, far more in mainstream poetic tradition than those we have looked at before. That Auden was not quite committed to this mode, however, is signaled by the poem's other obvious stylistic influence—Gertrude Stein. The two make an odd pair, to say the least, and not just in aural effect. The Yeatsian meditative voice that begins the poem implies a coherent lyric "I":

> It was Easter as I walked in the public gardens
> Hearing the frogs exhaling from the pond,
> Watching traffic of magnificent cloud
> Moving without anxiety on open sky. . . .   (*EA* 37)

But the idiom of Stein, with its gerunds, dropped articles, and absent subjects, works against the conventions of lyric point of view and subjectivity that Yeats reflects:

> "In grown man also, may see in face
> In his day-thinking and in his night-thinking
> Is wareness and is fear of other
> Alone in flesh, himself no friend."

Stein's influence here, as Mendelson observes, accords with Auden's theory of a post-Romantic, nonsymbolic poetry of the mind, but the style of Yeats implicitly roots poetry in the unity of mind with body.[26]

These discordances of style and point of view are bound up with the tension Mendelson identifies between "weaning" and "drowning," which symbolize the two models of change that the sequence offers. The first poem finds Auden in Berlin's public gardens, meditating on change during the "Season when lovers and writers find / An altering speech for altering things" (37). The subjective drama of the sequence commences when perception of the external world triggers memory and cognitive adjustment: the sight of a man weeping on a bench leads the speaker to recall "all of those whose death / Is necessary condition of the season's setting forth." Recalling the "success of others for comparison," in turn, leads the speaker to a crisis, "Making choice seem a necessary error."

The impetus of the meditation thus reflects one of Auden's journal passages: "Where there is conflict, free will is a necessity. Conflict occurs whenever two different stimuli are presented simultaneously. This is possible where there is (1) a co-ordinated nervous system, and (2) memory" (*EA* 297). The remainder of the sequence explores "choice," in Mendelson's words, as it has been presented by man's evolution "away from unconscious nature, after which there could be no turning back" (77). The second poem and most of the third reflect Auden's theory of mind evolving away from body, portraying this process as a psychologically traumatic birth:

> "Is first baby, warm in mother,
> Before born and is still mother,
> Time passes and now is other,
> Is knowledge in him now of other,
> Cries in cold air, himself no friend."

Consciousness of self, in this proto-Lacanian formulation, is born in consciousness of other and of self as other, "himself no friend." The argument here is analogous to the one Auden makes by way of animals in "To ask the hard question"—that the ultimate "natural" human condition is one of mind split from body. Gazing on the "ducks' indifference," the speaker realizes that the mind can only accept this self-alienation, choosing "To love my life, not as other, / Not as bird's life, not as child's, / 'Cannot,' I said, 'being no child now nor a bird' " (*EA* 39).

The trouble is that the third poem supplants this theory of mind's "weaning" from body with a hope of death. As the third poem ends, the speaker envisions summer giving way to autumn, the "frozen buzzard flipped down the weir / And carried out to sea": the detached, aerial view of the self-conscious mind, that is, will die. With this "forethought of death," he prays "that we may find ourselves at death / Not helplessly strange to the new conditions" (40). The last poem picks up the imagery of winter to offer a prophecy of death, which will drown diseased self-consciousness in nature. "Love," he says, "Needs death, death of the grain, our death, / Death of the old gang . . ." (40). The conjunction of sexual desire with death, in fact, has been lurking in the sequence for quite a while. In the second poem, for instance, after meditating on the self-consciousness that comes with birth ("himself no friend"), Auden diagnoses the attempt to seek consolation in bodily desire, "Perfunctorily affectionate in hired room," as "loving death." Sex is another form of the death wish, the desire to recover a comforting past:

> May see in dead,
> In face of dead that loving wish,
> As one returns from Africa to wife
> And his ancestral property in Wales. (38)

The third poem glosses the regression of homosexual love in evolutionary terms. The "frightened soul," Auden writes, "loves and love / Is insecure," for he fears that love is

> but a degenerate remnant
> Of something immense in the past but now
> Surviving only as the infectiousness of disease
> Or in the malicious caricature of drunkenness. . . . (39)

Both passages undercut the very theory the poem is arguing at those points—that the weaning of mind from body means growth. It is not simply that mind is not content with alienation from body, but that bodily desire—whether regressive or degenerate—has an entropy that pulls against the sense of such self-alienation as positive growth.

From a structural point of view, the sequence's resolution by symbolic recourse to death is satisfying enough. Indeed, it is hard to know how else Auden could have resolved a sequence so infused from the start with organic, seasonal tropes. It is perfectly reasonable, in fact, to see "1929" as working against his attempt to theorize advance, to see it instead as suggesting, like "Since you are going to begin to-day," that the only future is death. Such a reading would also have literary as well as theoretical authority. Jeff Nunokawa has analyzed literary antecedents for the link between same-sex desire and death that drives so much AIDS discourse. One of these is *The Picture of Dorian Gray;* more surprising is his persuasive case that *In Memoriam* stages the successful mourning for Arthur Hallam as the maturation of Tennyson's attachment beyond a homoerotic love, i.e. as the death of homoeroticism.[27] "1929" moves very much in this cultural orbit: its claim that "Love" requires "Death of the grain, our death" refers to a specific group of incurables.

But of course, as a linkage of homosexual desire with death, "Death of the grain" is a phrase with literary echoes besides Wilde and Tennyson (or Freud and degeneration theory). Auden is directly invoking a scandalous recent work—Gide's *Si le grain ne meurt,* first published in 1924 (see Mendelson, *Early* 77). This is more than an incidental allusion, for the title and the structure of Gide's autobiography implicitly liken his process of accepting his homosexuality to salvation by spiritual death and rebirth. His epigraph, from John 12:24, makes his analogy explicit: "except a corn of wheat fall into the ground and die, it abideth alone: but if it die, it bringeth forth much fruit." Like *Si le grain ne meurt,* "1929" overlays a dualistic geography on the psyche split by repression and desire—instead of Gide's France and North Africa, England and Germany. As the locus of Auden's meditation, Weimar Germany is therefore important, and not simply because it represented the potential liberation of desire. It is also because Germany's recent history offered a narrative of cultural apocalypse that could serve as an emblem and agent for personal change, as John Lehmann's account of Spender's attitudes toward Germany makes clear:

> In his view Germany, because of defeat and ruin, had escaped from the mortal sickness of Western civilization, and there youth had started to live again, free of the shackles of the past, a life without inhibition, inspired by hope, natural humanity and brotherhood in the springs of being. In England we were chained still by guilt, ossifying bourgeois conventions, and philistinism.
>
> (Lehmann 116)

In "1929," this idea of a new country of alien conditions first appears clearly in the third poem, when Auden has compared returning to Berlin, after a visit home, to the child's faltering attempt at growth by detaching from its mother:

> And as foreign settlers to strange country come,
> By mispronunciation of native words
> And by intermarriage create a new race
> And a new language, so may the soul
> Be weaned at last to independent delight.   (EA 39)

This stanza clearly looks backward to the figures of weaning in the sequence, but it also offers a notion of change as enabling survival in an initially alien environment. The next stanza elaborates this idea:

> Startled by the violent laugh of a jay
> I went from wood, from crunch underfoot,
> Air between stems as under water;
> As I shall leave the summer, see autumn come
>
> . . . .
> See frozen buzzard flipped down the weir
> And carried out to sea, leave autumn,
> See winter, winter for earth and us,
> A forethought of death that we may find ourselves at death
> Not helplessly strange to the new conditions.

This death invokes regression, the desire for resolution of tension that Auden associates with sexuality. But it is also transvalued into a figure for adaptive change in a new environment. In his journal, we recall, Auden opposes "mutation" to the death instinct of "habit": "Security. Habit. Deeper in the mine, or higher in the air. Satiety. Mutation. Persisting in his folly brings wisdom." Here, provoked "by the violent laugh of a jay," Auden prays that "we may find ourselves at death / Not helplessly strange to the new conditions." He envisions immersion in a new environment as leading to a change that would be spiritual, not medical—a cure that is the "folly" of man but the "wisdom" of God, John Layard's name for desire.

An apt term for this cure might be "Death By Water," for Auden's figure of sea-change seems rather Eliotic. The setting of this insight, as Auden walks amid "Air between stems as under water," recalls lines from the first poem, where he thinks of two boyfriends: "The happiness . . . of my friend Kurt Groote, / Absence of fear in Gerhart Meyer / From the sea, the truly strong man" (37). The end of the sequence recapitulates this symbolism, prophesying the "death of the old gang," "stiff underground," but then, "deep in the clear lake / The lolling bridegroom, beautiful, there" (40). This beautiful image resists interpretation. Christ as the bridegroom of the Apocalypse? Millais' Ophelia? It is hard to know, but in the context of the poem's symbolism, it suggests a new homosexual self reborn in (or of) the water: only after a personal apocalypse, akin to a cultural one such as Germany had undergone in the war, can the homosexual mutate from the paradigm of death in life to a condition of life in death—no longer "helplessly strange to the new conditions," but like one of Auden's Berlin boyfriends, Gerhart Meyer, "From the sea, the truly strong man."

In this reading, Auden is clearly using an orthodox symbolic apparatus, which undergirds not just *The Waste Land* but countless other canonical works, to eccentric ends. But while "the death of the grain" serves Gide quite well for giving symbolic meaning to his own experience, Auden's explorations of identity and self are more complex. "In the name of what God or what ideal do you forbid me to live according to my nature?" Gide asks at one point in *Si le grain ne meurt* (254), and it is not hard to see how he could find a story of death and rebirth in his sexual self-discovery. But his ethic of sincerity and his belief in natural identity are obviously quite foreign to Auden's sense of irremediable self-alienation in "1929" and many other poems considered here. If Auden's "lolling bridegroom" embodies a mutation that comes through "persisting in folly," it is perhaps a mistake to try to make too much sense of the image. It is certainly a mistake to try to reconcile the conflicting ideological and theoretical resonances of "death" in this poem. Auden's seasonal tropes, beginning with Easter in the first line, show him seeking symbolic reconciliation of life and death, self and nature, mind and body in conventional organicist typology. So does his use of a meditative mode Yeats used to reconcile his personal experience to the patterns of history. But "1929" resolves none of the theoretical problems Auden was engaged with at this time. After its fashion, it is a diagnostic text that analyzes disorder and imagines cure quite powerfully. But it does so, finally, by a kind of aesthetic sleight of hand that turns contradiction into paradox.

Its problems indicate the limits of Auden's diagnostic project as explored in his journal and his early poems. That project continued into the 1930s, but only because Auden had begun exploring alternative modes of analysis that foreground contradiction. A final passage from his 1929 journal points to Auden's interest in the *aesthetic* basis of these modes: "The error of Freud and most psychologists is making pleasure a negative thing, progress towards a state of rest. This is only one half of pleasure and the least important half. Creative pleasure is, like pain, an increase in tension" (*EA* 299). The idea that art should provoke "an increase in tension" is implicit in Auden's poetry of the closet, which suggests an erotics of textual irresolution. But with the arguable exception of "To ask the hard question is simple," his diagnostic poems typically seek truth in resolution. In the next chapter we will see how he turns the principle of aesthetic tension to analytical ends, proposing knowledge in irresolution, indulging the burlesque so that folly might bring wisdom. For in *Paid on Both Sides* and *The Orators,* Auden began to develop what amounts to a queer aesthetic, in our contemporary sense of the word "queer": an aesthetic that draws energy from the contradictions and incoherences of the homosexual subject.

Chapter 3

"HAVE YOU HEARD THIS ONE?":
QUEER REVOLUTION IN *PAID ON BOTH SIDES*
AND *THE ORATORS*

Paid on Both Sides (1928–29) and *The Orators* (1932) are the most ambitiously experimental and entertaining works Auden ever wrote. *Paid on Both Sides* is a Romeo-and-Juliet tragedy of love between two children of warring families, but as Isherwood once observed, "it is almost impossible to say whether the characters are epic heroes or members of a school O.T.C." (*Lions* 151–52). Matters are further complicated by a pivotal dream sequence—based on the folk drama of the mummers' play—which seems to culminate in a gay wedding. Subtitled "An English Study," *The Orators* incorporates imitations of everything from Old Irish poetry to Anglican hymns to Rimbaud and Stein, a parody of a school lecture on love and perversion, jokes about anal sex, geometric and genetic diagrams, and in the center, the diary of a queer revolutionary called the Airman, modeled on tribal tricksters of New Guinea.

As proof of Auden's imaginative appetite, these works are impressive, and they challenge easy summary. But their complexity is as much conceptual as formal and stylistic, and Auden's theories about the psychology and politics of same-sex relations shape them to a degree unmatched elsewhere in his work. *Paid on Both Sides* and *The Orators* involve a fusion of the diagnostician and the secret agent, for they function both as cultural critiques and as expressions of a subversive homosexuality. We have seen the various ways in which Auden's grapplings with sexuality are marked by certain contradictions: the concern for liberating expression and desire vs. the seductive powers of secrecy;

the sense that homosexuality is both regressive and progressive at the level of the subject and in culture at large. *Paid on Both Sides* and *The Orators* mark crucial aesthetic steps forward for Auden, for rather than taking contradiction as a condition to be resolved conceptually and artistically, these works embrace it.

To argue this is to invite the sort of response Auden voiced late in life when he wrote, "Psychological critics, do be more precise in your language: / symbols must not be confused with allegorical signs" (*CP* 857). It is one thing to note that *Paid on Both Sides* and *The Orators* are concerned with homoeroticism or homosociality, but quite another to say they are "really about" homosexuality or the predicament of the homosexual poet. I submit, however, that Auden was provoked by this very ambiguity—an uncertainty about the relation between his sexuality and his culture. These works operate, that is, in the no-man's land between minoritizing and universalizing models of same-sex desire and relations: theories that essentialize the homosexual as a distinct entity, and theories that see same-sex desire as a universal potentiality (see Sedgwick, *Epistemology* 85–90).

As in some of his shorter diagnostic poems, Auden's inability to be sure about such things contributes to the comic energy of these works. But in the wake of poststructuralism, we are perhaps better equipped to see uncertainty as conceptually valuable. More than anywhere else, in fact, *Paid on Both Sides* and *The Orators* show Auden deploying an aesthetic that prefigures queer studies in its interest in the subversive powers of theory and language. "The reinvention of systems," Harold Beaver has written, "begins with demolition, like the inner wall of a house which becomes an outer wall after wars and devastation" (115). "It is not enough," he argues,

> to work against ideology by pointing it out. Far more effective is subversion from within, sabotaging the machinery (like Soviet dissidents) by "making it grind so that it can be heard, so that it will not be innocent, so that it will lose in fact that beautiful mask of innocence and of being natural."[1]

Such views have informed the work of many recent queer theorists, particularly in questioning the essentialism and the assumptions of

normative heterosexuality that seem to have compromised gay and lesbian studies.[2] *Paid on Both Sides* and *The Orators* pursue a remarkably
similar agenda, even if Auden's intellectual sources were Freud and
Brecht, rather than Derrida and Barthes or Deleuze and Guattari. The
notorious difficulties of these works reflect his sensitivity to the tensions in a project of "demolition" and "reinvention" when same-sex
desire seems a universal and a marginal phenomenon, with both conservative effects and disruptive potential. On the one hand, Auden
imagines the homosexual poet as a revolutionary; on the other he sees
himself as Exhibit A of cultural degeneracy. As a later title for one of
the "Six Odes" that make up Book III of *The Orators* asks, "Which
Side Am I Supposed to Be On?"

From a hermeneutical point of view, the greatest challenge of these
works is their tonal and ideological indeterminacy—so much so that
critics have long been unsure whether to label *The Orators* communist,
fascist, or just plain muddled.[3] And since the Mortmerean England
these works portray recalls the world of public schools, some have
doubted whether Auden produced much more than clever schoolboy satire. Such questions come down, in effect, to whether Auden
was somehow "serious" or not—a critical question that is hardly free
of sexual politics. What these works offer, I argue, is a highly self-
conscious mode of political critique in which one of his major targets
is the seriousness that serves ideological conformity. "The joke," Auden
wrote in 1929, "includes its own contradiction. It is therefore the only
form of absolute statement" (*PDW* 461). At the heart of both *Paid on
Both Sides* and *The Orators* is a theory of queer art in which joking har-
nesses the very contradictions Auden sees as inevitably informing
homosexuality.

I

While *Paid on Both Sides* in its earliest form predates Auden's 1929
Berlin journal and many of the poems considered in the last chapter, it
participates in his effort to diagnose the psychic and cultural meanings
of same-sex desire. The play grew out of six lyrics written in the winter
and spring of 1927–28 and printed the following summer in his 1928

Poems.[4] Auden finished the first version shortly before his trip to Spa, Belgium, where he spent three weeks in analysis in the hope of curing his homosexuality so that he might marry. While he was fleetingly enthusiastic about the results,[5] they evidently did not take, and he broke off his engagement. He revised the play that fall in Berlin, and his second version incorporates John Layard's theories about disease and cure.

Paid on Both Sides is set in a Mortmerean northern England, and the plot follows John Nower and Anne Shaw, children of families who have feuded for years. The two fall in love, and their wedding promises an end to the murderous feud. But at the reception, Anne's brother Seth, urged on by their mother, kills John to avenge his earlier murder of their brother. The revised play opens with John's premature birth, when his mother learns that the Shaws have killed his father, who was on his way to visit "Layard." Having grown up to lead the Nower clan, John avenges his father by killing the patriarch of the Shaws. Auden's other major addition—John's dream after killing a Shaw spy (later revealed to be Anne's brother)—is designed to explain John's motives for marrying Anne. The dream implies that he identifies with the Spy, whose trial, execution, and resurrection in the dream dramatize John's psychic engagement with his doubts about the feud. After waking, he marries Anne Shaw, seeking to end the feud, but is killed in retribution for his execution of her brother, the Spy.

As an autobiographical commentary on the possibilities for cure, *Paid on Both Sides* seems cynical: Auden's hero manages to marry but not for long. His death points up a note of fatalism in one important comment in Auden's journal: "Freud's error is the limitation of the neurosis to the individual. The neurosis involves all society."[6] "Society" in this play, however, is basically the family writ large: these characters exist in a tribal culture where kinship governs all social relations and antagonisms. The plot, in effect, tells the story of John's effort to undo the biological principle that ontogeny recapitulates phylogeny: in seeking his own cure, he tries also to overturn a culture shaped by the tyranny of the past over the present. His psychic growth thus functions as a sign of the possibilities for social change.

The role of familial and homosocial bonds in this play seems appropriate to either of the models Isherwood cites for these characters—

Germanic epic heroes or schoolboys. Caught in an endless cycle of retribution, the Nowers and Shaws recall feuding clans from Germanic poetry. Auden's verse patently—and often beautifully—imitates Old English prosody, as in the first version's opening chorus, which echoes "The Wanderer": "Often the man, alone shut, shall consider / The killings in old winters, death of friends; / Sitting with stranger shall expect no good" (*PDW* 7). Then, in a weird but typical tonal shift, the first version of the play has characters enter who sound more like boys playing war games:

F."
> There are twenty men from Nattrass, sir, over the gap, coming at
> once.

WILLIAM.
> Have they seen us?

F."
> Not yet.

WILLIAM.
> We must get out. You go round by the copse and make for the
> Barbon road. We'll follow the old tramway. Keep low and run
> like hell.

>   (8)

The revised text heightens this public-school atmosphere, as when Kurt says to Culley, "I hear Chapman did the lake in eight," and Culley replies, "Yes, he is developing a very pretty style" (18). While the absurdity of such contrasts in tone is part of the fun, Auden's conflation of epic heroes and schoolboys is hard to read: is he satirizing primitive Germanic tribal culture, modern adolescent homosociality, or both? Is it even satire?

As we shall see, such questions get to the heart of what makes this play a theoretical and artistic advance in Auden's explorations of homosexuality. More immediately important is that the Nowers and Shaws reflect the theory of homosociality Freud describes in *Group Psychology and the Analysis of the Ego* (1921). His general argument is that group identification has an erotic basis, and his two main exam-

ples are the church and the military (*SE* 18, 93–99). Indeed, the plot of
Paid on Both Sides might seem taken right out of Freud:

> Love for women breaks through the group ties of race, of national di-
> visions, and of the social class system, and it thus produces important
> effects as a factor in civilization. It seems certain that homosexual love
> is far more compatible with group ties, even when it takes the shape
> of uninhibited sexual impulses—a remarkable fact, the explanation
> of which might carry us far.
>
> (141)

While Freud declines to pursue any such explanation, *Paid on Both
Sides* does so, the only difference being that Auden comes to see "*uninhibited* [homo]sexual impulses" as quite threatening to group ties. In
Freud's terms, the tribal structure of the Nowers and Shaws rests on
aim-inhibited libido, with male homosocial bonds cultivated through
group activities like games, which offer occasions for displaying and
admiring the male body. By falling in love with Anne Shaw, John
breaks through the "ties of national divisions" that enforce tribal unity.
His cryptic words to her at one point juxtapose heterosexual desire
with homoerotic memories of Audenesque landscape and school culture:

> On Cautley where a peregrine has nested, iced heather hurt the knuck-
> les. Fell on the ball near time, the rushing of forwards stopped. Good-
> bye now, he said, would open the swing doors. These I remember but
> not love till now.
>
> (*PDW* 9)

As in early poems like "I chose this lean country," homoeroticism is a
matter of pain, frustration, and loss ("Good-bye"); "love" is another
matter, and the haunting lyric John goes on to recite ("Some say that
handsome raider, still at large") personifies love as a messianic outlaw
who ends hatred and "silences the angry sons."

John's growth from homosocial group ties to heterosexual love
neatly follows Freud's trajectory of psychosexual stages. It also reflects

Auden's linkage of immaturity to the death instinct: the murderous feud rooted in ancestral hatreds offers graphic evidence of the death instinct at work. In the revised version of the play, John is literally born into the feud—his mother goes into labor when she learns of his father's murder. Joan's lament over her husband's corpse serves as an incantatory indoctrination of the infant John in her arms:

> Not from this life, not from this life is any
> To keep; sleep, day and play would not help there
> Dangerous to new ghost; new ghost learns from many
> Learns from old termers what death is, where.   (15)

As much as his dead father, John himself is the "new ghost" who will learn about the feud from veterans ("old termers," in the schoolboy idiom). He is ultimately identified not only with his dead father but with that death itself, and the end of Joan's lament draws out from loss the ethic of hate:

> Unforgetting is not to-day's forgetting
> For yesterday, not bedrid scorning,
> But a new begetting
> An unforgiving morning.

These lines might be paraphrased as saying that memory is neither escapist nostalgia nor elderly bitterness, but a way of binding future to past. But the heavy alliteration lends a sonorous drag to these lines, arresting forward movement, and they end in a kind of syntactic and aural inertia, "morning" haunted by its backward-looking echo, "mourning."

For all her efforts at inducing paternal identification, however, John's mother functions as the most powerful embodiment of continuity with the past. His father was killed, in fact, while traveling to meet "Layard"—a mission concerned with radical change, perhaps even ending the feud. John is left to be raised by his mother—*Joan*—and in his desire to avenge his father, he emulates her "unforgetting" and "unforgiving mo(u)rning." In later renouncing the feud, he is violating maternal authority (as his dream makes absurdly clear by having Joan guard the Spy with a giant baby-bottle). Ultimately, mothers are portrayed as the enforcers of hatred—it is Seth Shaw's mother who urges him to murder John at the end of the play.

Thus cultural arrested development in this play is clearly implicated in the psychic predicament of sons like John, for whom any effort at escaping the past is blocked by the mother. What is more complex is the relation between homosociality and homosexuality in the schoolboy/warrior ethos of the Nowers and Shaws. We have seen how Auden's shorter poems reflect a linkage spelled out in his 1929 journal between anxiety about masculinity and homosexuality: "All buggers suffer under the reproach, real or imaginary[,] of 'Call yourself a man' " (Mendelson, *Early* 59). *Paid on Both Sides* portrays a culture defined by this very anxiety. Like the Airman in *The Orators,* John has grown up with the strong mother + weak/absent father arrangement that is the stuff of Freudian cliché. Rather than taking human objects, however, same-sex desire is sublimated into homosocial group bonds and made to serve political ends. Paradoxically, this culture both exalts the paternal ideal of the aggressive male and, by making revenge for the father's death the duty of the son, enforces identification with the "unforgetting" mother—thus undercutting the son's emulation of the father. So the ongoing killings that would seem to express masculinity are never enough: to survive is to live in the world of women, to be feminized.

Written in a period when Auden was himself seeking to "cure" his homosexuality and marry, *Paid on Both Sides* reads like a grim prognosis on his chances for transcending arrested development. In a friend's copy of the play, he wrote: "A parable of English Middle Class (professional) family life 1907–1929," as if to mark both his beginning and his end (Mendelson, *Early* 47). More broadly, the play implies a cultural diagnosis very much like the one offered by Cyril Connolly in the 1930s:

Were I to deduce any system from my feelings on leaving Eton, it might be called *The Theory of Permanent Adolescence*. It is the theory that the experiences undergone by boys at the great public schools, their glories and disappointments, are so intense as to dominate their

lives and to arrest their development. From these it results that the
greater part of the ruling class remains adolescent, school-minded,
self-conscious, cowardly, sentimental and in the last analysis homosexual.

(Connolly 260)

The glibness of "in the last analysis" notwithstanding, such a view is
implied by *Paid on Both Sides* (and *The Orators,* as we shall see). Consider, for example, the elegiac words of the chorus just before John's
wedding:

> For where are Basley who won the Ten,
> Dickon so tarted by the House,
> Thomas who kept a sparrow-hawk?
>
> The clock strikes, it is time to go,
> The tongue ashamed, deceived by a shake of the hand.

(*PDW* 31)

The chorus reacts to John's rejection of old loyalties with an *ubi sunt*
lament for old boys that certainly sounds, as Connolly would put it,
"sentimental"—especially when we learn that "the Ten" was a traditional race at the Sedburgh School, which Auden's friend Gabriel Carritt had attended (*J* 242). Whether Auden meant us to sense a degenerate sentimentality here is hard to say. But it seems likely that he is
both indulging his own sentimentality about schoolboy life and leaving it open to critique. By the early 1930s, he was thinking and writing
about the pernicious social and psychic effects of the way England
educated its governing classes. In an essay we shall return to later,
"The Liberal Fascist" (1934), he claims that by making "honour" the
highest virtue, public schools induce a "backward" devolution of all
those emotions the authorities seek to suppress, "particularly the
sexual" (see *P* 59–60). Portraying a culture of schoolboy "honour,"
where morality is defined as loyalty to an institution, *Paid on Both Sides*
implies the beginning of such an argument: as stand-ins for modern
Englishmen of the governing class, the Nowers and Shaws suggest
that the public schools, with their games and Officers' Training Corps,

are institutions for making sure that the men who run the nation remain boys who are forever trying to prove themselves.

The historical context of this notion helps illuminate the play's concern with male aggression. As Hynes has argued, Auden's generation followed its predecessor in seeing parallels between school and life on the Western Front (see *Auden* 50–51). The major difference, however, was that while those on the Western Front might think back to school, Auden's generation had only the playing fields and war games. Anxiety about living up to the paternal ideal, then, would drive the effort to prove oneself a man, as in Isherwood's personal version of the War, "The Test," which in hindsight he saw as merely begging the question of his manhood (see Isherwood, *Lions* 56–58). One implication of all this is that the play amounts to a critique of the Auden group's own psychosexual arrested development, implicated as it is in a culturally conservative homosociality. In this regard it parallels many of the poems considered in chapter 2. But in adding the extraordinary dream sequence, Auden complicated the play's implications for the political meaning of same-sex desire. Even as it seems to portray a psychic cure that leads to John's marriage to Anne Shaw, it also suggests that "cure" means coming to terms with homosexuality, not overcoming it, and that self-conscious homosexual identity is the true force for revolution. The tension between these two views, in fact, is at the heart of what makes *Paid on Both Sides* a play built on contradiction.

II

I shall approach the dream sequence by way of a document dating from the spring of 1929, after the play had been revised. Compiled with Isherwood's help, Auden's "Preliminary Statement" is a convoluted, cryptic theoretical manifesto on what he calls "ritual drama." While it is unclear what project the "Statement" was designed to explain, it reflects many issues Auden had been thinking about in other contexts, including *Paid on Both Sides*.[7] About halfway through the hodgepodge of prose and verse that make up the "Statement," one finds this: "Of those carefully prepared and instructive prefaces. The soul reads between the lines" (*PDW* 460). In this case, it is rather easy to do so. The "Statement" is much concerned with the psychic sources of tragedy—which it explains in Layard's terms of "God" and "Satan"—as well as with "symptoms," "perversion," "cure," and "psychoanalysis." Auden theorizes "ritual drama" as enacting a contest between desire and repression, God and Satan, and in doing so he was not only crediting it with the curative power of psychoanalysis but proclaiming the theoretical and analytical potential of literary form.

Implicit in Auden's theory of ritual drama is his view that "creative pleasure" is not simply, as Freud would have it, "progress towards a state of rest," but "like pain, an increase in tension" (*EA* 299):

> Dramatic action is ritual. "Real" action is directed towards the satisfaction of an instinctive need of the actor who passes thereby from a state of excitement to a state of rest. Ritual is directed towards the stimulation of the spectator who passes thereby from a state of indifference to a state of acute awareness.
>
> (*PDW* 459)

Brecht's influence is clear both in Auden's emphasis on the alienation of the spectator and in a further claim: "Dramatic 'characters' are always abstractions." Subtitled "A Charade," *Paid on Both Sides* seems to fit with what Auden had in mind—drama that invites not identification with characters but interpretation provoked by the spectator's experience of cognitive and emotional tension. The "tragic emotion" associated with modern tragedy, a later entry states, "is aroused by the awareness that what is evil is potential good, that hate is love turned against itself" (460). That good and evil, love and hate, are bound together in this way is one kind of "awareness" that *Paid on Both Sides* aims to stimulate in the audience, and it does so in part through John's dream, an overtly symbolic play-within-a-play.

The warrior culture of the Nowers and Shaws rests on institutionalized hate, but John's dream suggests that the relation between hate and love is implicated in same-sex desire. In his dream, John speaks as prosecutor at the Spy's trial:

> We cannot betray the dead. As we pass their graves can we be deaf to the simple eloquence of their inscriptions, those who in the glory of

their early manhood gave up their lives for us? No, we must fight
to the finish.

(PDW 22)

In this echo of Great War rhetoric, John's homage to the dead brings
to the surface the sentimental homoeroticism that infuses tribal loyalty.
At the same time, it links homoeroticism with hatred of the enemy,
the imperative to "fight to the finish." Auden's plot as a whole works
out this notion on a large scale: John's marriage marks a turning away
from hatred of the Shaws to love. Same-sex desire is implicated in hatred of the enemy, while marriage symbolizes reconciliation.

But the formulation of this theory of hate in Auden's "Preliminary
Statement" is crucial. Hate is not simply a refusal of love but "love
turned against itself." A likely source for this idea is the work of Layard's one-time mentor, Homer Lane:

> The motive-power of goodness is love, and love is compulsory. . . .
> If [Man] hates, his behaviour is untrue to himself, to mankind and
> to the universe, but the energy is still love, for his act of hatred is love
> perverted.

(Lane 177)

John's dream portrays the cure of hate as the cure of "love perverted"—
or, as I shall argue, sexual perversion itself—so one psychoanalytic
reading of the dream is that it dramatizes John's growth from same-sex
to heterosexual object-choice. In this, perhaps, Auden was trying to
portray in drama a therapeutic outcome that he had failed to achieve
through analysis himself: a cure of homosexuality to permit marriage.
What complicates matters—and what makes the play so interesting—is
that Auden took to Lane's ideas (or Layard's version of them) in Berlin
largely because they seemed to sanction the embrace of homosexual
desire unfettered by the self-conscious mind: desire is, after all, the
meaning of "God" in Layard's system. And the logic of Lane's view of
hate is also the logic of Freud's theory of paranoia. As Freud extrapo-
lated from Schreber's case history, "the familiar principal forms of
paranoia can all be represented as contradictions of the single proposition: 'I (a man) *love him* (a man).'" These are the potential "contradic-

tions": " 'I do not *love* him—I *hate* him,' " a statement which is "transformed by *projection* into . . . '*He hates* (persecutes) *me*, which will justify me in hating him' "; and " 'I do not love *him*—I love *her.*' "[8] John's dream, in other words, implies through this logic of contradiction Freud's claim that "at the core of the conflict in cases of paranoia among males is a homosexual wishful phantasy of *loving a man* (62). The dream that "cures" John of tribal homoerotic attachments, so that he can marry, can also be read—quite contradictorily—as dramatizing his birth into "awareness" of his homosexuality and its political valences.

John's dream comes just after the ambush of Anne Shaw's father, undertaken to avenge the murder of John's father. The ambush is recounted by the returning raiders in quasi-Anglo-Saxon prosody whose alliteration, rhythm, and imagery suggest unmistakable phallic potency:

> Shot answered shot Bullets screamed
> Guns shook Hot in the hand
> Fighters lay Groaning on ground.
> . . . .
> Then Shaw knew We were too strong.
> . . . .
> There he died Nor any came
> Fighters home Nor wives shall go
> Smiling to bed They boast no more.   (*PDW* 20)

One raider who gets special mention is Stephen ("His first encounter Showed no fear / Wounded many"). Then, after this account, in one of the oddest moments in the play, Stephen abruptly declares, "A forward forward can never be a backward backward." Just as Stephen is being taken away to sleep it off, a captured Shaw spy appears. After a brief exchange, the Spy—Seth and Anne Shaw's brother, it turns out—is led off and executed. John falls asleep and dreams.

If we take the Spy as a figure for the closeted homosexual, his appearance here serves as a kind of dramatic gloss on Stephen's cryptic remark and even the raid itself. The erotic overtones in the account of the ambush recall "Control of the passes," whose closing lines are derived from the Anglo-Saxon "Wulf and Eadwacer": "They would shoot, of course, / Parting easily who were never joined" (*EA* 25). Here, the appearance of the Spy should confirm our sense of something homoerotic about all those weapons so "hot in the hand." In context, Stephen's apparently drunken outburst—"A forward forward can never be a backward backward"—suggests a deliberate denial of the homoerotic energy in their feuding aggression. A "forward forward" may be construed as someone of willfully determined prowess on the field of play or battle. "Backward" suggests the regression— ontogenetic and phylogenetic—Auden so often connects with homosexuality. By the logic of the double negative, a "backward backward" would be the inverted image of an invert. With paranoic contradiction, in other words, Stephen denies that the aggressive masculinity of the Nowers signifies a specifically homosexual reaction formation against doubts about manhood. He denies (thus begging the question) that aggression is an effort to "Call yourself a man"—as Auden's journal defines "buggery." The queer subtext of his remark then gets dramatic amplification with the appearance of the Spy. As the Spy is led off to be shot, Stephen calls after him, "Don't go, darling" (*PDW* 21).

As a figure of deceit and self-consciousness about political identity, the Spy provokes John's own crisis in the dream. "You know what we do to spies," John says before ordering his execution (20). But what *does* John want to do to the Spy? Alone onstage, having given the order, he is suddenly unsure:

> Always the following wind of history
> Of others' wisdom makes a buoyant air
> Till we come suddenly on pockets where
> Is nothing loud but us; where voices seem
> Abrupt, untrained, competing with no lie
> Our fathers shouted once.   (21)

Figuring inherited belief as a kind of motive force, John sees ideological crisis as finding oneself becalmed where "others' wisdom" and the paternal "lie" no longer operate. What "they never told us" about, he says, was "that soon-arriving day" when our acts and beliefs are no longer instinctive: "When to gaze longer and delighted on / A face or idea be impossible." His incipient ideological awakening is not yet a disavowal, but since it is instigated by the killing of the Spy—the epitome of secret disloyalty—his speech implies doubts that, brought into the open, would amount to treasonous identification with the enemy. He ends his soliloquy with an appeal to the death instinct, a loss of all consciousness and capacity for growth: "Yes, mineral were best: could I but see / These woods, these fields of green, this lively world / Sterile as moon."

As it happens, falling asleep allows the life instinct to assert itself through a dream that "stimulates awareness." The dream unfolds in psychosexual terms because political bonds here are rooted in desire and fear, love and hate. Auden's literary source for the dream was a 1923 study of the mummers' play by R.J.E. Tiddy. Influenced by Frazer's *The Golden Bough*, Tiddy argued that those elements common to the many extant versions of the Christmas mummers' play originated in pagan fertility ritual (Tiddy 70–71). The basic mummers' plot involved combat between two protagonists (usually St. George and another knight) and revival of the loser by a comic doctor. In Auden's version, John plays the role of St. George, and the Spy his opponent. Rather than armed combat, the contest becomes a trial presided over by Father Christmas (as in the mummers' play), with John as prosecutor, the Spy as defendant, and John's mother as the baby-bottle-wielding warden. After testimony of witnesses—Bo, Po, and the Man-Woman (all but Po standard mummers figures)—John shoots the Spy, who is then resurrected by the Doctor and his comic sidekick, the Boy. The cure is effected through the traditional mummer's play motif of tooth extraction.

The dream figures of "John" and "the Spy" fairly clearly enact the dreamer John's questioning of the feud. The shooting of the Spy in the dream is portrayed as an act of desperation, and his resurrection and reconciliation with John imply an unconscious process by which John overcomes the repression of political doubts about the feud. As a Christmas folk ritual, the mummers' play enacts the conflict between past and present, the old year and the new, and this organicist symbolism works nicely to suggest the promise of cultural rebirth in John's marriage to Anne Shaw after he wakes up.

Nevertheless, the psychosexual implications of the dream are not so tidy. In a play concerned with the political potentialities of desire, a trial is more than a useful metaphor for psychic conflict. If the Wilde trial is the classic case in point, Auden's trial also echoes wartime English fears of subversion through sex. There was Mata Hari, of course, but there were also conspiracy theories about treasonous homosexuals blackmailed by German spies. Such fears entered the legal arena in the 1918 libel trial of Pemberton Billing, an MP who had accused members of the Independent Theatre Society—then staging *Salome*—of belonging to "The First 47,000," a purported list of English homosexuals compiled by German agents. (Billing was acquitted of the libel charges; see Kettle; Hynes, *War* 223–26.) One implication of the dream is an idea elaborated in *The Orators,* that the social prosecution of deviance not only expresses fears of political infiltration but mimics the psychic dynamics of fear and repression. More importantly, it suggests that homophobia is not so much a fear of same-sex desire, but a fear of the secret self-identified homosexual. As long as it is diverted into the group, same-sex desire is safe—crucial even, for unit cohesion. But the Spy—which is to say, John himself—is on trial for having secretly detached his libido from the group, for which any attachment to specific objects is dangerous. Such detachments are even more threatening when the group is itself defined by common hatred of an enemy; the libido might, after all, find an object among the enemy. If hate is "a perversion of love" (Lane) or a "contradiction" of the statement "I love him" (Freud), the self-recognized homosexual threatens the ideology that hate is naturally justified by the moral otherness of the enemy.

Such an argument helps make sense out of the exceedingly cryptic testimony of the hostile witnesses against the Spy. They do not "accuse" the Spy per se (though he groans out loud after each one), but their testimony seems to be damaging because they metaphorically describe alternative ways to deal with incipient homosexual self-awareness. "By loss of memory we are reborn, / For memory is death," Bo says, and he goes on to describe living as in a dropout subculture: "On northern ridges / Where flags fly, seen and lost, denying rumour / We baffle proof, speakers of a strange tongue" (*PDW* 22–23). Po suggests a strategy of embracing psychic regression—not renouncing society but withdrawing from any real ideological commitment:

> Past victory is honour, to accept
> An island governorship, back to estates
> Explored as a child; coming at last to love
> Lost publicly, found secretly again
> In private flats, admitted to a sign.
> An understanding sorrow knows no more,
> Sits waiting for the lamp, far from those hills
> Where rifts open unfenced, mark of a fall,
> And flakes fall softly softly burying
> Deeper and deeper down her loving son.   (23)

Rather than going away, as Bo suggests, go back home to "estates explored as a child": embrace nostalgic regression. The speech lyrically encapsulates Freudian theory of the male homosexual's narcissistic identification with his mother, either or both of them lamenting the "loving son" being buried alive. In the midst of the soothing loss of consciousness, though, is an image of the closet, of love "found secretly again / In private flats, admitted to a sign."

What makes these speeches testimony against the Spy, and thus John the dreamer, is that they describe how same-sex desire, no longer sublimated into group identification, can provoke a secret free agency. The last, most devastating witness describes how desire becomes a free agent beyond the subject's control. The Man-Woman is traditionally a minor figure with little function in the mummers' play, whose cross-dressing can get some laughs. But Auden's source suggests that the Man-Woman may have roots in rituals to promote fertility by donning women's clothing (Tiddy 76–77). Auden's Man-Woman stands behind barbed wire, and Mendelson calls him-her a "personification of the repressed erotic impulse toward union and love which the feud has kept prisoned behind barbed wire, frozen out in the snow" (*Early* 51). He-she would seem therefore to prefigure the marriage of John and Anne, an emblem of heterosexual union and spirit of psychic wholeness. Couched in poetry as obscure as anything Auden ever wrote, his-her testimony exposes the childish psychic machinations that have blocked the way to health:

> Because I'm come it does not mean to hold
> An anniversary, think illness healed,
> As to renew the lease, consider costs
> Of derelict ironworks on deserted coasts.   (23)

Unlike Bo and Po, the Man-Woman is not concerned with how to live with homosexuality in the future, for no harmonious relation to the past is possible—neither blithe memory ("to hold / An anniversary") nor easy continuation ("to renew the lease"): there is just too much psychic decay. "Love," the Man-Woman says, was only "episodes, / Traffic in memoirs"—not only bookish artificiality but regression. "Refus[ing] to listen," he-she says, "you remained in woods," hiding away. Efforts to face up to desire led only to more evasive maneuvers: compulsive masturbation ("I lay with you; you made that an excuse / For playing with yourself"); reactive efforts at clean living ("So I was cold to make / No difference, but you were quickly meek"); manic excess ("You overworked yourself . . . Adored me for the chance"). The speech portrays an incapacity to confront homosexual desire in any effective way; it remains utterly inaccessible to conscious control, whose every tactic produces only another defensive maneuver. Far from the adhesive of group bonds, same-sex desire has become an agent of subversion in the self, eluding all attempts at containment or co-optation.

The whole tone of Man-Woman's speech is that of the diagnostician regretfully describing an incurable case; John declares, "I can't bear it" and shoots the Spy. The Man-Woman's diagnosis is then more succinctly put by the Doctor: "Um, yes. Very interesting. The conscious brain appears normal except under emotion. Fancy it. The Devil couldn't do that. This advances and retreats under control and poisons everything round it" (25). After some jokes from his boy helper, the Doctor gives the traditional mummers' play treatment, extracting a giant tooth from the body of the Spy, who then gets up. He and John plant a tree together in a gesture of reconciliation that prefigures John's marriage.

This "cure" is, to say the least, rather overdetermined, since Freud's and Groddeck's theories suggest various conflicting ways in which the tooth may be symbolically implicated in homosexuality.[9] It is easy to feel that the Spy's resurrection says less about Auden's serious concern with psychoanalytic cure than about his interest in having as much dramatic fun with the idea of cure as possible. The last words of John and the Spy, speaking together at the end of the dream, beg the question of how John has been cured: "Sharers of the same house / Attendants on the same machine / Rarely a word, in silence understood" (*PDW* 26). The tone connotes not resolution of the conflict so much as resignation. They share "the same house"—the body, perhaps—and tend "the same machine"—the psyche, and the image suggests not a cure of homosexuality (which would surely involve the erasure of the Spy) but a way of living with it as that which must never be named. Moreover, their scene of reconciliation at the end of the dream seems a great deal like a marriage. After the Spy is resurrected, a photographer takes his picture, and John rushes in from offstage like nothing so much as a bridegroom late for the ceremony: "I'm late, I'm late. Which way is it? I must hurry" (25). "Sametime sharers of the same house," the speech they deliver in alternating voices while planting the tree, reads like a recitation of wedding vows.

From this angle, the dream suggests a process of psychosexual growth obviously quite contrary to the trajectory of Auden's marriage plot—an exposition not of homosexual cure but of coming out to oneself. But these two alternatives merely crystallize the problem of reading the social and psychic meanings of same-sex desire in the play as a whole, where it is both a politically conservative force and a sign of subversive individuality. Such problems probably reflect in part the uncertainties of the period in which Auden wrote and revised the play: the first version—the "frame" plot—may reflect his earlier hopes for cure and marriage, while the later dream sequence, written after he had broken off the engagement and was living in Berlin, would reflect his doubts about any such cure, and indeed a growing acceptance of his homosexuality. One suspects that the mummers' play provided him with some flashy hocus-pocus to portray a psychosexual cure he could not theoretically define or otherwise portray.

The second version of the play, while far more interesting and entertaining than the first, seems much more problematic as an examination of the psychic and political meanings of homoeroticism, homosociality, and homosexuality. There is good reason, however, to see these interpretive difficulties not as problems but as signs that Auden was groping toward a more complex aesthetic and theoretical position than the first version of *Paid on Both Sides* had implied. Consider the final lyric in his 1928 *Poems*, which Auden inserted into the second version of *Paid on Both Sides* as a chorus after John's dream and before his marriage:

> To throw away the key and walk away
> Not abrupt exile, the neighbours asking why,
> But following a line with left and right
> An altered gradient at another rate
> Learns more than maps upon the whitewashed wall
> The hand put up to ask; and makes us well
> Without confession of the ill.
>
> . . . .
> The future shall fulfil a surer vow
>
> . . . .
> Not swooping at the surface still like gulls
> But with prolonged drowning shall develop gills.   (27)

In portraying cure as taking a journey, this lyric rejects the Freudian premise (as Auden took it) that a detached, analytical view—that of maps or birds—can release one from the past. "To throw away the key" is to abandon the effort to enter the past and treat it through the talking cure ("confession of the ill"). Instead Auden proposes deliberate but unstructured action, "following a line with left and right / An altered gradient at another rate."[10] The trope of "a line with left and right" supplants a linear model of (straight)forward growth and backward regression with one of alternating movement, ungoverned by teleological assumptions about the journey's end.[11] It is a positive figure of tension-in-movement from unresolved contradiction. Another term for such movement would be *crooked,* whose implications of duplicity and directional irresolution give it a force akin to the more recent usage of *queer.*

The last line of the stanza offers another figure for positive change from contradiction: "prolonged drowning shall develop gills." The same trope, we recall, functions in "1929" as a figure for change by mutation. And here, as Mendelson notes, the image of drowning prefigures the linkage Auden drew in his Berlin journal: "Satiety. Mutation. Persisting in folly brings wisdom" (*Early* 50). *Paid on Both Sides,* for all its atmosphere and tonalities of doom, is no less Audenesque in its elements of silliness—above all in the absurdity of John's dream-cure by tooth-extraction. In his "Preliminary Statement" on ritual drama, Auden's term for "cure-by-folly" is "joke": "The joke includes its own contradiction. It is therefore the only form of absolute statement" (*PDW* 461). Appropriately enough, this claim may be read in two contradictory ways (at least). First, the "contradiction" of a joke is meaningless: questions of its truth value are irrelevant, for a joke is not a truth statement. Second, a joke is the only absolutely true statement, for it alone implicitly recognizes that its own contradiction is also true. Auden was probably influenced here by Freud's claim that jokes, like dreams, employ representation by opposite.[12] He is not suggesting that contradiction should be resolved through analysis, however, but proposing the joke itself as a discursive source of meaning and value. He is far closer to Wilde's claim in "The Truth of Masks" that "A truth in art is that whose contradictory is also true" (Wilde 432).

But Auden wants to harness contradiction for the sake of therapeutic change. In describing "ritual drama," as we have seen, he says that it is "directed towards the stimulation of the spectator who passes thereby from a state of indifference to a state of acute awareness." Dramatic plot, like the joke, involves awareness of contradiction: "the assertion that God could not exist without Satan," that "what is evil is potential good, that hate is love turned against itself." As a diagnosis of personal and cultural disorder, *Paid on Both Sides* can be read in contradictory ways, and to recognize this potential is to see it as exemplifying not only ritual drama but psychoanalysis, as Auden defines it in his "Preliminary Statement":

People are in a room. Each is talking and listening. Part of what he hears makes him more like a saint, part more like a devil. The first is psychological truth, the second psychological falsehood. There is no other criterion. "Have you heard this one?" Sometimes his younger brother laughs, sometimes he opens the window, and sometimes he has one of his own to tell. That is psychoanalysis. There is nothing else.

(*PDW* 461)

Like ritual drama, psychoanalysis seeks to stimulate an "acute awareness" that will lead to some sort of response. "Have you heard this one?" is a way of introducing a story or a joke, and what the story or joke means will depend on how the listener responds—laughing, opening a window, telling another one.

The idea that artistic discourse, like psychoanalysis, realizes its potential through a provocative open-endedness informs not only *Paid on Both Sides* but Auden's later theories of art as "parable," "game of knowledge," and "analogy." Art, from this point of view, serves not as the bearer of singular truths but as a provocation to multiple, contradictory awarenesses that force us to "mutate" in response. If *Paid on Both Sides* dramatizes the sexual politics of "love turned against itself," its capacity for contradictory readings would be crucial to such a process. "God cannot exist without Satan," Auden wrote in the "Preliminary Statement," and while the terms and logic are Blakean, the meanings are Layard's, for whom God was desire and the Devil our conscious control of desire (see Isherwood, *Lions* 239). For Auden in Berlin, Layard's ideas implied that sexual liberation was a moral imperative, and *Paid on Both Sides* can be read in this way. The hate that leads John to kill the Spy springs from self-recognition, the realization that the sexual duplicity of the Spy is his own. By implication, the paranoic hate in this play can be undone only by a mutation of same-sex desire from homosociality to homosexuality, the release of desire from its repressive sublimation in group bonds dedicated to the murderous feud. By this logic, John should marry not Anne Shaw but her brother, the Spy—as, I suggest, he does in his dream. One could even read the outer "frame" drama itself as a coded tale of coming out—a tale of heinous love forbidden by the family, which is not just the plot of *Romeo and Juliet* but that of many a gay coming-of-age novel. To respond to the play this way would be to read it deliberately against the grain of its ostensible diagnosis of regressive homoeroticism and its prescription of heterosexual release. But such an antithetical reading would be taking it precisely as a "joke" in Auden's sense—as a statement that "includes its own contradiction": this is a play about curing homosexuality, and it is a play about curing homophobia, with its roots in anxiety about masculinity and aggression.

It is more than suggestive, therefore, that Auden declared in a letter to Stephen Spender about the play, "I am the Man-Woman." While Auden's Man-Woman does function as, in Mendelson's words, "a personification of the repressed erotic impulse toward union and love," the figure also recalls Proust's depiction of the homosexual as the "homme-femme" in *Sodome et Gomorrhe,* which Auden was reading in this period (see Mendelson, *Early* 51). In his 1929 journal Auden was equivocal about Proust's "analysis of the bugger." While commenting that Proust's "talk about the 'man-woman' seems astoundingly superficial and quite meaningless," he also wrote a long entry on "buggery" as a reaction to the cultural "segregation of maleness and femaleness": "For a long time education has enforced the idea that men are men and women women, quite different." Buggery "becomes an attempt to complete oneself. . . ." The entry is obscured by Auden's deletions, but the gist is clear: "The queer [?queen] is the . . . sensual repressed . . . in man . . . taking the female form, because these feelings have been called feminine."[13] Rather than reading the Man-Woman as prefiguring John and Anne's marriage, we might read their marriage as an allegory of the homosexual's "attempt to complete oneself," of man becoming man-woman, accepting the "sensual" world of the body.

If it is hard to know whether the homosexual is a figure for the heterosexual or vice versa, that might be Auden's ultimate point. To read *Paid on Both Sides* as a queer text would be to resist reconciling its contradictions, reading it both as a story of homosexual liberation and as a story of homosexual cure. As Auden wrote in his 1929 journal: " 'Normals' and 'perverts.' They're the same. Are sodulation and copotomy." Or, in its published version: "The pleasures of the English nation: / Copotomy and sodulation (*EA* 51)." Even if "normals" and "perverts" are "the same," however, Auden's terms are both crooked, marked as it were by "left and right": no sexual orientation implies that one can be self-identical; either way, one is queer.

III

On its publication in 1932, critics saw *The Orators* as a work that made Auden a poet to be attended to; one even called it "the most valuable contribution to English poetry since 'The Waste Land.' "[14] But critics were puzzled as well as impressed, and they have been notoriously uncertain about the politics of *The Orators*. At the time, Auden commented in a letter that it was "a stage in my conversion to communism" (Haffenden 122). But he was never fully converted, and when he introduced the third edition of *The Orators* (1966), he saw things differently: "My name on the title-page seems a pseudonym for someone else, someone talented but near the border of sanity, who might well, in a year or two, become a Nazi." Clarifying little about his conscious political identifications in 1932, he wrote, "My guess to-day is that my unconscious motive in writing it was therapeutic, to exorcise certain tendencies in myself by allowing them to run riot in phantasy" (*Orators* vii).

The "tendencies" Auden was overtly referring to were political, but we may wonder what else he might have had in mind. For *The Orators* is even more explicitly preoccupied with the homoerotics of political affiliation than *Paid on Both Sides,* and one cannot sort out whether it is fascist, communist, or something else without seeing how it portrays same-sex desire as a force both politically conservative and revolutionary.[15] By 1932, a sense of political crisis had only become more acute for Auden, and he was increasingly concerned with questions about the role of poetry and the poet in such a time. In this he was like many others in Britain, of course, and one reason his reputation began to grow so quickly after *The Orators* was that his worries about the relation between "public" and "private" dovetailed with those of his readers. But in considering the political role of the poet, Auden was specifically concerned, I shall argue, with the political role of the homosexual poet, and much of the complexity of *The Orators* reflects his effort to theorize and practice a queer aesthetic with a political conscience.

The idea that Auden was engaged with these issues at a conscious, deliberate level gains credence from the frequency with which *The Orators* prefigures concerns that have governed its own reception. The anxiety about whether Auden, a presumably leftist poet, was promoting fascism parallels the Airman's fears about complicity with "the enemy" in Book II. The messianic "He" of Book I has a "fondness for verbal puzzles," and the Airman describes how he uses practical jokes against the enemy. Moreover, as critics have noted, the Airman is homosexual,[16] and he is obsessed with how to distinguish himself from the enemy. *The Orators* is a text, in other words, consummately concerned with discursive operations and their implications for political identification.

This self-referentiality greatly enriches and complicates the analytical project that Auden presents himself as carrying out. Subtitled "An English Study," *The Orators* is most broadly a kind of anthropological examination of English culture and language, particularly the ways in which political power is exerted through rhetoric—public language used to subdue dissent and enforce group unity. What Auden sees rhetoric as performing at a linguistic level, he sees same-sex desire as doing at the psychosexual level: together they form a kind of political adhesive to preserve the governing class. *The Orators* implies not only that there is a homoerotic basis to fascism, but that the rhetorical and erotic workings of fascism are to be found in English culture.

To render such a critique as a homosexual poet, however, raises some knotty problems. How, for example, is it possible to expose rhetoric's coercive force except through means that have their own rhetorical aims? And if the governing class is constructed through homoerotic group bonds, what is the political position of the middle-class homosexual, educated in those very institutions that train that class? After all, homosexuality may be not so much a transgression as a crassly literal, bodily emulation of "normal" homosociality. Auden's problem of political opposition therefore entails an epistemological one, since there is no obvious position of true detachment from which to render any such critique: political complicity is also the complicity of subject with object, observer with observed.

The Orators explores this crux but also seeks to turn it to oppositional ends by exploiting the contradictory positionings of the homosexual. Against rhetorics that enforce epistemological order and social uniformity, Auden deploys an aesthetic of joking that exploits cognitive contradiction and social difference. This work frustrates critical analyses that depend on mutually exclusive binary terms (coherence/ incoherence, seriousness/ frivolity, fascism/antifascism, us/them), for it is questioning the politics of such conceptual orderings. In form and style it is relentlessly hybrid, and at its center is the hybrid of the homosexual trickster—the Airman of Book II.[17] The Airman's journal, which narrates his war of practical jokes against "the enemy," shows Auden theorizing and performing his own oppositional queer aesthetic, but such an aesthetic operates throughout *The Orators*. At the same time, in the demise of the Airman, Auden portrays the absurd limits of sexual-political theorizing. There are, ultimately, two intertwined "tendencies" Auden is diagnosing in himself here: his desire for totalizing sexual-political theories and systems, and his desire to believe in the political efficacy of purely discursive opposition.

Both such desires manifest themselves immediately in Book I. Auden once claimed that "The Initiates" was about a failed "revolutionary hero," but it is also about love and sickness (see Mendelson, *Early* 96). The middle sections of Book I ("Argument" and "Statement"), which more or less clearly explore the theme of revolution, are framed by two texts that link desire with moral and psychic disorder: "Address for a Prize-Day" and "Letter to a Wound." "The Initiates" as a whole, I shall argue, is about the leftist political pretensions of Auden and his group as products of all-male public schools.[18] Through parodies of official institutional rhetoric, scripture, and other forms of discourse, Auden both indulges a fantasy of queer revolution and diagnoses what he sees as its inevitable failure.

"Address for a Prize-Day" begins as rather typical schoolmaster rhetoric on the meaning of the past, only to modulate into a paranoic sermon on morality. The speaker diagnoses "England, this country of ours where nobody is well" (*EA* 62) by parsing schoolboys according to the three categories of improper lovers in Dante's *Purgatorio:* excessive, defective, and perverted lovers. While the first two can be saved, the perverted lovers can look forward only to the inevitable fate of the degenerate: "a protracted deathbed, attended by every circumstance of horror" (63). Like so many condemnations of degeneracy, this one urges active extinction of the incurables. They must "die without issue," he says, and he urges the other boys to thrust them into the "Black Hole" under the assembly hall. As he winds up his speech, the purge seems to begin: "Quick, guard that door. Stop that man. Good. Now boys hustle them, ready, steady—go" (64).

The "Address" expresses in parody the motives Auden analyzed in his essay "The Liberal Fascist," written for a 1934 anthology on public schools. Describing the "honour system" he had lived under at Gresham's School, Auden remarked, "The best reason I have for opposing Fascism is that at school I lived in a Fascist state." Gresham's honour system—banning swearing, smoking, and "indecency"—required boys to report any violators, so relied on "the only emotion that is fully developed in a boy of fourteen . . . the emotion of loyalty and honour" (*P* 59). The "Address" obviously critiques the ethos of "honour" by taking it to its pathological extreme—a pogrom against perverts. More than that, the "Address" implies that the seeds of fascism lie in the public-school ethos of group loyalty. The speaker never explains what is so dangerous about the perverted lovers, offering only a prognosis of "the hard death of those who never have and never could be loved" (*EA* 63). Their disease has in effect short-circuited the group bonds that preserve the institution.

What makes the "Address" so interesting, however, is that Auden is both indulging and interrogating his own analytical impulses. In his call to do away with the perverted lovers, the speaker actually misrepresents Dante, for the perverted lovers in *Purgatorio* are not irremediably damned. Auden's serious point is that disinterested analysis masks ideological interests. But he is also parodying his taste for psychosomatic and psychosexual diagnosis. The speaker offers elaborate descriptions of those who suffer from twisted love. "Excessive lovers" are Wordsworthian nature-lovers, identifiable by their taste for long walks and bird watching. "Defective lovers" collect bits of Audenesque industrial detritus. But the symptoms of the perverted lovers are inexplicable: "A slight proneness to influenza, perhaps, a fear of cows, traits easily misunderstood or dismissed," "extreme alarm" at "a simple geometrical figure," but basically they just somehow look sick. Auden brilliantly satirizes homophobia, pointing up how the pervert, by frustrating the categories that serve moral analysis, becomes a threateningly inexplicable otherness that can be dealt with only by being destroyed. At the same time, he is using comedy to ask whether his analytical bent is a form of paranoia about desire that reflects internalized homophobia. But while "Address" ends with an antihomosexual pogrom, the punishment of the perverted lovers—who are to be thrust into that Black Hole—is suggestively homoerotic. As Mendelson aptly puts it, what happens there is "a fatal parody of initiation," and "The Initiates" is of course the title of Book I (*Early* 98). The very image of the Black Hole is fraught with homoerotic implications: it suggests a site—both architectural and anatomical—for the mastering of nonconformists. Down below the oral, rhetorical arena of the assembly hall, a more physical enforcement of group unity takes place in an act that, in the Prize-Day speaker's own terms, is a ritual of perversion.

Or so the text implies: to suggest such a scenario is, of course, to read into the "Black Hole" and derive a narrative that continues beyond the "Address." Such gaps have the erotic quality of what Barthes calls variously "intermittence," "tear[s]," and "edges" (9–10). *The Orators* is full of moments like this, which eroticize readerly uncertainty in much the way Auden's poetry of the closet does. Such gaps—and the questions they raise—show Auden playing a sexual-political game with high modernist values of difficulty and obscurity. Like *The Waste Land* or Pound's *Cantos, The Orators* might be said to flaunt its modernism in the suppression of explicit transitions. One way to respond is to observe the constructedness of the whole. The manifest structure of *The Orators* is governed by genre: three "books" ("The Initiates," "Journal of an Airman," "Six Odes"), with "The Initiates" divided into "Address for a Prize-Day," "Argument," "Statement," and "Letter to a Wound." Many of these sections, in turn, are comprised of subsections in which Auden imitates (or parodies) a particular writer (e.g., Stein, Rimbaud, Lawrence), literary form (e.g., Old Irish versification, Pindaric Ode, Anglican hymn, ballad), or discursive practice (e.g., sermon, diary, love letter, scientific formula, riddle). This "English Study" offers itself, in other words, as an encyclopedic anthropological survey of a complex foreign culture.

Moreover, like *The Waste Land, The Orators* involves buried sources that might explain the whole mythologically. But part of Auden's joke is that these sources are far more obscure than J. G. Frazer and Jessie Weston, and in any case he doesn't provide notes. In creating Book II's Airman, Auden adapted John Layard's anthropological studies of New Guinea tribal tricksters, whose initiation rites supposedly involved death, resurrection, and anal insemination by ghosts. Such information would have seemed irresistible to Auden, one suspects, given his fascination with models of psychosexual growth and degeneration, death and rebirth, and ghosts. From one point of view, *The Orators* may be said to have an underlying dramatic coherence based on myth, with each book and the work as a whole telling a story of homosexual death and rebirth. But like his New Guinea model, the Airman is a trickster, and Auden's tropes of death and rebirth are also jokes about his own psychosexual fantasies and his love of theoretical systems. Thus a major target of parody in *The Orators* is high modernist Symbolism: the "mythical method" Eliot famously ascribed to *Ulysses* and was taken to be using in *The Waste Land*. This is, one might say, a queer parody of *The Waste Land*, in which Auden is satirizing the impulse—in himself and in others—to resolve private complexes by means of grand theoretical and symbolic orders.

Such a symbolic order comes into play immediately after the call to punish the perverted lovers at the end of "Address." "Argument" opens with images of death and rebirth: "Lo, I a skull show you, exuded from dyke when no pick was by pressure of bulbs: at Dalehead a light moving, lanterns for lambing. Before the forenoon of discussion, as the dawn-gust wrinkles the pools, I waken" (*EA* 64). Most neutrally put, what "Argument" proceeds to narrate is the return of the repressed perverts, reborn as a revolutionary movement. The joking contradiction lurking here is that the quasi-political, quasi-religious language of "Argument" expresses both a reaction against and a fulfillment of the punitive sodomitical impulses incited in "Address for a Prize-Day." In "The Liberal Fascist" Auden put it in serious terms:

> By appealing to [loyalty and honour] . . . you can suppress the expression of all those emotions, particularly the sexual, which are still undeveloped; like a modern dictator you can defeat almost any opposition from other parts of the psyche, but if you do, if you deny these other emotions their expression and development . . . they will not only never grow up, but they will go backwards, for human nature cannot stay still.
>
> (*P* 59)

Seen through the Freudian paradigm of psychosexual maturation, the authoritarian appeal to loyalty promotes exactly what it seeks to suppress; it forces sexuality "backwards"—producing the homosexual. "Argument" and "Statement" describe the consequences of this contradictory suppression and encouragement of same-sex desire in schools, as they construct the subjects of the governing class. In quasi-scriptural form, Auden narrates an uprising in which homoerotic drives erupt into attempted revolution. To use his later phrasing, this story jokingly "exorcises" his "tendency" to fantasize about queer avenging angels, showing his own regressive, protofascistic impulses.

Shaped by the very structures they attack, the rebels fail, and their failure offers both a diagnosis and a prognosis for those suffering, in Connolly's terms, from "permanent adolescence": the leftist, public-school-educated homosexual is implicated in the very culture and institutions he would oppose. The movement has a messianic leader who never appears directly to us, though He is described portentously by his followers:

> Speak the name only with meaning only for us, meaning Him, a call to our clearing. Secret the meeting in time and place, the time of the off-shore wind, the place where loyalty is divided. . . .
>
> On the concrete banks of baths, in the grassy squares of exercise, we are joined, brave in the long body, under His eye. . . .
>
> Walking in the mountains we were persons unknown to our parents, awarded them little, had a word of our own for our better shadow.
>
> (*EA* 64)

Taken straight, so to speak, this is a quasi-biblical account of a revolution led by a messiah: much as the church is the Body of Christ, this group is "joined, brave in the long body, under His eye."[19] However, this is also just a laughably mystical form of the standard gay adolescent coming-of-age narrative (minus bourgeois guilt): boy meets boy and realizes his true, "secret" identity, feels the erotic charge on the field and in the showers, and revels in his covert difference from parents. The schoolboy fantasy quality of all this implies that the homoerotic hero-worship of adolescence drives the desire for political strongmen—an idea as applicable to the left as to the right.

After describing such Mortmerean activities as building a torpedo base and visiting a mine, "Argument" offers a group litany and concludes by narrating the leader's sudden demise: "Suspicion of one of our number. . . . Friendly joking converting itself into a counterplot, the spore of fear. Then, in the hot weeks, the pavement blistering and the press muzzled, the sudden disaster, surprising as a comic turn" (*EA* 68). Like John Nower's betrayal of the feud, this moment involves a dangerous detachment of the libido from the group:

> If it were possible, yes, now certain. To meet Him alone on the narrow path, forcing a question, would show our unique knowledge. Would hide Him wounded in a cave, kneeling all night by His bed . . . wearing His cloak receive the mistaken stab, deliver His message, fall at His feet, He gripping our moribund hands, smiling. But never for us . . . a league of two or three waiting for low water to execute His will.
>
> (65)

Thus far, "Argument" has read like the collective expression of the group, but here an individuated *speaker* is coming to birth in fantasizing about exclusive bonds with the leader. In a moment of sexualized violence, he fantasizes merging with the wounded leader, as if to protect Him. But this fantasy is itself destructive of the group, for such exclusive erotic bonds would conflict with the aim-inhibited desire that drives the movement. At the last moment, the speaker renounces his fantasy, accepting the collective mission to "execute His will."

The first-person plural pronouns here imply that this fantasy is typical—one to which any initiate may be subject. The implication is that each member of the group carries the threat of individuation in overcoming inhibitions governing desire for the leader; indeed, such individuation is what seems to destroy Him toward the end of "Argument": "one of our number" is the perpetrator. With Him gone, the movement declines into furtive erotic individuality: "Love, that notable forked one, riding away from the farm, the ill word said, fought at the frozen dam, transforms itself to influenza and guilty rashes. Seduction of a postmistress on the lead roof of a church-tower, and an immature boy wrapping himself in a towel, ashamed at the public baths."[20] The discursive fallout of the leader's death is apparent in the next section, "Statement." Unlike the sometimes unfathomable tone of "Argument," "Statement" has the air of a scripture retrospectively codifying the leader's message (see Mendelson, *Early* 101). Its rhetorical aim, like that of "Address for a Prize-Day," is to assert orthodoxy and enforce group unity. But as John Boly has noted, "Statement" actually subverts itself by portraying extreme individuality (see "Portraits" 256–57). "To each an award," "Statement" declares, "suitable to his sex, his class and the power," yet the awards suggest utter difference: "One charms by thickness of wrist; one by variety of positions. . . . One delivers buns in a van, halting at houses" (*EA* 69). Similarly, the "fates" it describes are often ludicrous. As it reaches a rhetorical climax in Lawrentian prophetic tones, "Statement" collapses into absurd disconnection: "The leader shall be a fear; he shall protect from panic; the people shall reverence the carved stone under the oak-tree; the muscular shall lounge in bars; the puny shall keep diaries in classical Greek." The final decay into singularity is epitomized by "Letter to a Wound," an initiate's love letter to "the emptiness left in his psyche by the leader's departure" (Mendelson, *Early* 101). It is a deliciously smarmy, narcissistic paean to loss: "The surgeon was dead right. Nothing will ever part us. Good-night and God bless you, my dear" (*EA* 73).

As a story of failed rebellion, "The Initiates" implies that just as perverted love threatens the body politic with irreducible difference in "Address," the revolution born out of that pogrom is undone by desire that individuates. As in *Paid on Both Sides,* same-sex desire has contrary propensities: toward loss of self in group, and toward subversive individuation. Where *The Orators* goes further is in suggesting that an oppositional movement depends just as much upon a fascistic group ethos that requires sublimation of desire. All political groupings, dominant or resistant, involve the erotically and rhetorically charged subjection of individual to leader and group. Given that Auden is concerned specifically with the *homo*erotic nature of such bonds, the fascistic quality of the group movement in "The Initiates" implies that the would-be homosexual revolutionary identifies with his oppressor.

As fantasy, this is not politically subversive, for it reflects the homosexual's internalization of normative constructions of masculinity—in Auden's terms, the need of the bugger to call himself a man. Leo Bersani has made much the same point in analyzing post-Stonewall gay machismo: "If licking someone's leather boots turns you (and him) on, neither of you is making a statement subversive of macho masculinity. Parody is an erotic turn-off." By implication, Bersani writes,

> The dead seriousness of the gay commitment to machismo . . . means that gay men run the risk of idealizing and feeling inferior to certain representations of masculinity on the basis of which they are in fact judged and condemned. The logic of homosexual desire includes the potential for a loving identification with one's enemies.
>
> ("Is" 208)

From this point of view, the militant schoolboy antics of "The Initiates" implicate Auden's own political pretensions in the institutions of which he was a product; such fantasies of subversion are really politics by reaction formation.

"Letter to a Wound" has a further, more complicated meaning, however. In context one can read it as the fictional epistle of a neurotic initiate, exorcising Auden's fascistic fantasies of homosexual rebellion. But as a private joke on Auden's part, it enacts another form of political opposition in the rejection of seriousness. (Bersani's point, we recall, is not that parody is politically meaningless but that gay machismo is not really parodic.) Read as the epistle of an initiate, the letter describes a wound in the psyche. But if we know that Auden was treated in 1930 for an anal fissure, certain passages read rather differently: "Once, when a whore accosted me, I bowed, 'I deeply regret it, Madam, but I have a friend.' Once I carved on a seat in the park 'We have sat here. You'd better not' " (73). While Auden said that his injury did not come from sexual activity, he apparently enjoyed calling it in private the "Stigmata of Sodom" (Mendelson, *Early* 111).

However juvenile the joke, one can never read "Letter to a Wound" the same way afterward. It seems to be Auden's diagnosis of his homosexuality as neurotic self-infatuation, as the masochistic desire for subjugation by phallic masculinity. At the same time, "Letter to a Wound" also points to the subversive possibilities inherent in the constitution of secrecy surrounding this desire for subjugation. Like Auden's Mortmerean early poems, it turns private knowledge against the unknowing reader. And such gestures are made with a purpose, as the epigraph to *The Orators* suggests: "Private faces in public places / Are wiser and nicer / Than public faces in private places." "The Initiates" opens with rhetoric aiming to control the perverts who threaten the group; "Address for a Prize-Day" exemplifies public faces acutely troubled by certain people's private places. It closes with a text that introjects a private face into a public book, and in doing so covertly, Auden exploits social differences among readers at the expense of a unified "public." Those in the know will read "Letter to a Wound" differently from those who are not. Auden's epigraph celebrates not only private social groups but the techniques for mutual recognition in public places—in more recent slang, "gaydar."

Much of Auden's early poetry, as we have seen, confronts us with a private world, only to block our entrance: "Stranger, turn back again, frustrate and vexed: / This land, cut off, will not communicate" (*EA* 22). In portraying a failed revolution, "The Initiates" implies that the privacy of Mortmere is a debilitating form of discursive individuation whose political pretensions, as Boly argues, are ineffective and immature ("Portraits" 256). But the baroque obscurities of "The Initiates" also point to a different notion of socially oppositional writing, where immaturity has a different force. Twenty-five years after *The Orators*, Auden introduced John Ashbery's first book, *Some Trees*, observing:

> From Rimbaud down to Mr. Ashbery, an important school of modern poets has been concerned with the discovery that, in childhood largely, in dreams and daydreams entirely, the imaginative life of the human individual stubbornly continues to live by the old magical notions. Its world is one of sacred images and ritual acts . . . a numinous landscape inhabited by demons and strange beasts.
>
> (Ashbery 13)

The later Auden's religious idiom notwithstanding, his comments suggest that the very childishness of the fantasy of revolt in "The Initiates" critiques, like Ashbery's poetry or Rimbaud's, normative "adult" notions of reality and meaning. Indeed, the stylistic kinship of *Les Illuminations* and "The Initiates" is apparent. Here is Rimbaud:

> A swarm of gold leaves smothers the general's house. They're in the South. — You take the red road to reach the empty inn. The château's up for sale and the shutters are coming loose. — The priest must have taken away the key of the church. Around the park, the keepers' cottages are uninhabited. The fences are so high that you can only see the tree tops moving in the wind.
>
> (Rimbaud 217)

Here is Auden in *The Orators:*

> The young mother in the red kerchief suckling her child in the doorway, and the dog fleaing itself in the hot dust. Clatter of nails on the inn's flagged floor. The hare-lipped girl sent with as far as the second turning. Talk of generals in a panelled room translated into a bayonet thrust at a sunbrowned throat, wounds among wheat fields.
>
> (*EA* 65)

Both passages manipulate a tension between transparency of style and detail, on the one hand, and the absence of obvious connection among details on the other. The portentous weirdness of Auden's passage, so characteristic of his early poetry, comes from indeterminate significance in what is very precise imagery. As with much of Rimbaud's writing, the meaning of Auden's passage cannot be conceptualized in terms of determinate reference and signification, so in applying these standards to *The Orators,* many critics have found it obscure, confused about how serious it is, and immature.[21]

As argued in the introduction of this book, the charge of "immaturity" often serves as a code for "homosexuality" among Auden's critics.[22] But key elements of Auden's writing are precisely those cited by Freud in connecting the techniques of jokes ("Faulty thinking, displacements, absurdity, representation by opposite, etc.") with a child's linguistic play: "[The child] puts words together without regard to the condition that they make sense, in order to obtain from them the pleasurable effect of rhythm or rhyme. . . . A private language may even be constructed for use among playmates" (*SE* 8, 124, 125). "The Initiates" has the quality of a "private language" whose jokes are missed by those who are not native speakers. It is joking at the expense of the "public" reader—the *uninitiated*—who insists on reading with the adult attitude that language respect conventions of seriousness and noncontradiction. In its frequent opacities, its bizarre tone, its moments of sheer absurdity, "The Initiates" suggests that there are perspectives on and meanings within reality unavailable to some. From this point of view, Auden's serious critique of the futility of homosexual rebellion is only part of the point, and the question of whether this work is fascist, communist, or otherwise, is something of a critical red herring. For the real objects of Auden's assault are forms of systematic understanding threatened by the queer.

IV

In Book II of *The Orators*, "Journal of an Airman," the oppositional potential of writing becomes Auden's chief concern: this is, after all, a text whose title foregrounds its written status and implies a fictional author. I shall argue that the "Journal" is a coded study of writing as a revolutionary technique, in which flying is a metaphor for the power in sexual deviance for the queer poet. In the story of the Airman, Auden provides a biography of the queer poet and a theory of queer poetry as an antirhetorical mode. In comic form, Auden provides, in fact, the poetic theory behind *The Orators* as a whole—a theory of joking as a queer poetic.

In his revelatory 1977 essay on *The Orators*, Peter Firchow explains how Auden adapted John Layard's work as an anthropologist on the Bwili, sorcerers of Malekula, in New Guinea.[23] The crucial details, as offered by Layard, are these. A Bwili is initiated as a pubescent boy by another Bwili, who must be his maternal uncle. The boy is secluded from his family and abstains from sex with women. The climax of initiation involves a ritual of death and resurrection, in which he is progressively dismembered. If he manages to keep laughing while his limbs and head are cut off, his body reassembles and he becomes a

Bwili; if he fails, he dies (see Layard, "Malekula," 507–8). Moreover, during his initiation the boy is anally inseminated by ghosts. Having undergone ritual death and resurrection, the Bwili is, in Layard's words, "one with the world of the resurrected dead" (523). He can take the form of a bird and fly, or impersonate other animals, plants, and people, and as such he has all the powers of a ghost. In disguise he often plays jokes on people, sometimes composing songs about these jokes, and while he cannot be killed, he can kill others (509–10). Apart from these things, what probably interested Auden about the Bwili tricksters was Layard's Freudian analysis of them by analogy to epilepsy: "The purpose of epilepsy being to drown out one side—and that the adult side—of a conflict, the epileptic retains an infantile mentality, with the result that he is apt to be child-like in his tastes, irresponsible, roguish, and playful" (520). Layard in turn connects epilepsy with homosexuality as a disorder aimed at "the suppression of the adult side of the conflict" (524).

Like the Bwili, Auden's Airman has been initiated—seduced, it is implied—by his mother's brother, Uncle Henry: "It wasn't till I was sixteen and a half that he invited me to his flat. We had champagne for dinner. When I left I knew who and what he was—my real ancestor" (*EA* 85). Also like the Bwili, the Airman is involved with the dead—he worships his late Uncle Henry. Piloting planes is obviously Auden's modern version of the Bwili's ability to become a bird, and the Airman's poems recall an odd Bwili song Layard transcribes. The Airman is homosexual,[24] as well as a practical joker, and jokes are his main weapon against the enemy.

The Airman obsessively analyzes the enemy, but most tellingly by means of discursive habits: "Three terms of enemy speech—I mean—quite frankly—speaking as a scientist, etc."; "Three signs of an enemy letter—underlining—parentheses in brackets—careful obliteration of cancelled expressions" (81). These are signs of the enemy's mental distance on what he says or writes: in the Airman's terms, the enemy suffers from "self-regard"—Lawrentian self-consciousness—as opposed to healthy "self-care or minding one's own business" (73). Enemy "catchwords" are "insure now—keep smiling—safety first," for he minds other people's business, making them self-conscious about their future, other people's reactions, and above all, their own bodies (82).

The enemy perpetuates alienation of mind from body: "the enemy as philosopher," the Airman tells us, treats "intellect-will-sensation as real and separate entities" (76).

Since the enemy has elevated his own dysfunctions into a world-view, the Airman attacks by exposing the contingency of enemy ideas, revealing enemy truth as the mere objectification of "private associations":

> The enemy's sense of humour—verbal symbolism. Private associations (rhyming slang), but note that he is serious, the associations are constant. He means what *he* says.
>
> Practical jokes consist in upsetting these associations. They are in every sense contradictory and public, e.g. my bogus lecture to the London Truss Club.
>
> (78)

The enemy's governing ideologies are sincerity and seriousness ("He means what *he* says"), but his verbal tics ("I mean—quite frankly") bespeak his self-consciousness about language. His "sense of humour" shows that he actually reasons through "private associations," not logic. And the Airman's point is that the enemy *always* thinks this way: "the associations are constant. He means what *he* says." The enemy takes his private associations to be reality, so his "truth" is really just the collective agreement of those in charge. As Stan Smith puts it, "Foremost among the Airman's subversive activities . . . is the undermining of language, particularly in those oral public forms that posit an audience of participating equals" (*Auden* 62). The Airman's jokes rely on *in*sincerity and *un*seriousness, exposing enemy "truth" as consensus by revealing difference among those who seem equal and alike—"e.g. my bogus lecture to the London Truss Club," an oration no more serious or sincere than Auden's "Letter to a Wound."

The Airman's detached perspective on the enemy is symbolized by his flying—he has the diagnostic "hawk's view" of Auden's early work, the capacity to see a culture from without. As we shall see, the Airman eventually decides that such detachment is false, that he has been infected with enemy thinking, just as the uprising of "The Initiates" ended up mimicking the rhetorical modes of those it fought. But we must first see how the Airman's joking serves as Auden's model for a queer poetic.

Among the Airman's journal ruminations are a number of poems, all of which are highly coded and might well be called jokes. The most revealing one is a sestina Auden later gave a title that is itself a sexual joke—"Have a Good Time":

> We have brought you, they said, a map of the country;
> Here is the line that runs to the vats,
> This patch of green on the left is the wood,
> We've pencilled an arrow to point out the bay.
> No thank you, no tea; why look at the clock.
> Keep it? Of course. It goes with our love.   (*EA* 77)

As Blair has explained, the poem allegorizes the growth of the poet—a worker at the dyers' "vats." His elders advise him to "wind up the clock" and to "Keep fit by bathing in the bay," but to avoid the "flying trickster" who haunts the wood. In fact, though, the elders are the enemy, who treat "intellect-will-sensation as real and separate entities." The wood, Blair observes, signifies sensation, the bay a place to exercise the intellect, and the clock a device to assist the will (80). Defying his elders, the apprentice poet gazes at the divers in the bay and enters the wood, where he "Finds consummation . . . And sees for the first time the country," with "water in the wood and trees by the bay." He discovers, that is, that intellect, will, and sensation, are not discrete entities.

If we miss the suggestiveness of the poem's imagery, however, we become the butt of the joke. The warning against the "flying trickster," for example, recalls the antipathy of the Airman's mother toward his uncle, who was also a pilot. The "consummation" found in the wood may be psychic, but it is expressed with a word that has erotic overtones, just as "sensation" is figured in the sexy divers in the bay. To read the poem only as an allegory of the poet's growth actually requires divorcing intellect and will from sensation—thus contradicting the poem's point. It is another practical joke, in which the reader is forced into enemy thinking in order to decode the poem. To discover this is to realize that the enemy's version of "truth" requires bracketing out dangerous kinds of sensations (i.e., homoerotic ones), lest one admit that there is such a thing as the queer. Such jokes are a favorite pastime of the Airman, and his "Airman's Alphabet" extends this joking potential from A to Z, with much suggestiveness in between:

> COCKPIT—   Soft seat
> and support of soldier
> and hold for hero.
>
> . . . .
>
> JOYSTICK—   Pivot of power
> and responder to pressure
> and grip for the glove.   (79)

Like the secret agent, the Airman is a figure for the queer poet, whose special insight into social and cognitive means of domination has subversive potential. By implication, this power is rooted in the self-consciousness that comes with the closet. But looming here is a contradiction that undoes the Airman, for we have already seen how he idealizes *un*self-consciousness. It is the enemy, he says, who believes "man's only glory is to think" (78). "THE ENEMY IS A LEARNED NOT A NAIVE OBSERVER," he writes at one point, glossing "Naïve observation" as "insight," and "introspection" as "spying" (74). The enemy embodies "self-regard," not "self-care," and his overactive brain will make him pick out the oblique diagram in the Airman's *"Sure Test"* for identifying an enemy agent, not the obvious, symmetrical ones. In fact, the best word for the wrong diagram is *crooked,* for the Airman's analysis implies that the enemy suffers from sick homosexual self-consciousness. Of course, the Airman's incessant, pseudoscientific theorizing about the enemy and himself points to his own utter reliance on thought, his own self-regard. And diagramming the genealogy of enemy self-regard, the Airman unwittingly describes his own ancestry, which later he blithely traces to his maternal uncle: *"Note*—Self-regard . . . is a sex-linked disease. Man is the sufferer, woman the carrier. 'What a wonderful woman she is!' Not so fast: wait till you see her son" (73). This comment, of course, recalls the Freudian cliché of the homosexual's domineering mother, just as the diagnosis of enemy "self-regard" implies the roots of homosexuality in narcissism. Such theories are reduced to tools of homophobic policing in the hands of the Airman. Sure that he can, as it were, tell one a mile away, he reflects the notion that the depravity of the pervert is, as Foucault puts it, "written immodestly on his face and body" (*History* I, 43).

If homosexuality is an empowering difference for the Airman, it also defines the enemy's sickness. A corollary of this contradiction is that what produces the Airman's detachment also points to his complicity with the enemy, as seen in his periodic references to a strange problem with his hands. "Only once here, quite at the beginning, and I put it back. Uncle Sam, is he one too? He has the same backward-bending thumb that I have. I wonder. It's going to be alright. Courage. The daily exercise of the will in trivial tasks" (*EA* 79). The hint is that the Airman suffers from kleptomania, but kleptomania seems itself a code. In a 1932 review, Auden referred to "theft, that attempt to recover the lost or stolen treasure, love" (*P* 12), and this idea fits nicely with the hints at masturbation in the Airman's self-recriminations. Moreover, the Airman's "backward-bending thumb" recalls Auden's tropes of backwardness and crookedness. "Crook," of course, can also mean "thief." The Airman steals in spite of himself: his hands just will not follow orders. His kleptomania, in other words, is a symptom that implicates his homosexuality in the enemy split of "intellect-will-sensation."

The Airman's journal describes his increasing realization that he has been "infected" by the enemy, and the key moment is his dream about his lover, E. In the dream, a river separates him from E, who is tied to railroad tracks, a train on the way. Trying to save E, the Airman shouts to a ferryman (fairyman?), but his voice is drowned out by a crowd of football spectators behind him, and E is killed by the train. He then sees a newspaper photo of Uncle Henry, bordered in black, with the caption "I have crossed it" (85). The dream implies, as Boly puts it, that the Airman's "private self, which wants to save E, is repressed by . . . his public self, which heeds the roaring crowd ("Portraits" 253); the dream allegorizes his subjection to the closet, in other words, and implies his repression of his homosexuality by virtue of being a dream.

Suddenly, three days before he is due to launch his final attack on the enemy, the Airman figures out the dream:

Why, the words in my dream under Uncle's picture, "I HAVE CROSSED IT." To have been told the secret that will save everything and not to have listened. . . .

1. The power of the enemy is a function of our resistance, therefore

2. The only efficient way to destroy it—self-destruction, the sacrifice of all resistance. . . .

3. Conquest can only proceed by absorption of, i.e. infection by, the conquered. The true significance of my hands. "Do not imagine that you, no more than any other conqueror, escape the mark of grossness." They stole to force a hearing.

(EA 93)

His hands, that is, stole in order to tell him he was infected by the enemy; the harder he tried to control them, the more he proved that his mind and body were not one. The only way to overcome this enemy-induced split, he reasons, is total self-abnegation. Until now, the Airman has rejected the official verdict that his uncle's death was a suicide. But his uncle's words in the dream—"I have crossed it"— suggest that the verdict was right, that, as Mendelson puts it, "his uncle willingly crossed over the border that stood in the way of unity" (*Early* 109). The Airman puts his affairs in order, says goodbye to E, and flies off to die. His last words in the journal—"Hands in perfect order"—show his kleptomania cured.

Between the obscurities of the dream and the convolutions of the Airman's theories about subjectivity, it is rather hard to know what to make of all this. From the Airman's point of view, complicity with the enemy has finally vitiated his effort to subvert enemy single-mindedness and the ideology of univocality. Thus one implication concerns the double binds that impinge on a homosexual identity that assumes privilege in marginality, subversive power in detachment. The Airman sees himself as the descendant of his uncle, not his parents— the product of a crooked, deviating ancestry of tricksters. Yet the enemy disease of self-consciousness is passed on the same way— "Man is the sufferer, woman the carrier." And while he sees self-consciousness, the splitting of intellect-will-sensation, as the enemy disease, it is this kind of self-consciousness that gives him a sense of detachment on the enemy. The Airman's farewell letter to E suggests that homosexuality is the ultimate sign of infection with enemy self-consciousness, that it belies his pretension to organic self-integration. Since his desires are incurable, suicide is the only option, just as for his uncle. Such a conclusion would seem to reiterate the moral of "Address for a Prize-Day"—that death is the only end for perverts.

Rather than endorsing this notion, however, the death of the Airman represents Auden's recognition that a certain kind of oppositional homosexual poetic is self-defeating. What, after all, did the Airman's "bogus lecture to the London Truss Club" actually accomplish? Liberation and revolution, in other words, cannot come by fooling the censors: the enemy is still there. The Airman's suicide fulfills the fatalism of Auden's poetry of the closet, suggesting that the weapons of coding cannot liberate desire: ultimately they must destroy themselves by self-contradiction.

This is not to say, however, that Auden utterly rejects an oppositional queer poetic based on joking. To interpret the Airman's fate in this way is merely to replicate his basic acceptance of the enemy ideology of sincerity—an ideology he knows is belied by the enemy's every verbal tic. The enemy believes in univocality, that signifiers mean one thing, but the queer contradicts this proposition: this is what empowers the Airman's joking. Still, he persists in his ideal of self-integration, whose discursive analogue is sincerity. Since he is caught in an irresolvable contradiction, his sexuality shifts from a sign of insight to a sign of his own corruption, as if "straight" sexuality somehow meant *un*self-consciousness, sincerity, and unity of being. The Airman forgets that his uncle was a trickster. "I have crossed it" may mean that his uncle abandoned resistance and crossed over to the enemy. But as a dream about the Airman's repression of his love for E, it means that his uncle crossed over the river, overcoming the closet and accepting his homosexuality.

Auden is not, therefore, rejecting duplicity but portraying its limits as a political tool. It never occurs to the Airman that his uncle's words might be duplicitous. And in the end, his own "sacrifice of all resistance," his suicidal act of self-integration, is also duplicitous. Complete self-abnegation would surely mean doing nothing. Instead, in a gesture that is about as easy to read in Freudian terms as any image one could conceive of, he mans his plane and takes off—presumably to die explosively behind enemy lines. But this is not the first violent death of the queer in *The Orators*. The Airman's death is the final joke of Book II—not his own, but his creator's: he is "reborn" in Book III as a figure named "Wystan," who comes "round from the morphia" in the first ode.

V

The "Six Odes" that comprise Book III mark a significant formal shift not only in *The Orators* but in Auden's career. "The Initiates" and "Journal of an Airman" epitomize the Mortmerean, coded poetic of Auden's early work: figuratively complex, stylistically tough, resistant to the reader in so many ways. But in declaring a conventional generic allegiance, the odes portray the poet as addressing us *in propria persona,* on matters of personal or public import—for that is what odes do. The question of their political implications is no simpler to answer than in the rest of *The Orators,* for the question of Auden's seriousness here is just as acute. Is he looking for a leader at the end of the first ode? Does he really hope, in the words of the fourth, that some day "All of the women and most of the men / Shall work with their hands and not think again" (*EA* 105)? While the Airman's trouble with his hands makes it hard to take these lines seriously, *The Orators* is full of motifs of antibourgeois revolt, and the Airman is hardly a reassuring example of the life of the mind.

Some critics have exonerated Auden by arguing that he is not really the speaker of the odes but stands apart laughing and expecting us to laugh too; alternatively, one may simply see Auden as politically uncertain.[25] But the odes are problematic only if we forget what *The Orators* has been suggesting thus far: attempts to make words signify and refer univocally, free of contradiction, are really exertions of rhetorical power, and such attempts inevitably leave room for contradictions to undo them. The Airman uses this realization, even if he is destroyed in trying to save his own identity from self-contradiction. He dies in the process, but he is reborn, as it were, in the odes, as "Auden," a different poet with different responses to these problems.

In naming his poems generically, Auden conveyed—as his earlier writing did not do—a self-consciousness about literary form as involving publicly defined conventions. These are not odes *on* anything very precise, to be sure, but the middle four are odes dedicated *to* various people: Gabriel Carritt, Edward Upward, John Warner (Rex Warner's infant son), and Auden's pupils. While such people might not be known to the general reader, the odes are not coterie poetry in the manner of Auden's earlier writing, for they ask to be read as public performances. They take up themes treated already—leadership, group movements, political change—but they hardly resolve any of these issues, and they are not seriously meant to. In their flaunting of formal artifice, they represent a significant shift in how Auden negotiated the relation between public and private as a homosexual poet. From "Control of the passes" through "Journal of an Airman," Auden tended to use the public/private dichotomy as a source for power over the uninitiated reader, seeking to turn marginality into a politically subversive condition. The odes certainly involve private topicality, but Auden is overtly betraying his cliquishness here as he has never done before, precisely because he is "speaking as himself" in poems with explicit personal dedications, poems in which formal artifice is not a weapon but a source of pleasure in eccentricity.

Exploring personal references suggests that the private does not function in the odes as a realm of privileged knowledge and marginality. The first ode, "Watching in three planes from a room," has Auden dreaming in the recovery ward after the operation alluded to in "Letter to a Wound." People wander in and out of the poem speaking ominously—a "night-nurse," "the Headmaster," and two friends. "Stephen signalled from the sand dunes like a wooden madman / 'Destroy this temple' " (95). Even if we know that the line alludes to Spender's novel title, an emblem for the eroticized male body, the tone here (both Spender's and Auden's) remains obscure. In the next stanza, we are told that "It did fall," but not what "fall" means. Then,

> In cold Europe, in the middle of Autumn destruction,
> Christopher stood, his face grown lined with wincing
> In front of ignorance—"Tell the English," he shivered,
>   "Man is a spirit."

The tone here is so ambiguous that one cannot be sure whether something profound is being conveyed or something trivial posing as profundity. As Michael O'Neill and Gareth Reeves have observed, the ode "makes play of its cliquishness" by utterly indulging what the Airman calls "self-regard" (103). In a serious reading of these voices, "Destroy this temple" and "Tell the English, Man is a Spirit" would diagnose the self-regard of Auden and his group. But if one reads the ode this way, the grandeur of its ending, spoken by a beggar, is ludicrous:

> "Have you heard of someone swifter than Syrian horses?
> Has he thrown the bully of Corinth in the sanded circle?
> Has he crossed the Isthmus already? Is he seeking brilliant
>   Athens and us?"

To wonder whether these lines herald a social savior or demon, a fascist leader or a communist, misses their absurdity in context. We can read them seriously only if we take seriously the rhetoric of Stephen and Christopher (as recalled by "Wystan" coming out of the morphine), or if we see their generational "self-regard" as requiring so mythic a savior. The verses are put in the mouth of a beggar, but they are cast in the pretentious allusiveness of schoolboy classicism. One cannot be sure whether private worries are being raised to a level of public importance, or public concerns undercut by the silly self-importance of the private.

Such uncertainties follow from each of the next five odes. In the sixth ode—"Not, Father, further do prolong"—Auden's fun in parodying the convoluted inversions of hymn syntax is quite at odds with the poem's plea for clarifying deliverance by a savior who will "with ray disarm, / Illumine, and not kill" (110). Even as every "maddened set we foot" ostensibly bespeaks moral sickness, Auden is showing off his prosodic virtuosity. The message of the ode is not so different from his well-known 1929 sonnet "Petition" ("Sir, no man's enemy, forgiving all"), asking some deity/psychoanalyst to "look shining at / New styles of architecture, a change of heart" (*EA* 36). But "Petition" can be read *seriously* to a degree that his 1932 ode cannot. Like the drag queen donning gender codes in order to flaunt his/her femininity, the ode's formal garb of supplication, so precisely but ludicrously arranged, undermines any sense that the poet is really asking for salvation.

One way to describe the formal shifts reflected in the odes is by analogy to a mode long favored in gay culture: camp. As Susan Sontag famously wrote, camp is "esoteric—something of a private code, a badge of identity even, among small urban cliques" (275). Auden's early poetry and *The Orators* thus far certainly employ private codes to communicate to a coterie. But in the odes, it is not secret information that expresses their cliquishness so much as style itself. The tonal ambiguity of this poetry derives from the irony that one critic sees as defining camp: "incongruous contrast between an individual or thing and its context or association" (Babuscio 41). Such incongruities register in Auden's mixture of lofty and low subject matter and diction. Beyond this, these odes depend on an incongruity between private and public instigated by their dedications themselves. The second ode expresses a rhapsodic worship of power and the male body that one might read as fascistic, but it is addressed to Gabriel Carritt as ex-rugby player— "Captain of Sedburgh School XV, Spring 1927." The fourth ode welcomes a social savior that might be a fascist hero, but that savior, the poem's dedicatee, is John Warner, infant son of Auden's friend Rex Warner. Both the triumphant rugby players, "Joy docked in every duct" (98), and the infant John Warner embody union of mind and body, what the Airman calls "self-care." But their elevation to heroic stature in such mannered idioms hardly advances serious political analysis.

Ultimately, the odes show Auden letting go of fantasies about the inherent subversive power of homosexuality. This shift has a number of important implications for his evolution as a homosexual poet. In killing off the Airman, Auden in effect abandoned a dream of a homosexual identity that would be both oppositional and essentialist. In spite of his use of practical jokes "in every sense contradictory and public," the Airman still believes that he can fight the enemy from a position of detachment made possible because he has a coherent, essential self free from implication in the enemy. The later Auden spoke of *The Orators* as "exorcising certain tendencies" in himself: one of these, we might extrapolate, is the tendency toward essentialist fantasizing. Such fantasizing undergirds the ethic of sexual liberation that motivates so much of Auden's early work, both the contestatory, Mortmerean variety and his diagnostic mode. The odes, by contrast, flaunt the implication of same-sex desire in fascist group affiliations, immaturity, and self-regard—publicly indulging the kind of pleasure Auden took in his childish joking about the "Stigmata of Sodom." Their frivolity marks not just Auden's realization but his acceptance of the political and psychic contradictions of homosexuality.

At the same time, the odes suggest a disenchantment with the political possibilities of discursive opposition, given the inescapability of complicity. The Airman carries out his jokes, but the enemy remains undefeated, just as the group movement of "The Initiates" ultimately collapses. Auden's shift to a less avant-garde poetic in the odes and in his subsequent work in the 1930s coincided with a dropping away of the motifs of embattlement that had characterized his work thus far. His poetry, in other words, no longer sought to enact a war for liberation of desire in the way it had been. Certainly there is a sense at the end of *The Orators* that Auden is questioning the political efficacy of its aesthetics of contradiction. " 'O where are you going?' " asks the "reader" in the Epilogue, and the "rider" answers, " 'Out of this house' "—by which one might read, "Out of this book" (110).

Auden did not give up addressing politics in his poetry, exploring the relation between public and private, or negotiating how he might write about homosexuality in light of these things. But the odes herald a more accessible, less avant-garde poetry, formally more conventional than what he had been writing. A work like "Letter to Lord Byron" marks in many ways a far more conservative strategy for a homosexual poet. Similarly, Auden's subsequent love poetry, epitomized by the 1937 "Lay your sleeping head, my love," makes itself available to universalizing responses in a way that "Control of the passes" does not. There is much to see about how works like these reflect negotiations of public and private enforced by Auden's sense of his position as a homosexual poet. But these are the works not of the would-be queer revolutionary, the trickster trying desperately to be the outsider. This is Auden writing instead as the insider/outsider, cultivating possibilities for critique from within.

Chapter 4

"WHAT WE SEE DEPENDS ON WHO'S OBSERVING": POLITICS AND AUTHORITY IN THE 1930S

In its obsession with alternative ancestry, *The Orators* served Auden as a tribute to a literary queer uncle of his own: Arthur Rimbaud. While Rimbaud was something of a formal influence, more broadly he formed a prototype of the socially oppositional artist, as Auden acknowledged in a 1938 sonnet:

> But in that child the rhetorician's lie
> Burst like a pipe: the cold had made a poet.
>
> Drinks bought him by his weak and lyric friend
> His senses systematically deranged,
> To all accustomed nonsense put an end. . . .[1]

As Paul Schmidt has argued of Rimbaud, so we may say of the early Auden: homosexuality is one of the "*disorderings of the senses* which free us from our everyday perceptions of the world."[2] The verbal derangements of *The Orators* strive for just such disruptions, projecting through the lens of sexual deviance a crooked world to resist the official lies of adult reality. Still, if *The Orators* locates the absolutely modern poet in the queer boy, it also discovers Rimbaud's limits as a model. The last poem of *Une saison en enfer*, "Adieu," was one source Auden used for the Airman's suicide: in killing off his trickster, Auden conceded that his own avant-garde queer poetic might explode rhetoric, but it failed the test of worldly efficacy.[3]

"Rimbaud" is one of five sonnets from December 1938 in which Auden used portraiture to think about the homosexual artist. "Edward Lear" honors another childish poet of "nonsense," who fled social humiliation into the "prodigious welcome" of his work (*EA* 239); "The Composer" and "The Novelist," modeled on Benjamin Britten and on Isherwood, find in music and fiction the consolations at risk in the historical world. By contrast, "A. E. Housman" is a witty autopsy on the corpus of a closeted scholar-poet whose "private lust" was "something to do with violence and the poor" (238). Of these sonnets, "Rimbaud" is the most admiring and the most troubled, for it treads closest to Auden's own career. Rimbaud's "declination"—his abandonment of art— is portrayed as surrender to the enemy: "Now, galloping through Africa, he dreamed / Of a new self, the son, the engineer, / His truth acceptable to lying men" (238). Rimbaud's career, that is, makes for a cautionary tale of worldly ambition as a failure of nerve, and the desire to grow up as the final sign of arrested development. In 1934, Maxim Gorki had declared to the First All-Union Congress of Soviet Writers, "The proletarian state must educate thousands of first-rate 'masters of culture,' and 'engineers of souls'" (265). Drafted as Auden was about to leave England, "Rimbaud" insinuates that in playing engineer to the hopes of the English literary left, its author had himself trafficked in "truth acceptable to lying men."[4]

Auden's fraught relations with the left in the 1930s have had extensive study, and it is clear that he was less committed than many realized at the time.[5] We are by now used to seeing his notorious reaction against political art and the left (his disowning of "Spain," for example) as the culmination of longstanding ideological uncertainties. So it is easy to read his career as following a trajectory away from the hermetic insularity of the 1930 *Poems,* through a phase of political engagement epitomized by "Spain," and leading to odes like "In Memory of W. B. Yeats" and "September 1, 1939." From this angle, the greatness of the latter poems is that in a time of historical crisis Auden transcended party, at once conceding art's weakness ("poetry makes nothing happen") and retrieving it as a source of positive humanism ("We must love one another or die"). But to read "September 1, 1939" and know that the dive on Fifty-Second Street was a gay bar (as Harold Norse claims) is to find a personal resonance for the mirrors and drink that

Auden used to symbolize "human" self-deceptions (see Norse 78–79). And no less than the elegy for Yeats, "Rimbaud" is a poem of self-judgment, but one in which sexual politics are not fully absorbed into a universalizing humanist idiom. It suggests that Auden saw his political and aesthetic choices in the 1930s as transactions in a currency of truth and lies belonging to sexual as well as to party politics.

This chapter explores how homosexuality informed Auden's political identifications in the 1930s, and how, as he became the preeminent poet of the English left, he sought new ways to address politics as a homosexual poet. As coding is to Auden's earliest poetry, and joking to *The Orators,* so "parable" is to this stage in his career: a term that focuses the intersections of form, sociology, and sexuality. Parable has become a keyword for Auden's critics because it points up his desire for political art distinct from propaganda. "You cannot tell people what to do," he wrote in 1935, "you can only tell them parables; and that is what art really is, particular stories of particular people and experiences, from which each according to his immediate and peculiar needs may draw his own conclusions" (*P* 103). The risk for political art, Auden implies, lies in an authoritarian erasure of human particularity for the sake of a common cause—a view that suggests one reason he never quite embraced communism. The concept of parable helped him discover how art might preserve differences, so that his poetry could accommodate both his own particularities as a homosexual poet and those of his readers. Parable would be a way of rendering private experience into usable art—as Auden does, in fact, in his portrait sonnets of Rimbaud et al.: these are Auden's readings "according to his immediate and peculiar needs," and parables for readers to use according to theirs.

The first part of this chapter considers Auden's more directly political poems from the early to mid-1930s, showing how sexual politics complicated his efforts to write from an explicitly leftist stance. The poems in question suggest that his difficulties in promoting a leftist vision of the future indicated fundamental uncertainties about how a bourgeois homosexual poet might identify with the working class. Such doubts were not just his own; as the Auden group grew in prominence, it raised anxieties on the left and the right about the masculinity and sexuality of the political writer. In this context, Auden's "Letter to Lord Byron" (1936) forms a remarkable political and sexual apologia. Modeled on *Don Juan,* this poem critiques serious political art as embodying a totalitarian masculinity. The self-described "confession" of an "intellectual of the middle classes," it renders homosexual experience parabolically—as an eccentric life whose meaning for the times is left for the reader to construct.

This chapter ends by examining Auden's theories of parable-art in "Psychology and Art To-day" and "The Good Life" (1935), which mark a major transition in his understanding of poetry as a game of knowledge. For here Auden theorized his movement away from an agonistic view of the relation between homosexual poet and reader. Rather than a struggle between quasi-erotic enemy agents, he portrays parable-art as a means of antiauthoritarian discovery for both poet and reader. This model theorizes what Auden was doing in his greatest poetry of the 1930s—not only in "Letter to Lord Byron" but in poems like "Our hunting fathers" and, as chapter 5 shows, his love lyrics: practicing poetry as a game of knowledge between virtual intimates.

I

The last poem before the "Epilogue" of *Look, Stranger!* (1936)[6] addresses the public duties of the writer. "August for the people and their favourite islands"—a 1935 birthday poem for Isherwood—begins as an informal meditation on tourists "liv[ing] their dreams of freedom" by the sea (*EA* 155). Auden then observes how Isherwood's work and his own have evolved over nine years of friendship. From the vantage point of 1935, their Mortmerean aesthetic looks boyishly insular—a tourism of social crisis:

> Our hopes were set still on the spies' career,
> Prizing the glasses and the old felt hat,
> And all the secrets we discovered were
> Extraordinary and false; for this one coughed
> And it was gasworks coke, and that one laughed
> And it was snow in bedrooms; many wore wigs,
> The coastguard signalled messages of love,
> The enemy were sighted from the Norman tower. (156)

Auden asks "pardon for these and every flabby fancy"—the "lure" of "private joking in a panelled room," "the whisper in the double bed." These are mere escapism in a time of "Scandal," "Falsehood," "Greed," and other capitalized and capitalist evils. In 1935, "this hour of crisis and dismay," he therefore enjoins Isherwood to "warn us from the colours and the consolations," to "Make action urgent and its nature clear" (157).

This poem exemplifies qualities new to Auden's work since *The Orators* but well in evidence in *Look, Stranger!*: discursive fluency, an idiom and form in the mainstream of poetic tradition, and accessible topicality. It is undoubtedly true that Auden's stature increased as others of his age and class became similarly worried about politics and sympathetic to the left. But his reputation also reflected his cultivation of less forbidding forms for rendering political worries. The use of personified abstractions—"Greed," "Falsehood," and so on—is one way of gesturing toward a common world with the reader, and if they recall Pope, his use of the meditative landscape poem owes much to Wordsworth. In trying to write about a common world, that is, Auden employed a common literary heritage.

Significantly, his meditative poems tend to treat love and sex only in passing, as experiences of pleasurable but irresponsible insularity. "August for the people," for example, alludes to a visit with Isherwood to the Baltic (Rügen Island—a popular gay resort, though one could not guess that from the poem itself), recalling their fantasy that "one fearless kiss would cure / The million fevers."[7] The same theme is taken up in "Here on the cropped grass of the narrow ridge I stand": "Gross Hunger took on more hands every month," "Europe grew anxious about her health," "business shivered in a banker's winter"—the slump came, in other words—"While we were kissing" (*EA* 142). And this idea forms the structural and moral pivot of "Out on the lawn I lie in bed": we "look up" at the moon, "and with a sigh endure / The tyrannies of love," but "do not care to know, / Where Poland draws her Eastern bow, / What violence is done" (137). Love is beautiful but inconsequential in these poems—an occasion for pathos in the face of the larger crisis—and little in Auden's writing here forces the reader to consider, much less confront, the kind of love Auden is talking about. It is not that he is writing about "universal" love. (As we shall see in the next chapter, his love poems of the 1930s typically associate the delusional escapism of homosexual love with the insularity of narcissism, and even with authoritarianism.) Rather, in these poems Auden is more concerned to conjure a commonality with his middle-class readers.

Nevertheless, the position of "August for the people" just before the "Epilogue" of *Look, Stranger!* implies that Auden was dismissing not just one-time fantasies of playing secret agent, but more recent poems like those we have been considering. And this poem's act of self-critique takes on an unobtrusive but real sexual undertone. The signs of worldly crisis, Auden writes, were unseen by the "close-set eyes of the mother's boy," and he proposes a curative sublimation of eros in Isherwood's "strict and adult pen." Auden thus concedes his own failure to urge or clarify "action" amid his own "flabby fancy," and intentionally or not, his clever phallic wordplay reinforces the point. The poem, in other words, is symptom as well as diagnosis. Auden worries again and again in the 1930s about poetry's public obligations, but in practice his subject is his own inability to address politics meaningfully. To "make action urgent and its nature clear" would require both knowledge of action and a relation to an audience that would make such urging compelling. Even the most powerful poems of *Look, Stranger!*—poems like "Out on the lawn I lie in bed" and "Here on the cropped grass of the narrow ridge I stand," which movingly portray the times as compelling a political conscience—are quite unspecific about "action." The beautiful title poem focuses on ships that "diverge on urgent voluntary errands" and hopes that "the full view / Indeed may enter" (157–58). But just as in "The Watershed," Auden calls the reader "stranger," implicitly conceding that poet and reader lack a common "view." He *hopes* for "the full view"—encompassing everything, open to all—rather than offering it, and its absence coincides with his inability to "make action urgent and its nature clear."

Part of Auden's problem, one might say, was that he had so thoroughly exposed the dangers of rhetoric, but he was also confronting difficult issues involving the relation between class politics and sexual politics. The more directly the poems in *Look, Stranger!* try to imagine a possible political future, the more clearly "love" figures as a saving force. Auden invokes it as a kind of marriage of Freudian eros and

Marxist revolutionary consciousness. But the act of appealing to love as a quasi-magical power instigates a crisis of difference, in which homosexuality becomes a stumbling block to commonality with the masses who must form the basis of a leftist vision of the future. The "Prologue" to *Look, Stranger!* is the first example of this kind of prayer: "O Love, the interest itself in thoughtless heaven." Auden prays that we may realize an "eternal tie" with England, but he elides messy questions of who "we" are, what kind of "love" we are talking about, and what sort of "tie" with England we have. The crisis is troped as an economic and spiritual asphyxiation: a "dream" once living in the soil, which "sprouted" chimneys in Lancashire and furnaces in Dumbarton, has receded, leaving England high and dry, its people "too much alone" (*EA* 119). Our ancestors were "affectionate people," but Auden hints at psychosexual dysfunction: "the seed in their loins were hostile." Such overtones ultimately compromise the poem's ending, with its prophecy of "Some possible dream" moving "out of the Future into actual History." Far from addressing actual history, the poem retreats to the mythic Arthurian past via a stirring, grammatically obscure simile of Merlin sailing north from the Mediterranean toward Britain, driving "For the virgin roadsteads of our hearts an unwavering keel." It is difficult to make sense of the interplay of the patriotic and the erotic in this arresting line. That social change has something to do with rekindled eros is clear. But the mingled notes of impregnation and punishment imply that we are on the wrong side of history, that our hearts need violent therapy—perhaps the "death of the grain" prophesied in "1929."

Who, then, are "we"? It is telling that the poem first prays that Love "Make simpler daily the beating of man's heart." Auden wrote the line in 1932, and the poem appeared a year later in *New Country*, Michael Roberts's formative anthology. I turn now to two other poems he included in *New Country* and revised for *Look, Stranger!*.[8] Their problems indicate Auden's poetic difficulty in defining the relation between contemporary history and his heart. Here he tries directly to bridge the gap between the "I" or "we" of the poem and something larger, and these poems are very much about how—and to what—men's hearts beat.

"The chimneys are smoking, the crocus is out in the border" (later placed at the numerical center of *Look, Stranger!*) is something of a landscape poem, a love poem, and a political poem, and it sounds a lot like Arnold's "Dover Beach." Dating from 1932, it straddles the resistant poetic of Auden's earlier work and the looser, more accessible poems we have been considering. His most determined effort to combine leftist politics and sexual politics in a post-*Orators* mode, it is also the most syntactically tortured poem he included in *Look, Stranger!*. The poem's opening images of renewal are followed by a line that associates social rebirth with public speech: "Like a sea god the political orator lands at the pier."[9] (The fact that after *The Orators* Auden could unironically figure an orator as a savior presages problems.) The effect of these lines is to suggest a time of promising natural and political energy, and in its *New Country* version, this is a "communist orator" (*EA* 421). Then the speaker abruptly steps back, and the verses shorten:

> But, O, my magnet, my pomp, my beauty
> More telling to heart than the sea,
> Than Europe or my own home town
> To-day is parted from me
> And I stand on our world alone.   (116–17)

It is not being literal-minded to wonder: how can "*I* stand on *our* world *alone*"? For this kind of difficulty ultimately thwarts Auden's gestures of political affiliation. As the poem proceeds, he makes increasingly obscure distinctions, even as he tries to assert a parallel between personal erotic concerns and social crisis.

Much of the difficulty comes from a confusing mixture of registers and styles. When concerned with "us"—the lovers—Auden uses the coded idiom of his earlier work. While once we seemed to enjoy nature's blessing, "Now lakes and holes in the mountains remind us of error, / Strolling in the valley we are uncertain of the trees." Their "shadow falls upon us; / Are they spies on the human heart. . . ?" The blend of paranoia and desire has a Mortmerean ring; so do the cryptic lines about a "game . . . which tends to become like a war / The contest of the Whites with the Reds for the carried thing / Divided in secret among us" (about which, more shortly). The stanza goes on to imply self-realization in sexual coupling:

That power which gave us our lives
Gave us, we found when we met,
Out of the complex to be reassembled
Pieces that fit,
Whereat with love we trembled.

These lines rework the conceit of Auden's poetry of the closet, where sexual power and interpretive knowing are tropes for each other; here, "we" seem to get it together successfully. But the poem as a whole is too beholden to gamey obliquities for its larger agenda to be convincing or successful—that of linking the personal and political. Since the poem also evokes historical time and space, we cannot help trying to apply them to the closeted land of Auden country. Are the Whites and Reds opposing teams in a school game? Factions in the Russian Civil War? Refugees from Lewis Carroll? The "white death," we are soon told, "has his own idea of us," so perhaps "we" are being placed in the degenerate party of the death wish. But given the "communist orator" of the first stanza in the 1933 *New Country* version, perhaps Auden is alluding to Russian revolutionary blocs. Such questions involve readerly identification—figuring out what the pronouns refer to, whether possible echoes and patterns in imagery are really there, and if so, what they mean. The poem resembles the odes of Book III in *The Orators,* but its tone is not that of political camp. Quite serious issues of political identification seem at stake: both Auden's own effort to define his political commitments, and the reader's perception of them.

The crux of the poem—whether personal, erotic crisis is of a piece with social crisis—utterly overwhelms sense in the fifth stanza. Auden writes that "our hour of unity makes us aware of two worlds"—a line whose obscurity is only compounded by semantic and syntactic knots in the rest of the stanza.[10] The overall thrust is that a sense of division has arisen at a moment of erotic unity, with the lovers' despair implicating them in "the white death." Such division afflicts "the masters of harbours, the colliers, and us." But Auden's failure to clarify what all "the divided" have in common suggests his doubt that the lovers' crisis is an expression of anything larger.

The poem's conclusion resolves little, but it does so revealingly. The final stanzas make a last stab at defining the relation between erotic and worldly crisis, and they do so through coded reference to homo-sexuality:

> And since our desire cannot take that route which is straightest,
> Let us choose the crooked, so implicating these acres,
> These millions in whom already the wish to be one
>> Like a burglar is stealthily moving,
>> That these, on the new façade of a bank
>> Employed, or conferring at health resort,
>> May, by circumstance linked,
>> More clearly act our thought.
>
> Then dance, the boatmen, virgins, camera-men and us
> Round goal-post, wind-gauge, pylon or bobbing buoy;
> For our joy abounding is, though it hide underground,
>> As insect or camouflaged cruiser
>> For fear of death sham dead,
>> Is quick, is real, is quick to answer
>> The bird-like sucking tread
>> Of the quick dancer.

The masses already "wish to be one," but for now the wish lurks in the criminal political unconscious. Fortunately, *we* are conscious of their wish so must help *them* "act our thought." The logic of this patroniz-ing notion is that the lovers are specially gifted in subterfuge: the stanzas seek to turn the crookedness of homosexuality and the closet to positive political account. Contradiction lurks here, between the lovers' inability to take "the straightest" route, and their freedom to "choose the crooked."[11] But the overall point is that by "implicating" the larger world, the lovers' criminal deviance, willingly embraced, can spark a desire for political unity as yet unrealized (unreal *and* unrecog-nized) among the masses.

Commanding celebration, the last stanza declares "our joy" to be "real" and alive. If it "hide underground," that is only because open ex-pression is illegal. It "sham[s] dead," like "insect or camouflaged cruiser"—or closeted desire. But Auden has not solved the problems he has raised. "Boatmen, virgins, camera-men" can all dance with us because we are "implicating these acres"—England—but the burden of this hope rests on the capacity of "implicating" to link the predicament of the lovers with that of the body politic. It is tempting to think the word succeeds by its own richness of semantic implication: to involve; to entwine; to entangle in crime. But as yet unaddicted to the *OED*, Auden probably did not intend one obsolete meaning of "implicate"— to *confuse* (*OED* 1.b)—and his word choice bespeaks radical confusion (as well as confused radicalism).

The questions at stake here are these: What political connection does a bourgeois male homosexual *as such* have with the proletariat? Is there a politically meaningful identity between his own desires for erotic connection and progressive working-class solidarity? To be sure, Auden dodges—as middle-class leftists often did in the 1930s— the matter of whether the masses actually felt "already the wish to be one"; his answer is, in essence, "They do but don't know it": they are latent leftists. This elision allows him to pose the closet as an asset for the homosexual who would be a political radical. Measured by theory or praxis, this is an odd idea, and the reader today may find it an amazingly ingenious rationalization of the closet. But the poem's use of coding to consider these matters also highlights the comparative freedom of post-Stonewall life. For all his difficulties, Auden seriously raises questions that gay and lesbian people began to ask in significant numbers only in the 1970s, in seeking alliances with the New Left.

While "The chimneys are smoking" seeks to resolve these questions in poetic argument, the more famous poem just before it in *Look, Stranger!* uses more slippery means. Also dating from 1932, "Brothers, who when the sirens roar" helped establish Auden's leftist credentials, not least because earlier versions, including the *New Country* text, began with "Comrades" and bore the title "A Communist to Others." For *Look, Stranger!*, Auden changed "Comrades" to "Brothers," dropped the title, and cut six stanzas. Three of these had concluded the poem with a striking, turgid claim of erotic connection between the speaker and his brothers/comrades. (Both words are used in the last stanza.) Whether for aesthetic or political reasons, Auden never reprinted it after 1937, scrawling, "O God what rubbish" on the printer's copy when preparing his *Collected Poems* in 1943 (Spears 154).

Critics largely agree. But it is worth noting the effect "A Communist to Others" had in its time. Julian Symons, who recalls memorizing it in 1932, has described its power:

> For the many like me who thought social change not merely desirable but inevitable, much of Auden's work appeared prophetic. Some of the prophecies were hard to understand, but "A Communist to Others" seemed straightforward: an appeal to join the Party. We never doubted that the poet was himself a Party member, and indeed that (mistaken) belief was reasonable enough. (Auden, *Map* 178)

The writer John Cornford, who *was* a Party member and died fighting in Spain in 1937, wrote in 1933 that Auden had gone beyond the bourgeois fashion of leftist rhetoric to write a poem genuinely revolutionary in "form" (Haffenden 11).

Cornford may have been responding to Auden's facility with light verse, especially the Burns stanza, whose "radical and democratic ancestry," in Stan Smith's words, Auden may well have been invoking.[12] Certainly its tail rhymes and rhythm let him spew vitriol at "double dealers" with entertaining force:

> Let fever sweat them till they tremble,
> Cramp rack their limbs till they resemble
>   Cartoons by Goya:
> Their daughters sterile be in rut,
> May cancer rot their herring gut,
> The circular madness on them shut,
>   Or paranoia.   (*EA* 123)

Auden is attacking modern schoolmasters, who have traded the whip for subtler ways of "Making a weakened generation / Completely neuter" (422). The tone typifies his stance toward all his targets: county gentry who find workers "a nasty sight" (421); mystics who preach "fasting, prayer, and contemplation" to "the starving" (122); wise men defending the status quo with the "nicely balanced view"; liberal Cambridge thinkers who use theory to show that "wealth and poverty are merely / Mental pictures" (123); and a host of "splendid people," including the "Unhappy poet . . . whose only / Real emotion is feeling lonely / When suns are setting" (422).

Auden's talent for anarchic harangue carries things along until the turn from attack to prophecy. The basic problem—acutely so in the *New Country* version—is that the speaking voice is unstable. To call it "leftist" is to gloss over the labile identifications of this voice, which throws around "We" and "You" with vituperative abandon. As Cunningham has noted, the pronouns make it difficult "to decide who is speaking and to whom" (Auden, *Map* 182). Critics have labored to make sense of them, some concluding that there is no sense to be made.[13] But as in "The chimneys are smoking," problems in grammatical identification bespeak questions of political identification and sexual identity.

The poem starts by telling the speaker's comrades/brothers that "We know" their troubles, that "The fears that hurt you hurt us too." "On you our interests are set," the voice continues, and the rest of the poem enumerates the evils of the oppressor class. But early on, strange slippages occur. Having claimed such a deep bond with the workers, this is how the speaking voice describes their plight:

> We know the terrifying brink
> From which in dreams you nightly shrink.
> "I shall be sacked without," you think,
> > "A testimonial."   (121)

The absurdity of this idea only begs questions of who we are and how well we can identify with the proletariat. In its *New Country* version, the title labels the speaker "A Communist," and the workers are called "Comrades." But it is hard to imagine the dedicated party member describing workers' fears in such terms, or continuing this way:

> We cannot put on airs with you
> The fears that hurt you hurt us too
> > Only we say
> That like all nightmares these are fake
> If you would help us we could make
> Our eyes to open, and awake
> > Shall find night day.

Since the subject has been the *workers'* nightmares, one expects to hear that with their help "we could make / *Your* eyes to open" (see Cunningham 222). In citing "our" predicament, the poem shows itself concerned more with the speaker's anxieties and enemies than with workers. Such self-doubt hardly seems right for the bourgeois party-member, who, as Cunningham notes, would typically have evinced "greater confidence and faith in superior political wisdom" (Auden, *Map* 183). Auden's 1936 revisions helped by not naming the speaker as communist, but at the cost of muddling the political or class identification of the poem's sentiments. The instabilities of point of view in the *New Country* text might be taken as Auden's devious dramatization of his own complicity.[14] The poem, then, could be read as a queer subversion of the ideology of individuality taken for granted by bourgeois leftists. But while *The Orators* offers countless motifs of contradiction and self-referentiality, idiom, tone, and sheer rhythmic momentum discourage such readings here. As Cunningham has said, "A Communist to Others" seems deeply confused, not clever, and its confusion indicates Auden's ideological uncertainty.[15]

But sexual politics shed light on this confusion. First, Auden's jabs sometimes have a sexual element. He calls Cambridge social theorists "a host of columbines and pathics"—the latter, of course, a standard term for the passive sodomite. Liberal intellectuals thus have an affinity with the victims of modern schoolmasters ("a weakened generation / Completely neuter") and with the mental masturbation of the "Unhappy poet," whose "thoughts like castaways find ease / In endless petting." All this suggests a degenerate, overeducated, pampered middle class from which the speaker stands virilely apart.

Nevertheless, Auden ends the *New Country* version by having the speaker tell the lonely poet, "You need us more than you suppose" and "Return, be tender." The last stanza expands into a universal erotic appeal:

> Comrades to whom our thoughts return,
> Brothers for whom our bowels yearn
>   When words are over;
> Remember that in each direction
> Love outside our own election

Holds us in unseen connection:
> O trust that ever.   (*EA* 422)

There is much to wince at here. The image of yearning bowels is one kind of badness; the flat, vague pleading of the last line is another. But in invoking an eros beyond words and will, the stanza tries to cure the incoherence of the poem's speaking voice. "Love outside our own election / Holds us in unseen connection": the lines concede the failure of elective political affinities but appeal to a collective, adhesive force below and beyond consciousness.

This maneuver recalls the assertion of an unconscious "wish to be one" driving the people in "The chimneys are smoking": a definition of mass progressivism by analogy to dissident eros. In fact, Auden has used semantic and grammatical methods for eliding differences throughout the poem. His use of apostrophe is crucial. "Comrades" and "Brothers" are not exact synonyms. "Comrades" bears an obvious connotation of communist affiliation; the capacity of "Brothers" to do so is context-dependent. Used together, "Brothers" gains a political cast, and "Comrades" a bodily, familial, even spiritual quality. Further minglings occur as "thoughts" for comrades mutate into bodily yearnings "When words are over." Auden took the image of yearning bowels, evidently, from Gerald Heard's communism of love (as opposed to what Heard saw as Marx's communism of hate); Heard's *The Social Substance of Religion* links eros with the communitarian "love feast" of the early church, rather than with sex.[16] But few readers were likely to think of Heard, and the line in question has an indefinite but intense homoeroticism, albeit expressed with an odd anatomical precision.

The discomfort one feels in reading this stanza is very much to the point. Early on, the speaker tells his brothers/comrades, "The fears that hurt you hurt us too." The poem fails to prove this, but it is telling that a painful image of *homo*-erotic yearning occurs just as Auden tries to assert a grounding link between "us" and "you." For this poem tries to claim a homology between classes, between the speaking voice and "others"—a homology Auden wants both to affirm and to conjure by words like "comrade" and "brother" and "love." The poem confesses more than it knows in admitting that "yearning" begins "When words are over": poetry cannot make the differences go away;

desire is all too easy to see as signifying lack. The homology of political hopes and homosexual desire is not convincingly an identity, as the last line concedes: "O trust that ever."

Auden avoided many problems by cutting the closing stanzas and dropping the title for *Look, Stranger!*, but the resulting poem effectively buries its connections with the sexual politics of middle-class leftist expression in the 1930s. Given the role of *New Country* in promoting a public sense of Auden as leading a coherent leftist literary movement, it is significant that homoerotic language appears frequently in other poems in the volume.[17] This chapter cannot offer a full treatment of sexual politics in the construction of the Auden group as a leftist movement. But a brief look at other passages from the *New Country* anthology will help foreground the very different sexual-political workings of "Letter to Lord Byron."

Immediately following Auden's poems are several by Richard Goodman, whose work recalls Auden's in idiom and homoerotic suggestiveness. "Ode to a Dead Comrade" elegizes a fellow traveler thus: "Comrade, the sun to-day . . . stands erect with joy . . . and we, in step with it, / come to new frontiers, cancel out remorse" (Roberts 217). "The Squadrons" has planes "throbbing with strength" and "bright with desire" in the manner of the "Airman's Alphabet" of *The Orators* (218), and "Ode in Autumn" praises the "solidarity" of earth to an ungendered "lover" (221). Auden is invoked twice by name in *New Country*. The more famous instance comes from C. Day-Lewis's *The Magnetic Mountain,* its flying imagery sounding straight out of *The Orators:* "Look west, Wystan, lone flyer, birdman, my bully boy!" (223). Auden figures also in Charles Madge's "Letter to the Intelligentsia," which chronicles a recovery from middle-class male adolescence in Auden's diagnostic manner. Sick in bed, Madge could think only of "Winchester" (his public school) and "complicate the web / Of those occult relations; diagnose the ebb / And flow of passion." Then came the cure:

> But there waited for me in the summer morning,
> Auden, fiercely. I read, shuddered and knew
> And all the world's stationary things
> In silence moved to take up new positions. (231–32)

Coming to political consciousness here is like sexual awakening, with Auden as the hero of discovery; the passage recalls the Airman's encounter with his Uncle Henry. "It was untrue," Madge writes a few lines later, "The easy doctrine which separated things." The "new positions" of "things" are seen at the poem's end in an erotic revolution that abolishes diseased self-consciousness: "Theory and practice once in contact, see / The sparks fly. Comrades, yours fraternally. . ." (233).

The final poem in *New Country*—indeed its closing text—is Rex Warner's "Hymn"; its refrain runs, "All Power / to lovers of life, to workers, to the hammer, the sickle, the blood." Bodily fluids and political desires erupt in a flood of militantly polymorphous perversity:

> The splendid body is private, and calls for more.
> No toy; not for a boy; but man to man, man to girl
> runs blood, sweat oozes; each of us has a share.
> All flesh is a flag and a secret code. Ring bells, then! (254)

Warner is careful to note that the call of the "body" is "not for a boy," but this Lawrentian vision has been mediated by Auden. While we might blame Auden for creating a fashion—many have—his own contributions to *New Country* strive with difficulty to express the mutual infusion of political hopes and bodily desire that others find so easy to render poetically. For Madge and Warner—neither of whom self-identified as homosexual—false consciousness "separated things" that eros could readily bring together; for Auden, sexual self-awareness was a barrier to easy identification with the proletariat. By 1937, when "Letter to Lord Byron" appeared, Auden had stopped writing poems like "A Communist to Others" and "The chimneys are smoking." For by then, he had become England's preeminent poet of the left (soon to be awarded the King's Gold Medal for Poetry), and his public stature vastly complicated writing as a bourgeois leftist poet and a homosexual one.

II

In its opening stanzas, "Letter to Lord Byron" presents itself as a confession: a guilty revelation of the personal. But like *Don Juan*, Auden's epistle offers many other things: news of the day, poets' shoptalk, potted history, gossip, and innuendo. It is also an act of identification with Byron—another homage to a queer uncle—and the meanings of this gesture involve Auden's reception as a leftist and homosexual writer in the 1930s. The mode of confession recalls Freud, but we might also think (as in *Paid on Both Sides*) in juridical terms, for Auden's ideological purity is one preoccupation of the poem. The virtues he ascribes to Byron are the traits that some critics implied had compromised Auden as a political poet: immaturity, inauthenticity, and superficiality. "Letter to Lord Byron," however, transvalues such terms to critique the coercive dangers of political art. This critique is then enacted by the parabolic autobiography Auden recounts—a story shot through with sexual suggestion, whose larger meaning requires the reader to weigh this poet's eccentricity and typicality.

For Auden to imitate Byron in the 1930s was also to make a willfully unfashionable poetic gesture: "T. S. Eliot, I am sad to find, / Damns you with: 'an uninteresting mind' " (*P* 250). Auden defends Byron by asserting the value of light verse ("Only on varied diet can we live") and by using him to authorize the coexistence of genuine political concerns with comic art. Auden had traveled to the Spanish Civil War in early 1937; in May and again in July, Faber issued "Spain" as a pamphlet to raise money for medical aid to the Republic. "Letter to Lord Byron" had already been written before Auden's trip to Spain, but it was first published only in August 1937 in *Letters from Iceland,* commissioned by Faber in 1936 and coauthored by Louis MacNeice. Published after "Spain," therefore, "Letter to Lord Byron" served at the time as something of a commentary on Auden's recent political activism. His travel book must have seemed as far from "the struggle" as geographically marginal Iceland was from Spain—"that arid square" where "Our fever's menacing shapes / are precise and alive."[18] At one point Auden writes, as Wordsworth did of Milton, "Byron, thou should'st be living at this hour! / What would you do, I wonder, if you were?" (214). Byron would never have gone to Iceland. But he might have gone to Spain as he went to Greece, and for readers in 1937, his invocation must have resonated with Auden's recent trip to the Spanish Civil War. It was, in other words, Byron's grappling with the relations *between* the personal and political, public and private, seri-

ous and comic, that made him useful to Auden at this point in the
1930s.

Introducing Byron for a selected edition in 1966, Auden remarked
that *Don Juan* formed a kind of self-defense:

> Aware that he was believed by many to be the heartless seducer and
> atheist of the legend, Byron says, as it were, to his accusers: "The leg-
> endary Don Juan does not exist. I will show you what the life of a
> man who gets the reputation for being a Don Juan is really like."
>
> (Byron, *Selected,* xxi–xxii).

In other words, the meanings of *Don Juan* are functions of those given
to "Byron" by his readers. Earlier in his introduction, Auden connects
the melancholic Byronic hero to Byron's physical deformity and to "extraordinary happenings, probably sexual, of which he dare not speak
openly" (x). This is coyly unspecific, but one hears an echo of the traditional locution for sodomy as the sin "not to be named among men."
Auden's "Letter" names neither the scandals of Byron's life nor his bisexuality, but they serve as open secrets and, in effect, as honorable and
honored antecedents for Auden's own sexual eccentricity.

Auden begins by admitting himself well aware of the sort of fan
mail Byron must get from "perfect strangers": "Sometimes sly hints at
a platonic pash, / And sometimes, though I think this rather crude, /
The correspondent's photo in the rude" (*P* 179). The pretense is that
Auden (who had received nude photos from one fan)[19] will not be so
forward: he too knows the presumptive, presumptuous intimacy readers can feel. But Auden also recognizes Byron as a master manipulator
of self-revelation and public rumor, and his own charade of propriety
soon evaporates:

> For since the British Isles went Protestant
>   A church confession is too high for most.
> But still confession is a human want,
>   So Englishmen must make theirs now by post
>   And authors hear them over breakfast toast.
>   For, failing them, there's nothing but the wall
>   Of public lavatories on which to scrawl.

No nude photos, perhaps, but self-revelation nonetheless: the last lines suggest what they disclaim. This fan letter in light verse will have the intimacy and appeal of confession by "the perfect stranger"—private speech in a public accommodation.

Such writing makes a strategic response to Auden's reception as a homosexual leftist. While nothing in his life came close to Byron's public shaming, real forces of sexual knowledge did shape views of his politics. Julian Symons has said, "Auden's early readers were divided between those who knew him or had heard tales about his unusual sexual and personal habits, and the larger number who like me knew of him only through the poems." But what one "knew" was not so simple: "I don't think the homosexual currents in Spender and Auden disturbed many of us then, although a certain Rupert Brookeian gush about some of Spender's lines . . . rocked one back on one's heels occasionally. There was comradeship but no gush about Auden." (Auden, *Map* 178–79; Symons then quotes the beginning of "A Communist to Others").

Symons was less temperate in the 1930s, however, praising Dylan Thomas for not being a "Pylon-Pitworks-Pansy poet" (Cunningham 401); Julian Bell spelled out the implicit critique:

> The idealized hero; the Proletarian, the Worker, of the cartoons and posters, ruggedly Grecian, stripped to the waist, muscular, with hammer or axe in hand . . . a wish-fulfilment, after all, of the scrawny, scraggy, embittered little proletarian intellectual who has pushed his way to the top by using his wits rather than his muscles.
>
> (Cunningham 169)

Auden and Isherwood were not proletarian, and if anything, their eroticizing of the worker typified bourgeois homosexual tastes. What is striking is how automatically, for Bell, psychology trumped politics, so that the truth was that leftist homosexual writers were not really interested in politics. For right-wing Roy Campbell, writing in *Flowering Rifle* (1939), Franco's victory in Spain signified much the same for English literary leftists:

> Their "Progress" is to shunt along a track
> Where "Left" means left-behind and "Front" means back.

> When was a Front so definitely split
> As this fat Rump they have mistook for it,
> And shown us little else as we advance
> Our proper *Front* from Portugal to France:
> And if they're facing "Front"-wards, I'll not quiz
> What must the tail be like, if that's the phyz?
> With them, for opposites we have to hunt—
> "Backwards"'s the word, when Popular the "Front."   (21)

In adopting Auden's favorite codes, Campbell assumed some readers could get the joke. So did Hugh MacDiarmid in his "Third Hymn to Lenin" (1938), lumping the Auden group with the editor of *New Country:* "Michael Roberts and All Angels: Auden, Spender, those bhoyos, / All yellow twicers . . . / Unlike these pseudos I am *of*—not *for*—the working classes" (29). This piece of invective concisely brands the Auden group as a pretty-boy coterie of pretenders.[20]

The most influential critic of Auden's political authenticity was George Orwell (himself adept at masquerade). Most famously, in "Inside the Whale" (1940) Orwell attacked Auden's line in "Spain" about "The conscious acceptance of guilt in the necessary murder":

> It could only be written by a person to whom murder is at most a *word*. Personally I would not speak so lightly of murder. . . . Mr. Auden's brand of amoralism is only possible if you are the kind of person who is always somewhere else when the trigger is pulled. So much of left-wing thought is a kind of playing with fire by people who don't even know that fire is hot.
>
> (*Inside* 36–37)

Auden's assertion of "necessary murder," in other words, is false moral bravado born of true physical cowardice—the playacting of a boy, not a man (who would know what he is talking about). The passage reworks gibes in *The Road to Wigan Pier* (1937) at Auden as a "gutless Kipling" and at "Nancy poets" who know nothing about the real men who work in mines. To be a real political writer, for Orwell, you have to be a real man first; Auden and company are neither real nor men.[21]

For Auden, Byron functions as a locus of contraries that stand against categories of essential authenticity, maturity, and masculinity. Byron's great "invention," Auden says, was a style: "You are the master of the airy manner" (*P* 250). For "serious thought you never said you aimed at," instead cultivating a muse "gay and witty . . . neither prostitute nor frump" (249). At the same time, Byron's butch image lets Auden combine sexy tribute with a swipe at one 1930s he-man writer: "A poet, swimmer, peer, and man of action, / —It beats Roy Campbell's record by a mile— / You offer every possible attraction" (249). In sum, Auden sees Byron as a *performer* in life and art—a model for how the homosexual writer can address politics in the 1930s.

In bringing Byron up to date in Part II, Auden grapples with the social realities that define not only the crisis of modernity but the limits of modern heroism. The "average man" has changed since the Regency; John Bull is gone—"passed away at Ypres and Passchendaele," replaced by Disney's "little Mickey with the hidden grudge" (213). Modern man can see himself only as antihero: " 'I am like you,' he says, 'and you, and you, / I love my life, I love the home-fires, have / To keep them burning. Heroes never do." It is in response to this attitude that Auden exclaims, "Byron, thou should'st be living at this hour! / What would you do, I wonder, if you were?" What he would *not* do is to be found among those "hearing honest Oswald's call" (Oswald Mosley, leader of Britain's fascists). To be sure, "Suggestions have been made that the Teutonic / Führer-Prinzip would have appealed to you / As being the true heir to the Byronic" (214). Auden's words belie the notion. "Teutonic" and "Byronic" rhyme neatly but comically (and Byronically), and those who believe in such correspondences lose themselves in the mythopoetic echo chamber of fascist rhetoric. They miss the Byronic/Audenesque wit that lurks in the tautology of "*true* heir to the Byronic":

> You liked to be the centre of attention,
> > The gay Prince Charming of the fairy story,
> Who tamed the Dragon by his intervention.
> > In modern warfare though it's just as gory,
> > There isn't any individual glory;
> The Prince must be anonymous, observant,
> A kind of lab-boy, or a civil servant.   (214–15)

The elements of Auden's political critique coincide here with a queer reading of Byron. The fascist "honest Oswald" cannot be the "true heir to the Byronic," for "the Byronic" was a role Byron performed. Rather than the ancestor of the hypermasculine fascist, he played the "gay Prince Charming of the fairy story." Auden's wording, rich in sexual overtones, ascribes a radical inauthenticity, immaturity, and effeminacy to Byron's heroism. The "man-of-action" who outdid Roy Campbell and his kind was a man of acting, not a heroic "real man" but a "gay Prince Charming" who showed that masculine activism was a performance.

Behind Auden's comments on heroism is an argument about the threat to individual freedom of political saviors. In an age of social leveling, the "Prince" must assume a mask that lets him pass "anonymous, observant." If "A kind of lab-boy, or a civil servant" seems less compelling than the Byronic hero, truly dramatic personae are the great modern danger, for real immaturity lies in naïve fantasies of political salvation. The evil that Byron fought lives on—"ogre, dragon, what you will": "Sometimes he seems to sleep, but will not fail / In every age to rear up to defend / Each dying force of history to the end" (215). Byron knew him, for he has always existed: "He comes in dreams at puberty to man, / To scare him back to childhood if he can." Salvationist social movements are, Auden implies, a political wet dream:

> Banker or landlord, booking-clerk or Pope,
>   Whenever he's lost faith in choice and thought,
> When a man sees the future without hope,
>   Whenever he endorses Hobbes' report
> "The life of man is nasty, brutish, short,"
> The dragon rises from his garden border
> And promises to set up law and order.

This is real immaturity, Auden implies—when "a man" is arrested at political pubescence, swallowing promised salvation from the coercive dragon disguised as a liberating hero. The mark of Byron's authentic maturity as a political poet was his awareness of the roles he played—a self-consciousness poets need in an age of dark oratorical temptations to abolish political choice for others or relinquish them oneself.

Although it was written before "Spain," "Letter to Lord Byron" suggests that Auden's later retraction of that poem expressed a sense that he was guilty of giving in to such temptations. Auden's reading of Byron reflects critically on the kind of polemics practiced there: even as "Spain" presents the Spanish Civil War as the reader's "choice" and "decision," the deck of "History" is poetically stacked with inevitability. The same critique applies to Auden's efforts to combine leftist political hopes and homosexual desire in "A Communist to Others" and "The chimneys are smoking." For such attempted homologies bespeak a desire for some higher power to eradicate particularity and individual agency in favor of sameness and a common political agenda. "Letter to Lord Byron" does not critique the left as explicitly as it does the right, but like *Don Juan,* it reflects deep disillusion about the power of liberatory politics.[22] It is Jane Austen, not Marx, whom Auden credits with the ability to "Reveal so frankly and with such sobriety / The economic basis of society" (*P* 182). And the serious confidence of "Spain" in "Tomorrow" is contrasted here by a witty cynicism: "The Great Utopia, free of all complexes, / The Withered State is, at the moment, such / A dream as that of being both the sexes" (356).

Auden's simile neatly epitomizes the way sexual politics shape political critique in "Letter to Lord Byron." The "Great Utopia" of the "Withered State" is a Marxist fantasy of androgynous but sterile sameness, our eccentric particularities gone. This fantasy of identity giving way to identicality is not only impossible, Auden implies, but dangerous, and through a comic autobiography in Part IV, he offers a parabolic critique of this dream, making homosexuality his defining eccentricity. The expressed purpose is to bring Byron up to date: "A child may ask when our strange epoch passes, / During a history lesson, 'Please, sir, what's / An intellectual of the middle classes?' " (326). Because "the part can stand as symbol for the whole," Auden presents himself as a representative child of the bourgeois professional class. Yet the constant subtext is that he isn't. His passport notes "no distinctive markings anywhere," but he cites the "large brown mole" on his "right cheek" (327); he knows that " 'Daunty, Gouty, Shopkeeper' " are the truly great, but his own literary heroes are children's writers, queer, or both: "Firbank, Potter, Carroll, Lear" (328).

Like Byron, Auden is capitalizing on his reputation even as he pretends to be confessing his guilt:

> I've lately had a confidential warning
>   That Isherwood is publishing next season
> A book about us all. I call that treason.
>   I must be quick if I'm to get my oar in
>   Before his revelations bring the law in.

Isherwood's 1938 "autobiographical novel," *Lions and Shadows: An Education in the Twenties,* did indeed offer a veiled account of the Auden group in the 1920s and 30s. Auden's charge of "treason" suggests that Isherwood would out them, that this "book about us all" would tell all, upsetting the poise of secrecy and suggestion they had cultivated. But Auden's outrage is belied by a couplet confessing (with an unscrupulous rhyme) his own willingness to make such use of their lives for himself here.

Behind Auden's cynicism about literary capital is a moral about eccentricity and social opprobrium:

> Goddess of bossy underlings, Normality!
>   What murders are committed in thy name!
> Totalitarian is thy state Reality,
>   Reeking of antiseptics and the shame
>   Of faces that all look and feel the same.   (331)

The face Auden presents in this section is at once typical of the middle class and shameless in suggesting his dirty abnormality. Flouting Normality, Auden locates the bourgeois value of health in the camp of totalitarian ogres. His own "slogan," he writes, is "Let each child have that's in our care / As much neurosis as the child can bear." Byron exemplified the point:

> "Es neiget die weisen zu schönem sich."
>   Your lordship's brow that never wore a hat

> Should thank your lordship's foot that did the trick.
>   Your mother in a temper cried, "Lame Brat!"
>   Posterity should thank her much for that.
> Had she been sweet she surely would have taken
> Juan away and saved your moral bacon.   (356)

"The wise are susceptible to the beautiful," wrote Hölderlin in "Sokrates und Alcibiades" (Fuller 208); Byron's career, Auden suggests, was set in motion by the almost perfect beauty of his body, and the subtext of Greek love is telling. Auden admits he hardly rivals Byron's beauty, but he offers a childhood full of hints of neurosis and perversion. His "first remark at school did all it could / To shake a matron's monumental poise; / 'I like to see the various types of boys' " (P 330). The implied tendencies are in play when Auden turns a comment on his parents into a witty Freudian riff on identification, object-choice, and erotic postures toward authority:

> We imitate our loves: well, neighbours say
>   I grow more like my mother every day.
> I don't like business men. I know a Prot
> Will never really kneel, but only squat.   (329)

"We all grow up the same way, more or less," Auden remarks: in portraying his youth as the typically deviant experience of his generation, he brings out the latent contradiction in this line.

The bildungsroman Auden offers is also a tale of sexual and aesthetic education. He declines to go into detail about public school but refers the reader to "the Greek Anthology, / And all the spicier bits of Anthropology."[23] At Oxford, Auden and his friends were "a sort of poor relation / To that debauched, eccentric generation / That grew up with their fathers at the War"—legendary figures like Brian Howard and Harold Acton, who "made new glosses on the noun Amor" (333). After Oxford, "to Berlin, not Carthage, I was sent," Auden writes, but reader of Eliot though he was, he came under the nontraditional tutelage of John Layard:

Part came from Lane, and part from D. H. Lawrence;
>   Gide, though I didn't know it then, gave part.
They taught me to express my deep abhorrence
>   If I caught anyone preferring Art
>   To Life and Love and being Pure-in-Heart.
I lived with crooks but seldom was molested;
The Pure-in-Heart can never be arrested.

He's gay; no bludgeonings of chance can spoil it,
>   The Pure-in-Heart loves all men on a par,
And has no trouble with his private toilet. . . .   (333–34)

As we saw in chapter 2, this passage provides a nostalgic picture of free
love in Weimar Berlin. But Auden is also marking the distance he has
come since 1928–29: being "Pure-in-Heart," he insinuates, was learned
behavior. Ultimately, Auden implies, this poem's Byronic model of
identity is really *more* "gay" in its embrace of neurosis and perversion
for the sake of "Art."

As a sexual apologia, this autobiography proceeds by questioning
the grounds of accusation. Where Wilde tried (and failed) to defend
himself by asserting the purity of Greek love, Auden virtually pleads
no contest: like Byron's, his writing is inextricable from his abnormality. Instead, Auden mounts his defense by intimating the hypocrisy
of the prosecution:

I know—the fact is really not unnerving—
>   That what is done is done, that no past dies,
That what we see depends on who's observing,
>   And what we think on our activities.
>   That envy warps the virgin as she dries
But "Post coitum, homo tristis" means
The lover must go carefully with the greens.   (335)

Coming near the end of Part IV, when Auden has finished narrating
his life, this stanza opens with the mock-stoic resignation of the confessed defendant, only to undo a simple notion of "fact." He may be
guilty of being cavalier about his cavalier past, but the thoughts of oth-

ers are no less implicated in their own "activities." Like envious virgins, they are "warped" as they spy on what (or whom) he does. But he can be patient, for he has a worldly wisdom about grappling with the shock of first-timers.

Teasing as it is, this passage gets at the essence of Auden's sexual-political self-defense. "I hate pomposits and all authority," he writes in Part IV: the posturing of "the cultured smug minority." He professes what might be called anarchism, but he is willing to admit it verges on quietism:

> "Perpetual revolution," left-wing friends
> Tell me, "in counter-revolution ends.
> Your fate will be to linger on outcast
> A selfish pink old Liberal to the last."   (328)

The charge here ascribed to "left-wing friends" relies at base on the same diagnosis that critics like Campbell, MacDiarmid, and Orwell were making in the 1930s: the homosexual leftist was not red but pink, his dissidence politically flaccid. Auden does not reassert his leftist credentials in reply, for his point concerns how deeply the discourse of political commitment has been soiled by cant. Instead he turns the charge of fakery against his accusers:

> "No, I am that I am, and those that level
>   At my abuses reckon up their own.
>   I may be straight though they, themselves, are bevel."
>   So Shakespeare said, but Shakespeare must have known.
>   I daren't say that except when I'm alone,
>   Must hear in silence till I turn my toes up,
> "It's such a pity Wystan never grows up."

The effect of these lines (excised, like many of the more suggestive stanzas in Part IV, from later reprintings) comes from the deviousness of their own levelings. The concluding verses are patently untrue: Auden is not enduring the charge of arrested development in silence. His point is that such carping at the softness of his commitment is not "on the level"—it only points up his critics' insecurity. (In Wilde's terms,

such criticism adds up to unintended psychosexual autobiography.)
Auden is co-opting innuendo, indulging the cheap but gratifying pleasure of saying, "It takes one to know one."

As a commentary on politics in 1930s literary culture, however, the
stanza has a more serious point: the obsession with sexuality as an index to authenticity of political commitment is self-compromising and
not to be trusted. Auden is laying bare the assumptions about art that
his critics take for granted, and he does this by invoking an irreproach-
able authority in order to defend his own sexual and political re-
proachability. Sonnet 121 (" 'Tis better to be vile than vile esteemed") is
about public reputation; in the verses quoted, Shakespeare employs
Auden's favorite trope of crookedness as a defense against charges by
those "frailer spies, / Which in their wills count bad what I think
good" (104). The sheer immodesty of recruiting Shakespeare here is
crucial. It is one thing to identify with Byron, but *Shakespeare?* Auden
gives what amounts to a queer reading of the quoted lines and of their
author by turning the logic of "It takes one to know one" on Shakespeare himself: "So Shakespeare said, but Shakespeare must have
known." The retort patently invited is "So Auden said, but Auden
must have known." But then, the speaker of *that* statement becomes
subject to it too: "So you say, but. . . ." The point is partly that in
playing this game with his own accusers, Auden can muster a blithe indifference to their attacks—the Byronic "airy manner." At the same
time, he expresses cynicism about the very discourse of authentic political commitment: his own beveled words, Auden implies, hardly reflect a singular, constitutional crookedness. When hypocrisy is the illness of the age, the only recourse is the unashamed duplicity of *Don
Juan* or of poetry like this—playing with serious issues like a "gay
Prince Charming."[24]

Such a posture is eminently Byronic, and *Don Juan* itself offers an
ancestral type for this moment that illuminates its larger sexual, political, and literary meanings. Embedded in Canto III of *Don Juan* is Byron's ballad "The Isles of Greece." Sung by a fictive modern Greek
poet at the banquet of Don Juan and Haidée, the ballad's call for commitment to Greek nationalism is offered to Byron's readers as a form
of expression impossible in an age of political cant such as their own.
The ballad marks an attack on political apostasy including, Jerome

McGann has argued, Byron's own "forms of ideological backsliding and dishonesty" (*Beauty* 279). "Thus sung, or would, or could, or should have sung, / The modern Greek, in tolerable verse," Byron comments of the ballad's singer:

> His strain display'd some feeling—right or wrong;
>   And feeling, in a poet, is the source
> Of others' feeling; but they are such liars,
> And take all colours—like the hands of dyers.
>
>   (*Complete* V: 192)

For Byron, the political hopes poetry can excite are dishonest: such feeling is the derivative coloring readers get from poets, and poets themselves are just as guilty. Byron's allusion to Shakespeare's sonnet III ("O, for my sake do you with fortune chide") bespeaks such susceptibility: citing the "public means" by which he has made his "livelihood," Shakespeare writes, "Thence comes it that my name receives a brand, / And almost thence my nature is subdued / To what it works in, like the dyer's hand" (96). Like Shakespeare, Byron is concerned with the infectious, self-infecting color of false feeling that poetry accrues from its use as public currency, but his particular target is the mutual debasement of politics and poetry.

In *The Dyer's Hand,* of course, Auden himself later adopted Shakespeare's simile for his own concern with the moral stakes of art.[25] So too in "Letter to Lord Byron," reference to Shakespeare serves to raise questions of the use and abuse of poetic duplicity. "So Shakespeare said, but Shakespeare must have known": the line marks Auden's self-designation as the homosexual student of Shakespeare and heir to Byron. What he knows as well as they is that a low, dishonest age leaves no true defense against what others count bad in politics or sexuality. But dishonesty is not the same thing as masquerade, and "Letter to Lord Byron" proposes that poetry might be a mode of productive crookedness distinct from the canted, coercive words of ideological correctness. This is not the work of a "gay Prince Charming of the fairy story," however winning Auden's performance: he is Byron in a lesser guise, "a kind of civil servant." But nor is he guilty of the authoritarianism of those who would impose their truths on the reader eager to be told what must be done. The life this poem relates may be read as the tale of a generic "intellectual of the middle classes," or as the more colorful story of "a selfish pink old Liberal to the last." These choices exist because, as Auden puts it, "what we see depends on who's observing."

III

Recognizing the importance of the term "parable" for Auden's work, critics have understood it as evidence of his search for a political role for art that would not reduce it to propaganda.[26] What "Letter to Lord Byron" suggests is that Auden's desire for an antiauthoritarian mode was bound up with a sense that human difference is a special problem for the homosexual poet in the modern age. Until Romanticism, "Each poet knew for whom he had to write, / Because their life was still the same as his" (P 253): high-brow or low, the poet belonged to a community. The Industrial Revolution changed things, however; Wordsworthianism notwithstanding, the poet since then has left society for "the Poet's Party" (254). Auden tells the same story in his 1937 introduction to *The Oxford Book of Light Verse:* "As the old social community broke up, artists were driven to the examination of their own feelings and to the company of other artists. They became introspective, obscure, and highbrow" (433). The "modern poet," therefore, faces the problem of "how to find or form a genuine community" (436).

This diagnosis of modernity recalls the views of Eliot and Yeats in the 1930s, but unlike them, Auden distrusted nostalgic politics and Symbolist aesthetics as ways of reconjuring social cohesion. "Letter to Lord Byron" entertains the idea that light verse itself might recreate community, for Auden's poem has the qualities he ascribes to the work of Byron, Chaucer, and Pope in *The Oxford Book of Light Verse:* "Poetry intended to be read, but having for its subject-matter the everyday social life of its period or the experiences of the poet as an ordinary human being" (431). The form may be different, but like folk songs and nonsense verse, such writing presumes a continuity of interest between poet and reader.

But while it certainly qualifies as light verse, "Letter to Lord Byron" does not seek sentimentally to recover a premodern sense of community.[27] "Art, if it doesn't start there, at least ends," Auden writes in Part III, "In an attempt to entertain our friends." But the "first problem is to realise what / Peculiar friends the modern artist's got" (252). Clearly much of the "Letter" seeks to entertain friends. Just as clearly, it addresses a wider audience, and much of the fun comes from playing with his friends' peculiarities and his own—especially sexual ones. In the various meanings of "peculiar" lies the problem with poetry as a vehicle for recovering community: what is particular to Auden is also what is odd. His eccentricity—literally, divergence from the center of things—would vitiate his poetry as a vehicle for envisioning renewed community. "Letter to Lord Byron," however, posits eccentricity itself as the source of art's political value in the modern age—what a more recent critical vocabulary would term "difference" or "alterity." In inviting readers—*any* readers—to hear his "confession," Auden proposes that reading itself is an activity of consciously realizing our own particularities by discovering the writer's.

"Letter to Lord Byron" marks, therefore, the most elaborate embodiment of Auden's views on parable in "Psychology and Art Today" and "The Good Life," both published in 1935. The former essay seeks to explain Freud's value for modern writing, while the latter is a comparative analysis of psychology, communism, and Christianity. These are complicated essays—full of provocative ideas, assertively theoretical, but despite their numbered subsections, quite unsystematic. Auden is trying to synthesize Freudian and Marxist critiques of the liberal tradition, as Buell has noted (167), but he is also working out more personal concerns about the function of poetry in the modern age.

At the heart of each essay is the assumption that the modern subject is a site of radical differences. "The Good Life" puts it this way:

The development of self-consciousness in man marked a break with the rest of the organic world. . . . As D. H. Lawrence wrote, in *Psycho-Analysis and the Unconscious,* Adam and Eve fell, not because they had sex or even because they committed the sexual act, but because they became aware of their sex and of the possibility of the act.

When sex became to them a mental object . . . they were cursed and cast out of Eden. Then man became self-responsible; he entered on his own career.

(*P* 113–14)

While Auden's concern with self-consciousness recalls his 1929 Berlin journal, his views had changed. Earlier he celebrated the birth of self-consciousness as bringing freedom from connection to others, including the need to write symbolic poetry; such a view lent theoretical force to his poetry of the closet. Here, the gap between the conscious mind and bodily desire makes us ethically "self-responsible": Auden no longer welcomes this alienation as a sign of our evolution away from Nature, as he had in 1929, nor does he idealize a return to unself-conscious unity-of-being. In "Psychology and Art To-Day," he portrays such a hope as politically disastrous:

The danger of Lawrence's writing is the ease with which his teaching, "trust the unconscious," by which he means the impersonal unconscious, may be read as meaning, "let your personal unconscious have its fling," i.e. the *acte gratuit* of André Gide. In practice, and particularly in personal relations, this itself may have a liberating effect for the individual. "If the fool would persist in his folly he would become wise." But folly is folly all the same and a piece of advice like "Anger is just. Justice is never just," which in private life is a plea for emotional honesty, is rotten political advice, where it means "Beat up those who disagree with you."

(*P* 102)

First among Auden's targets is his own embrace of Lawrence and Gide, via John Layard. This ethic of sexual liberation, he implies, is implicated in the coercive politics of fascism. In *Paid on Both Sides* and *The Orators* he explored joking as a way to subvert the authority of group psychology and rhetoric. Here Auden portrays "folly" as complicit in political coercion: in the public domain, it leads not to a transforming recognition of contradiction, but to a violent imposition of one person's "personal unconscious" on others.

Instead of indulging desire, transvaluing good and evil, Auden now argues we must understand it consciously. "What we call evil is something that was once good but has been outgrown," he writes in "The Good Life": "Ignorance begets the moralistic censor as the only means of control. Impulses which are denied expression remain undeveloped in the personal unconscious" (114). While this is a conventional Freudian articulation of the split subject, Auden is also generalizing from his longstanding view of homosexuality as a condition of arrested development. In both essays, he sees cure as proceeding from an interaction between conscious subjects, a process he terms "confession": "Cure consists in taking away the guilt feeling, in the forgiveness of sins, by confession, the re-living of the experience, and by absolution, understanding its significance" ("Psychology and Art Today"; 102–3). It is the specificity of one's "guilt" and "experience" that psychology addresses, for it is "opposed to all generalisations. Force people to hold a generalisation, and there will come a time when a situation will arise to which it does not apply" (103).

It is at this point that Auden invokes "parable" to describe noncoercive modes of cure that acknowledge difference: "You cannot tell people what to do, you can only tell them parables; and that is what art really is, particular stories of particular people and experiences, from which each according to his immediate and peculiar needs may draw his own conclusions" (103; for the corresponding passage in "The Good Life," see *P* 115). We can now see why "parable" becomes Auden's crucial term. First, it helps him synthesize Freud, Marx, and Christianity. He is able to suggest the political value of art through the echo of Marx in "each according to his immediate and peculiar needs." Parable also allows him to link psychoanalysis and Christianity as modes that work through confessional storytelling. By claiming that the value of each lies in a form of expression—stories of particularity that are parables for others to adapt in different ways—he is able to find a social value in individual experience.

The formal implications of "parable" are crucial here, for the semantic and figurative valences of this term are in keeping with Auden's habitual ways of thinking about homosexuality. In *The Orators*, the Airman outlines a mad science of deviation for understanding identity: the enemy can be detected by his preference for crooked geometry, and the Airman's real ancestry follows not a straight line from his parents but a crooked one through his uncle. "Letter to Lord Byron" renounces the goddess "Normality" in poetry and politics as in love; it is a poem well aware of its own eccentricity in emulating the Byron of *Don Juan* in the 1930s. Its semiserious obliquities, which capitalize on innuendo and public image, seek to derive community from comic recognition of difference in an age of lowest-common-denominator politics. If, from a social angle, a subject constitutes an isolate of particularity—a point in time and space—each subject is also comprised of differences; what psychoanalysis terms the unconscious is the sum of a subject's guilty particularities. Coercive mass politics overcome repression through direct appeal to prohibited impulses—an *acte gratuit* writ large—but collapse the subject's particularities into the collective sameness of the state.[28] But the poet, who can write as one such isolate to others, salvages particularities by linking them not as points on straight lines, but through the crooked gestures of parabolic verses.

The parabolic value of particularity motivates some of Auden's best-known shorter poems from the 1930s, from the darkly comic ballads of "Victor," "James Honeyman," and "Miss Gee," to "Musée des Beaux Arts," which meditates on the marginality of suffering that defined its "human position" for the Old Masters. I end this chapter by turning to "Our Hunting Fathers" (1934), which graphs with stunning parabolic concision the relations between sexuality and politics. Here is its first stanza:

> Our hunting fathers told the story
>   Of the sadness of the creatures,
> Pitied the limits and the lack
>   Set in their finished features;
> Saw in the lion's intolerant look,
> Behind the quarry's dying glare,
> Love raging for the personal glory
>   That reason's gift would add,
> The liberal appetite and power,
>   The rightness of a god.   (*EA* 151)

As Mendelson has observed, this stanza presents the Victorian view of humanity's evolution from the level of animals, arrested in their "finished" forms, to its "god"-like capacity for "conscious rational love" (*Early* 215). Auden retells this tale, however, to demystify it. Our "fathers" failed to detect the irony that they were expressing their superiority to animals in the act of their own hunting. In fact, Auden implies that this belief in humanity as the apex of evolution was a kind of narcissistic projection onto nature—a hunting for humanity's self-image. Lurking in the last lines is the notion that the 1930s saw a disturbing rehabilitation of divine "rightness": the "liberal appetite and power" celebrated in liberalism, deified in fascism, only begged the question of whether human freedom from animal "limits" signified divinity.

The second stanza addresses these implied ironies, and its underlying metaphor is that of deviation from the line of our hunting fathers:

> Who nurtured in that fine tradition
>   Predicted the result,
> Guessed love by nature suited to
>   The intricate ways of guilt?
> That human ligaments could so
> His southern gestures modify,
> And make it his mature ambition
>   To think no thought but ours,
> To hunger, work illegally,
>   And be anonymous?

With its quotation from Lenin (as Auden thought) in the last two lines, this stanza suggests that forward-looking politics *are* an outgrowth of love and reason, but not in the way liberalism had envisioned.[29] As Anthony Hecht has noted, Auden used these words in a 1934 review of Liddell Hart's biography of T. E. Lawrence (Hecht 58–59). Arguing that "the Western-romantic conception of personal love is a neurotic symptom, only inflaming our loneliness," Auden saw Lawrence as witnessing to the lesson that only "a kind of asceticism" can lead "back to real intimacy":

> The self must learn to be indifferent; as Lenin said "To go hungry, work illegally and be anonymous." Lawrence's enlistment in the Air

Force and Rimbaud's adoption of a trading career are essentially similar. "One must be absolutely modern."

(P 62)

Auden is extolling not sublimation but conscious absorption in a
cause, the "synthesis of feeling and reason, act and thought" exemplified by Lawrence and Lenin. "Our Hunting Fathers" does suggest this
argument, as Hecht observes: "modified" by our will, love can now
"think no thought but ours," expressing itself not in instinctive "southern gestures" (a witty trope for genital sexuality) but in deliberate asceticism ("to hunger") and undercover activism ("work illegally," "be
anonymous"). The connections we have failed to make through romantic love can be made through politics.

"Our Hunting Fathers" ventures these ideas far more obliquely than
Auden's review, however. The second stanza takes the form of a question, not a call to action, and while it reads like a rhetorical question—
"Who could have predicted"—the effect is quite different. A rhetorical
question takes its answer as self-evident; by foregrounding agreement
between questioner and auditor, it evokes commonality. But Auden's
syntax demands some very close reading indeed to arrive at a para-
phrase like the one outlined above, and the tone of his question is by
no means self-evident either. The first-person plurals in the poem—
"Our hunting fathers," "no thought but ours"—assert a commonality
between poet and reader. But the climactic verses make a claim less
self-evident than apparently circular. Love's once instinctive "southern
gestures" have been "modified" by "human ligaments" so as to "think
no thought but ours," and this "thought" is then defined, via buried
communist allusion, in terms of a hidden agenda.

This poem, in other words, pulls continually against its rhetorical
gestures of commonality; in doing so it foregrounds for the reader the
tendentiousness of such gestures—the possible points in the poet's experience or thoughts where these words originate. It seems clear that
he is grappling here, as in "A Communist to Others" and "The chimneys are smoking," with the relation between homosexuality and leftist
politics; "To hunger, work illegally, / And be anonymous," after all,
makes an apt slogan for life in the sexual underground. And from this
angle, the story the poem tells can be read as a parable about homo-

sexuality as a deviation from "our fathers": for them, the marriage between reason and love defined humanity's superiority to animals, but
also its place in a natural order; for us, love is "by nature" a convoluted
matter of guilt (therefore quite *un*natural) and self-conscious "gestures." Ours is not the "rightness of a god" but, to our liberal fathers, a
wrongness: a condition of unnameable, outlawed desire of which leftist activism is the "mature ambition."

This reading helps explain why "Our Hunting Fathers" cuts against
its own rhetorical gestures of commonality, for it suggests that Auden
is hazarding a parallel between sexual and political dissidence not so as
to collapse them into each other but in order to question the relation
between them. He does not assert that Love "holds us in unseen connection" or use "we" to elide differences that would threaten a polemical leftist agenda. Rather, the effect of this poem is to foreground his
own self-questioning—to carry it out both intimately and publicly and
thus to instigate a similar process in readers. If Love is "by nature
suited to / The intricate ways of guilt," that idea can yield very different
conclusions. It can mean that our self-denying political choices, ratio-
nally arrived at, are ways of curing the neuroses of our private lives, as
Auden proposes in his comments on T. E. Lawrence. But it can also
mean that professions of leftist affinity are not acts of true dissidence
but contrived gestures—guilty displacements of private fears and desires.

"Our Hunting Fathers" does not tell us which meaning Auden
intends, and what it implies about poetic gestures should make us
doubt whether he even knew. Instead it testifies to his own uncertainties. It confesses them in a poetic form that bears the traces of his own
particularity as a homosexual poet self-consciously sympathetic to the
left—positing a relation between eros in private and public, but not
drawing a straight line between them. Auden does not tell us "To
hunger, work illegally, / And be anonymous"; he asks what it means to
say this, offering self-contemplation in parabolic form. And he was attracted to parable not simply because it might accommodate difference
between the homosexual poet and his readers, but because he saw the
negotiation of sameness and difference as the ethical challenge of
homosexual love itself.

Chapter 5

"TELL ME THE TRUTH ABOUT LOVE": CONFESSIONAL LYRIC AND LOVERS' DISCOURSE

The 1994 film *Four Weddings and a Funeral* has probably done more to popularize Auden than any other recent event. It is also an instructive moment in his reception, for where the academy has often praised his work for its universality, the film invokes him as a gay sage: before reciting "Funeral Blues" at his lover's funeral, the character Matthew prefaces it by calling Auden "another splendid bugger" like the late Gareth.

This scene makes visible a number of significant occlusions in Auden's love poetry, including those he himself instigated. This lyric first appeared in Auden and Isherwood's play *The Ascent of F6* (1936), recited to "A Blues" at the death of James Ransom, the protagonist's brother (see *PDW* 350–51). The version used in the film dates from 1938 and gained the title "Funeral Blues" in *Another Time* (1940). Included there as one of "Four Cabaret Songs for Miss Hedli Anderson," it is presented as an exercise in light verse. As Mendelson notes, its dedication to Benjamin Britten's favorite soprano was a form of disguise Auden used only for love poems with masculine pronouns (*Later* 32). By putting the text in the voice of a gay male character, *Four Weddings and a Funeral* outs the poem, much as Matthew uses it to affirm before the mourners the romantic nature of his relationship with Gareth. Auden's words become a poignant utterance about the public unspeakability of gay love:

> Let aeroplanes circle moaning overhead
> Scribbling on the sky the message He Is Dead,

Put crêpe bows round the white necks of the public doves,
Let the traffic policemen wear black cotton gloves.

(*EA* 163)

In cinematic context, such extravagance is not just an effect of the conventions of light verse, or an expression of anguish that the world goes
blithely on—a feeling hardly limited, of course, to gay mourners. For
these campy pleas for public ritual point up a gap between gay romantic loss and official forms of lament.

To read "Funeral Blues" as expressing a universal sense of the un-
fairness of death is to be so taken by Auden's facility with romantic
commonplace as to be deaf to its sexual-political implications. For its
part, *Four Weddings and a Funeral* risks another illusion in recovering
Auden as a master of gay pathos. Perhaps his most touching line came
with the 1938 revision: "I thought that love would last forever; I was
wrong." Auden was evidently responding not to death but to the end
of the affair that had generated most of his love poetry since 1932 (see
Mendelson, *Later* 32). But while it is almost irresistible to see the
poem as voicing utter desolation at a breakup, impermanence had
always haunted Auden's love poems. "Certainty" and "fidelity," in
his famous words, are delusions of lovers "in their ordinary swoon"
(*EA* 207). From this angle, "Funeral Blues" might sound contrived or
even cruel, since it mourned someone still living. But the poem might
also be read as a confession that grief can be a self-indulgent performance, as manipulative of oneself as it is of others. Rather than obscuring the personal, Auden's title invites moral reflection: grieving
can indeed be "Funeral Blues"—a way of acting out romantic pathos.

Both universalizing and "gay-positive" readings of "Funeral Blues"
find it confirming what we—however "we" may be defined—already
feel: we sentimentally construe the mourning voice as echoing our
own desires. To read the poem instead as Auden's private response to
the end of a homosexual love affair is to see its expression of grief as a
means for reflection on love. We have seen how Auden used "parable"
to articulate the social value of poetry as an antiuniversalizing form,
and this chapter extends my concern with his poetic theory. My largest
claim is that Auden came to treat poetry itself as a kind of lovers' discourse: a site of intimate relation between poet and reader in all their

particularities. Poetry would be an erotic "game of knowledge," as Auden writes in the 1948 essay "Squares and Oblongs": "a bringing to consciousness . . . of emotions and their hidden relationships" (173).

Early and late, Auden's poems treat erotic relations as raising problems of emotional coercion and freedom—problems, I shall argue, that can be clarified only by attending to his sense of the psychology of homosexual love and to his ways of rendering it in poetry. Part I of this chapter explores how Auden's love poems of the 1930s use Plato's *Symposium* and Shakespeare's *Sonnets* as culturally legitimating resources for expressing homosexual love, and for analyzing relations between an older poet/lover and a younger beloved. Ever aware of political authoritarianism, these early love poems typically operate as confessions of an erotic will to power. The one just end Auden seems able to imagine is loss: only thus can the beloved escape emotional coercion, born of the lover's desire to absorb his beloved's particularity into a totalitarian fantasy of "Universal love and hope" (*EA* 207).

The remainder of the chapter examines Auden's love poetry after he met and fell in love with Chester Kallman in 1939. Their enduring, troubled life together and apart has inspired two book-length memoirs, and in this regard, scholars and critics have helped to illuminate Auden as a homosexual poet.[1] I focus specifically on his preoccupation with fidelity and freedom—sexual and emotional—in his love poems to Kallman and in his later writings about love and poetry. Almost from the start, Auden was writing poems that welcomed an escape from the sexual and emotional faithlessness that had obsessed him in the 1930s. When it soon became clear that Kallman could not or would not consider himself married, Auden experienced what he later called "The Crisis," affecting his views of love, his writing, and his religious beliefs. As a love poet, the later Auden is often pained, painful to read, and remarkably candid. Yet the *meanings* of this candor are not simple. For in conceding infidelity and duplicity—his own and Kallman's—Auden's later love poems seek to be faithful to the complex truths of their love, but also to honor the plurality of wandering eros as something sacred. To see Auden treating poetry as a kind of virtual lovers' discourse is to see him playing a game of knowledge with Kallman, with others who occasioned his love, and ultimately with every reader, who is invited to become "Thou" to the poet's "I."

I

The poems Auden wrote for Benjamin Britten offer a useful way into his early love poetry, for this relationship is far better documented than the one that generated most of his love poems of the 1930s. If Britten's own artistic gifts were as prodigious as Auden's, his letters and diaries after they met in 1935 repeatedly express inadequacy in the face of what he saw as Auden's artistic and political maturity (see Britten 378–81). By 1942, they had parted as friends and collaborators, largely, it seems, because of the domineering qualities that had first made Auden so compelling.[2] A telling moment came in January 1942, when he wrote to diagnose Britten's "attraction to thin-as-a-board-juveniles, i.e. to the sexless and innocent" as the sign of the damaging sway of "Order" and "Bourgeois Convention" (see Britten 1015–16). Britten did not appreciate this, and the relationship ended. But Auden had always been ready to psychoanalyze his friends, and Britten's shyness, age (he was six years Auden's junior), and closetedness seemed at the start to invite mentoring. Isherwood recalls: "No doubt both [Auden and I] tried to bring him out, if he seemed to us to need it. We were extraordinarily interfering in this respect—as bossy as a pair of self-assured psychiatrists—he wasn't a doctor's son and I wasn't an ex-medical student for nothing."[3]

In Isherwood and Auden, Britten had two gay uncles, and in "Underneath the abject willow" (1936)—one of "Two Songs" dedicated to Britten in *Look, Stranger!*—we see Auden adapting the *carpe diem* mode for a text of gay initiation:

> Underneath the abject willow,
>   Lover, sulk no more;
> Act from thought should quickly follow:
>   What is thinking for?   (*EA* 160)

Commanding "Strike and you shall conquer," the lyric equates release from repression with self-discovery. There is little verbal complexity to the poem, which argues for an essential gay (not *queer*) self to be freed from the closet:

> Geese in flocks above you flying
>   Their direction know;
> Brooks beneath the thin ice flowing
>   To their oceans go;
> Coldest love will warm to action,
>   Walk then, come,
>   No longer numb,
> Into your satisfaction.

Gay identity figures here as part of nature: a form of being with its own natural end. Rather than a perversion from true sexual aims, homosexual consummation means "satisfaction"—happiness, completion—of a gay self.

Such would be the initiatory lesson of the poem, with its dedication "for Benjamin Britten." Auden gave him the lyric in March 1936; later that year Britten wrote a score for it that his diary described as "very light & Victorian in mood!" (Carpenter, *Britten* 79). Donald Mitchell has seen this setting as an effort to distance Auden's message by turning the poem into "a brisk—jaunty, even—impersonal and highly mannered polka-like dance," scored for *two* voices (164). The setting, in other words, hardly seems to convey the kind of release that the text preaches. Britten "could not have made it clearer," Mitchell writes, "that he declined to emerge as the song's protagonist, despite the dedication." But he probably knew Auden well enough to suspect that this avuncular advice poem might mask a seduction poem—that when Auden wrote "Walk, then, come, / No longer numb, / Into your satisfaction," he was not just concerned with a young man in the closet. If so, the poem's expressivist lesson about gay selfhood would be belied by ulterior motives.[4] The line "What is thinking for?" seems, coming from someone who wrote "To ask the hard question is simple" and "Our hunting fathers," just that: a *line*. In turn, Britten's contrived setting may well indicate not a refusal of Auden's advice, but a sense that the poem's surface candor might be deceptive.

"Night covers up the rigid land," the second poem Auden dedicated to Britten in March 1936, seems, in Peter Pears's words, like the work not "of a received lover, rather of a rejected one" (Carpenter, *Britten* 82):

> The wounded pride for which I weep
>   You cannot staunch, nor I
> Control the moments of your sleep,
>   Nor hear the name you cry,
>
> Whose life is lucky in your eyes,
>   And precious is the bed
> As to his utter fancy lies
>   The dark caressive head.   (*EA* 162)

These lines seem to acknowledge Britten as an independent erotic subject whose "eyes" do not look to Auden. But the wordplay is quite busy. Applied to Auden's rival (whoever that may have been), "lucky" suggests Britten's sexual good fortune. But it is qualified by the narcissistic overtones of "in your eyes"; Auden then rhymes "eyes," in fine Petrarchan fashion, with "lies," tugging "fancy" toward delusion. The last stanzas may indict Auden for erotic folly, but they predict Britten's "fall":

> For each love to its aim is true,
>   And all kinds seek their own;
> You love your life and I love you,
>   So I must lie alone.
>
> O hurry to the fêted spot
>   Of your deliberate fall;
> For now my dream of you cannot
>   Refer to you at all.

As in "Underneath the abject willow," Auden portrays Britten's desire as inevitable, "true" to "its aim." Because this "aim" is someone else, Auden's star-crossed love must let Britten go, no longer trying to make his own "dream" of love "refer to you at all." The elusive tone—compassionate or self-pitying? accepting or bitter?—comes from Auden's manipulation of double meanings (e.g., lie) and dark phonic overtones (e.g., fêted/fated) amid soothing alliteration. The love proffered is anything but true to a singular aim. "You love your life and I love you, / So I must lie alone": we expect "But," not "So." "So" makes sense only if we see the pathos of the "and" conjoining Auden's love and Britten's indifference. "Lie" is just right: the poet's solitude reflects not a wish to be alone, only avowed resignation.

We may see "Night covers up the rigid land" as a passive-aggressive gesture on Auden's part or as a rueful acknowledgement of Britten's erotic independence; alternatively, we may see it as a formal exercise Auden shared with another artist. Such choices, and the interpretive uncertainty they indicate, have two sources: the impossibility of drawing a straight line between historical/biographical information and poetic intentionality; and a verbal complexity that serves to dramatize moral and psychic ambiguities in the speaking voice. The prototypes for this kind of love poem are Petrarchan—above all Shakespeare, whom Auden had emulated in his love poetry before.[5] "Night covers up the rigid land" is rather reminiscent, in fact, of sonnet 87 ("Farewell, thou art too dear for my possessing"), where tonal uncertainty builds to a couplet replete with sexual wordplay: "Thus have I had thee as a dream doth flatter: / In sleep a king, but waking no such matter" (Shakespeare 76). Auden quotes this very couplet in his 1964 introduction to the Signet Classic edition of the *Sonnets,* a crucial document for understanding his own love poetry from the 1930s onward. For in sorting out sex and eros in Shakespeare, he was writing criticism as oblique autobiography.

A major aim of Auden's essay is to argue that Shakespeare's sexuality should not matter to the reader. Like Dante's *Vita Nuova* and Plato's *Symposium,* Auden says, the sonnets to the young man relate a "mystical" experience—a "Vision of Eros . . . concerned with a single person, who is revealed to the subject as being of infinite sacred importance" (*FA* 101). The beloved is "felt to be infinitely superior to the lover," and to such an experience it does not "make any sense to apply . . . terms like heterosexual or homosexual," which refer to "profane" experiences of "philia" and "lust." Noting that the Dark Lady sonnets are inarguably about sexual infatuation, Auden discounts the first 126 as evidence of Shakespeare's homosexuality. He prefers the word "mystery" to "aberration," implying that genital difference (or sameness) is meaningless at the metasexual level of eros with which Shakespeare was concerned.[6]

Whether Auden believed this is another matter; so is the larger cultural meaning of his remarks. About the time he wrote his essay, he told Igor Stravinsky that "it won't do just yet to admit that the top Bard was a member of the Homintern" (see Pequigney 79–80, Bruce Smith 231). So when Auden pokes fun at those who enlist Shakespeare as "patron saint of the Homintern," one might suspect him of acceding to propriety when his gut instinct was otherwise (*FA* 99). However, Stravinsky also recalls Auden saying on the same occasion that Beethoven was "queer" and Rilke was "the greatest Lesbian poet since Sappho." This need not mean that Auden did not believe Shakespeare homosexual, but it does weaken the case of those who would charge Auden with simple hypocrisy.[7]

Auden's beliefs may simply be beyond recovery, of course, but they may also have been unsettled or complex. There is, however, another way to illuminate his essay on the *Sonnets* and, by implication, his own love poetry. Auden does declare himself "certain" that "Shakespeare must have been horrified when [the sonnets] were published," for "sodomy was still a capital offense" (105). Such a statement clearly implies that whatever Shakespeare actually felt, he knew how his poems might be read, and that Auden could read them this way too. The question of how his own comments might be read is also, I suggest, something Auden is concerned with. With this in mind, his comments on the "Vision of Eros" seem less a way of sidestepping Shakespeare's sexuality than an echo of Oscar Wilde's own obliquities. Peter Stallybrass has argued that "one primary site in the formation of sexualities was the post-Enlightenment formation of 'literature,' " in which the *Sonnets* "played a central role" (102). "The Portrait of Mr. W. H." was a signal text in this history, according to Alan Sinfield: in invoking Renaissance Neoplatonism and friendship, Wilde implied that "there is something of importance to gay men in Shakespeare," but "not to be claimed at the expense of the fluidity of sexuality, in both personal and cultural terms" (*Wilde* 19). Wilde presents the tale of Shakespeare's infatuation with the boy actor Willie Hughes as a tantalizing but dangerous fiction. Auden was also concerned to reject reductive sexual essentialism, but his claims about the Vision of Eros align him with Wilde's effort to sanctify same-sex love by way of the idealism of "Greek Love."[8]

All this bears importantly on a sixteen-poem sequence, including twelve sonnets, that Auden sent Isherwood in 1934.[9] For while these poems deal with what he later termed the Vision of Eros, they also show homosexuality provoking a crisis of skepticism about any such vision. These lyrics focus on the relationship mourned in "Funeral Blues," which began in the summer of 1933, when Auden was teaching at the Downs School in the West Midlands (see Carpenter, *Auden* 157–59). They address an adolescent boy who is sexually mature but toward whom the poet poses as an elder in erotic wisdom and experience. The predatory potential in the relationship is something Auden is keenly aware of—in part, one assumes, because of his job as a teacher: "The fruit in which your parents hid you, boy, / Their death, is summer perfect: at its core / You grow already" (*EA* 148). The textual fate of this sonnet is exemplary; it appeared in *New Verse* in 1934 but not in Auden's collections during his lifetime. The sequence as a whole was never published as such, and those poems Auden did print were dispersed in *Look, Stranger!* (1936) and *Another Time* (1940). But it seems clear that to Isherwood, he was showing himself to be emulating Shakespeare.

For commercial publication, one value of sonnet form would be precisely its conventionality—the addressee's gender may be occluded by "you," and even when not, it can be taken merely as a matter of a poet imitating Shakespeare. But Auden's private dissemination of these poems is the social analogue to what comes across as their intense emotional enclosure. In his study of homosexuality and Elizabethan literary culture, Bruce R. Smith argues that Shakespeare's sonnets serve as "homologs to private life" (233): they carry out in poetry what Foucault terms the practice of *scientia sexualis,* with its "procedures for telling the truth of sex."[10] In the sonnets, Smith writes, "speaker and listener are bound together in a pact of secrecy," the bond of "secret sharers" (233). While Smith does not equate secrecy in Shakespeare's sonnets with the closet, the sense of enclosure in Auden's early love poems—whose sexual component is quite clear—asks to be read this way. "Yes, we are out of sight and earshot here," he writes of a secret rendezvous (*EA* 149). Auden thus reanimates the sonnet's traditional traffic with secrecy, finding modern sexual-political meaning, as it were, in the Elizabethan usage of *closet* for private chamber.[11] Where

his earlier poetry used secrecy as a weapon against the outsider, here
the poem becomes an erotic space of potential self-revelation: sonnets
that are not just pretty rooms but safe-houses.

The overall trajectory of the sequence conveys a sense of the boy's
birth, under the poet's tutelage, from erotic innocence into a conscious
loving subject. But from the very start, Auden's posture of erotic authority is qualified. The first poem ("The earth turns over, our side
feels the cold") finds the poet in a bedroom in his parents' house at
holiday time, and it portrays erotic vision as a suspect route to wish-
fulfillment:

> Your portrait hangs before me on the wall
> And there what view I wish for, I shall find,
>
> . . . .
> Through the blue irises the heaven of failures,
> The mirror world where logic is reversed,
> Where age becomes the handsome child at last,
> The glass sea parted for the country sailors.   (*EA* 145)

As the pun on "irises" suggests, Auden's gaze at the boy's image is
a narcissistic look in his own glass, transforming his age into the
boy's youth, the glass of separation into a sea of adolescent erotic adventure. Auden's later title for the poem, "Through the Looking-
Glass," fits with the more surreal images in the poem. But by implying
that the mirror opens on a left-handed world, so to speak, it hints at
sinister potential in homoerotic fantasy. The poet's love is unspeakable:
"You are a valley or a river bend, / The one an aunt refers to as a
friend. . . ." "False" is Auden's judgment on such subterfuge. Mean-
while, in "Love's daytime kingdom which I say you rule," "Yours is the
only name expressive there, / And family affection the one in cypher."
Here, eros mounts fascistic displays of abjection to repress its sexual
basis and elevate the boy as an image of its own purity:

> The total state where all must wear your badges,
> Keep order perfect as a naval school:
> Noble emotions organised and massed
> Line the straight flood-lit tracks of memory

> To cheer your image as it flashes by;
> All lust at once informed on and suppressed.

"Such dreams are amorous; they are indeed," Auden continues, but these figures of total submission to the beloved really express covert autoeroticism: "no one but myself is loved in these."

The poem hopes for abnegation of will as an escape from this double bind: "Gale of desire may blow / Sailor and ship past the illusive reef, / And I yet land to celebrate with you . . ." (146). Beyond the self-gratifying, totalitarian state of eros, Auden imagines "Birth of a natural order and of love," the two lovers "Free to our favours, all our titles gone." It is a beautiful ending, hoping for a "natural order" that would be a state of anarchy—a condition and polity without "titles" of authority. But the grammar of this hope is entirely optative, awaiting a lucky "gale of desire." What the sequence narrates instead is imprisonment in the power dynamics of homoerotic obsession.

The implied setting of this poem—Auden's bedroom in his parents' house—shows how secrecy licenses both fantasy and self-examination, only to become a hall of mirrors in which the truth about eros becomes harder to pin down. The next poem (the first sonnet in the sequence), which finds the poet/lover in bed with the boy, ingeniously uses sonnet form to render this sense of enclosure:

> Turn not towards me lest I turn to you:
> Stretch not your hands towards your harm and me
> Lest, waking, you should feel the need I do
> To offer love's preposterous guarantee
> That the stars watch us, that there are no poor,
> No boyish weakness justifying scorn,
> To cancel off from the forgotten score
> The foiled caresses from which thought was born.
>
> (*EA* 146)

The birth of love, Auden warns, brings an impulse to indulge absurd Petrarchan figures for its cosmic gravity. The charm of the warning is that it purports to confess the lover's own "need" to say such things, thus shame at his own potential "harm" to the boy. The dramatic and rhetorical situation is typical of Auden's early love poems, where the beloved is morally unconscious and either absent or literally asleep. With his latent capacity for self-love, he is like a strip of unexposed film, a passive medium that when brought to light will instantly, fatally reproduce the poet's own erotic and rhetorical will to power. At work is a narcissistic logic whose force depends on this being homosexual love: the poet sees in the boy a younger version of himself. The first verse may be construed in several ways. "Do not look at me, lest I look at you and indulge my wish-fulfilling fantasies," but also "Do not look at me, lest I become an image of yourself that you fall in love with."[12] Coming to consciousness as a lover brings a propensity and susceptibility to lies, for either reading suggests that the Vision of Eros narcissistically effaces the difference of the other—his particularity. The sonnet ends in a position of safety only by circling back to its beginning, the boy still asleep: "He [i.e. Love] means to do no mischief but he would. / Love would content us: that is untrue. / Turn not towards me lest I turn to you."

As the sequence unfolds, the poet/lover increasingly finds the greatest danger within the charmed circle of secret sharers. "On the provincial lawn I watch you play" sees the boy as one who innocently finds "The future like a promised picnic still" (147). "Will love refuse the power to exploit," it asks, "Or you the power which corrupts the heart?" The next sonnet—"At the far end of the enormous room"—gives the answer:

> It is an enemy that sighs for you:
> Love has one wish and that is, not to be.
> Had you been never beautiful nor true
> He would not have been born and I were free
> From one whose whispers shall go on and on
> Till you are false and all your beauties gone.   (147)

On one level these lines seek to undeceive the boy, to tell him what he does not yet know—that time steals both beauty and truth. But the poet's sense of the boy's innocence is entangled in his own disingenuousness: like the god "Love" personified here, he is an "enemy that sighs" for a boy still "true." With its aural ghosts—*lies, eyes, I[s]*—the phrase "sighs for you" neatly implies that the boy's innocence is a turn-on, blurring the line between passion and compassion, exploitation and sympathy. Love's one wish—its *only* one—is the entirely selfish wish "not to be": not to be born, but failing that, to be satisfied to death by its victims. The Vision of Eros is exposed as narcissistic delusion; the lover is intent on finding his lost innocence in the boy, knowing at the same time that this innocence is a function not of the boy but of his own seeing.

Rhetorically, the enclosure of the sonnet becomes a kind of mirrored confessional booth. Again, Auden's poems are clarified by Smith's remarks on Shakespeare. "As a way of putting sex into discourse," Smith argues, "confession . . . individualizes the speaker, it assumes that he or she speaks to some kind of authority figure, and it sets as the goal of his or her speaking a revelation of truth" (233). Smith applies to the *Sonnets* Foucault's views of Platonic *eros paidagogos*—educational love—which "problematized" male bonds "through reflection on the relation itself."[13] In *The Symposium*, Foucault argues, Greek concerns about erotic conduct and courtship are transformed into a philosophical question: "What is love in its very being?" (*History* 2, 229–33). Plato reacts to cultural worries about the freeborn boy as a passive "object of pleasure" by making him a conscious, active *sub*ject—a "lover of the master of truth" (Socrates)—and by making eros "a relation to truth" (242).

Whether Foucault is right about Plato, this understanding of *eros paidagogos* aptly conveys Auden's concern with authority and truth in his love poems. In "The Good Life" (1935), he prefaces his statements about noncoercive, curative "parable" with the following claims about guilty self-consciousness:

> What can be loved can be cured. The two chief barriers are ignorance and fear. Ignorance must be overcome by confession—i.e. drawing attention to unnoticed parts of the field of experience; fear by the exercise of *caritas* or *eros paidogogos* [sic].   (*P* 114)

This passage helps explain what Auden was doing at roughly the same time in his love poetry. By virtue of youth and apparent moral innocence, the boy is an authority figure to whom the guilty poet confesses; by virtue of age, experience, and convention, the poet/lover is an authority figure, empowered to cure erotic ignorance and fear, to help the love object to become a conscious subject. The crisis of Auden's sequence is that the moral authority of the poet/teacher/lover proceeds from awareness of his own guilt. Someday, Auden writes, "you will know what people mean by looking" (*EA* 148), but as yet the boy lacks the duplicity to detect predatory desire in others. And becoming a conscious erotic subject means learning the hard way that things are not what they seem, in others or in oneself: "Soon enough you will / Enter the zone where casualties begin" (146); "It is an enemy that sighs for you" (147); "Some you will beckon closer and be sorry" (148); "Are you aware what weapon you are loading, / To what that teasing talk is quietly leading?" (149).

The ultimate deception, Auden suggests, lies in the motives of the would-be master of truth as he seeks to teach the boy about deceit: "For only beauty still can make him kind, / Make teachers from the errors of his mind / Or surgeons from the vices of his heart" (148). As the Shakespearean sexual overtones of "kind" would imply, even the poet's wish to tell the truth of his falsehood diverges from good intentions. The truths these love poems tell about desire are ultimately ones of falsehood and faithlessness. Formally, Auden crosses the visionary eros of Shakespeare's sonnets to the young man with the sexual realism and linguistic games of the Dark Lady sonnets. The cynicism of sonnet 138 ("When my love swears she is made of truth") lurks in Auden's "Dear to me now and longer than a summer" (*EA* 149–50). Verbally, the boy is no longer innocent or awkwardly inhibited—"prisoned in the tower of a stammer." The imperative grammar of the poet/lover signals desperation: "Through sharpened sense peer into my life / With insight and loathing," he demands. At the same time he wants the boy to play the innocent:

> sigh and sign
> Interpret simply like an animal
> That finds the fenced-in pasture very green,
> No hint of malice in the trainer's call.   (*EA* 149)

The poet asks the boy to remain an unconscious animal to himself as trainer. In asking this, he is both confessing and asking for abandonment to narcissistic delusion. "Elsewhere these hands have hurt, these lips betrayed, / This will has quarrelled under different names," Auden writes, and by now hands, lips, and will (another word with sexual overtones in Shakespeare) could belong to either party. The sonnet ends with a desperate plea, at once utterly undeceived and wanting to be deceived: "See in my eyes the look you look to see; / I may be false but O be true to me" (150). For the boy to "be true" at this late date would demand acting, not sincerity, and on the poet's part as well. This sonnet marks the rhetorical limit of Auden's confessional mode, for the truth it reveals is the truth of lying: the honest confession of a desire for lies. It is *eros paidagogos* whose only remaining authority comes in the revelation of moral self-contradiction.[14]

This revelation assumes political form in the second-to-last lyric in the sequence, "Easily, my dear, you move, easily your head" (152–54). An initially subdued contemplation of the sleeping boy modulates into a monstrous erotic vision, expressing the totalitarian implications lurking in the sequence all along. Love feels safe from outside threats, but only because it ignores violence and power: "Looking and loving our behaviours pass / The stones, the steels and the polished glass," the poet declares; "and in the policed unlucky city / Lucky his [i.e. Love's] bed" (152). The poem proceeds to locate authoritarianism in visionary eros itself. Love "Makes worlds as innocent as Beatrix Potter's" only to call up "Such images . . . As vanity cannot dispel nor bless":

> Hitler and Mussolini in their wooing poses
> Churchill acknowledging the voters' greeting
> Roosevelt at the microphone, Van der Lubbe laughing
> And our first meeting.   (153)

In the context of the sequence, such sudden topicality suggests both the falsity of the lovers' sense of seclusion from the world and the appetite of Eros for annexing the world to his own fantasies. Love "through our private stuff must work / His public spirit," Auden writes, creepily implying that our physical relations—our bodily fluids, even—serve a larger agenda. Foretold in "The earth turns over," the coercions of visionary love now find grotesque release: "Be deaf," Auden tells the boy,

> To what I hear and wish I did not:
> The voice of love saying lightly, brightly,—
> "Be Lubbe, Be Hitler, but be my good
> Daily, nightly."

The fantasy of eternal love is unmasked as a yearning for erotic law and order, a willing abdication of freedom: private love is the local incarnation of the politics of dominance and submission. "Will you," the lover asks the boy, "Forfeit the beautiful interest and fall / Where the engaging face is the face of the betrayer, / And the pang is all?" He himself has, of course, and the final lines are directed at both of them:

> And the heart repeats though we would not hearken:
> "Yours is the choice, to whom the gods awarded
> The language of learning and the language of love,
> Crooked to move as a moneybug or a cancer
> Or straight as a dove."

These lines see only one escape from the dynamics of dominance and submission: we may choose to move "crooked" or "straight," embracing cancerous possessiveness or dovelike *caritas*.[15] "Crooked" and "straight" certainly function as more than sexual code words, but they are code words nonetheless.[16] As such, they suggest that homosexual love cannot but be crooked—ethically and psychologically self-directed. The final lesson of *eros paidagogos* is that it must come to an end: "the language of learning" and "the language of love" are ultimately at odds.

How to "move straight" is imagined in the final poem, "Love had him fast, although he fought for breath." As Mendelson shows, this sonnet (later titled "Meiosis") allegorizes a sperm cell released by ejaculation to fertilize an ovum (see *Early* 228). The sestet apostrophizes the embryo, where ontogeny recapitulates phylogeny but perhaps with a difference:

> Cities and years constricted to your scope,
> All sorrow simplified, though almost all
> Shall be as subtle when you are as tall:
> Yet clearly in that "almost" all his hope
> That hopeful falsehood cannot stem with love
> The flood on which all move and wish to move.   (*EA* 150)

As a conclusion to the sequence, this sonnet imagines the boy as having "chosen the straight," fulfilling the injunction to procreate in Shakespeare's early sonnets. The only way out of the narcissistic circularity of homosexual love, Auden seems to imply, is to reject it entirely. The sonnet represents the poet/teacher/lover, therefore, as having made his own choice to forswear erotic authority, allowing the boy to "move straight."

Such a resolution is deeply problematic, with its tropes of evolutionary progress and rhyming of "love" and "move." These elements recall the comedic, heterosexual conclusion to *In Memoriam,* with Tennyson's stately invocation of that Love "To which the whole creation moves."[17] But the hopeful rhythms of Auden's last line hardly resolve the tangled syntax. "All sorrow" is "simplified" in the genetic "constriction" of the boy to his sperm cell, but "almost all / Shall be as subtle when you are as tall." Here, nothing is simple, and the expansive "All" diminishes as it echoes through "almost all," "Shall" and "tall," " 'almost' all," and finally, "falsehood." "Hope" is undercut by "hopeful falsehood"; to "move" on the "flood" of the life force is qualified as a "wish to move." In the context of the sequence, the sonnet bespeaks skepticism about any consoling natural resolution to the involutions of homosexual love. The "hope," it appears, is that heterosexual consummation for the boy will "simplify" eros, but the crookedness of Auden's syntax begs the question of whether this is not just another "hopeful falsehood." Auden's other sonnets are often complex, but here verbal intricacy is pressed hard for schematic conclusion.

Auden may have forced his sequence to a close, but the relationship went on to inspire some of his greatest love poetry, including the famous "Lay your sleeping head, my love" (1937). If this is, as Mendelson claims, "the first English poem in which a lover proclaims, in moral terms and during a shared night of love, his own faithlessness"

(*Early* 233), it is also an exercise in *eros paidagogos,* teaching a lesson in
the purely ideal status of "certainty" and "fidelity" in a transitory relationship. The poem's pathos reflects an elegant reworking of the major
concern in Auden's earlier poems to this boy: the gap between the
poet/lover's rhetorical pretensions, born of a momentary Vision of
Eros, and the reality that the boy will not remain an innocent "child":

> Lay your sleeping head, my love,
> Human on my faithless arm;
> Time and fevers burn away
> Individual beauty from
> Thoughtful children, and the grave
> Proves the child ephemeral:
> But in my arms till break of day
> Let the living creature lie,
> Mortal, guilty, but to me
> The entirely beautiful.   (*EA* 207).

Almost every adjective here confesses transience: sleeping, human,
faithless, ephemeral, mortal, guilty. If the boy is "entirely beautiful,"
that is only because he can "lie" asleep: the lover indulges the Vision of
Eros but knows it is a function of the moment. "Soul and body know
no bounds," begins the second stanza: physical union is also metaphysical, ascending the Platonic Ladder of Love toward "the vision
Venus sends, / Of supernatural sympathy, / Universal love and hope."
But the marriage of physical and metaphysical is ironized. It is
"Grave"—solemn—but given the earlier use of "grave" as a noun, also
fatal. And it is the mundane effect of an "ordinary swoon."

   Auden's essay on Shakespeare notwithstanding, the Vision of Eros
in this poem does not transcend terms like heterosexual and homosexual but remains a matter of "profane" sexual experience. To assert
that "Acquaintance with the sex of the particular beloved is irrelevant"
here, since "A love poem is a love poem," is to abdicate critical and historical knowledge.[18] The poem's fame certainly reflects our freedom to
imagine the beloved as female, but Auden's emphasis on faithlessness
follows from his psychological and ethical concerns with narcissism
and deceit in homosexual love. Apart from a brief period after meeting

Chester Kallman, he seems to have been unable to imagine homo-sexual love *except* as given to infidelity and some measure of loss.

The poem can, of course, be made to yield a moral about the transi-toriness of love—a moral so conventional that it is easy to take it as Auden's "deeper" meaning. Consciously to universalize the poem, however, is to perform a critical gesture mirroring the lover's wishful-ness, but subtracting his clearsightedness to leave unalloyed sentimen-tality:

> Beauty, midnight, vision dies:
> Let the winds of dawn that blow
> Softly round your dreaming head
> Such a day of sweetness show
> Eye and knocking heart may bless,
> Find the mortal world enough;
> Noons of dryness see you fed
> By the involuntary powers,
> Nights of insult let you pass
> Watched by every human love.

This stanza's pathos is inseparable from its explicitness about the im-possibility of what the lover wishes: he would have the Vision of Eros that dies at midnight extend magically to the day. "Let the winds of dawn that blow": in all the verses that follow, "Let" confesses itself touchingly impotent, imagining a wish that the poet/lover knows well is contrary to fact. Since the vision cannot last, he prays that the boy may "Find the mortal world enough"—that quotidian things may sat-isfy. Even so, there *will* be "nights of insult": those who experience such love do not always pass safely. For the poet/lover to pretend otherwise would be to use pseudoinnocent language unfaithful to facts and to his own faithlessness.

By the same token, to take the poem as an expression of the tran-sience of *all* love is to elide the sexual-political specificity of its dra-matic scenario, indulging "supernatural sympathy" and "Universal love and hope" of another sort by pretending that the conditions under which heterosexual and homosexual love are experienced are the same. The poem certainly conveys the wish for "Universal love and hope," but it is also about the powerlessness of sympathy to make wishes come true. The effect of the poem, therefore, is not that of Keatsian or modernist paradox, reconciling time and eternity; nor does the poem resolve itself into a Petrarchan conceit about how poetry defeats change and preserves love forever. Instead, its poignancy comes from the poet/lover's awareness of the impossibility of such resolutions.

Rather than reconciling time and timelessness, the poem balances stasis and change, and Auden exploits the temporal unfolding of its verses to suggest that this is a precarious poise that can last only in the safe-house of art or the bedroom. The first two stanzas, broadly speaking, focus on the present moment. The third foresees separation. The fourth expresses not faith, but good wishes for a future whose arrival means the moment is gone. In addition, each stanza exploits imagery and sound to interfuse temporal and spatial precariousness. The first is rich in aural patterns: rhymes (away, day), half-rhymes (day, lie, me), internal rhymes (guilty, me, entirely), alliteration (lie, love, let, living, lie; love, fevers, grave, proves, living; time, arm, arms; mortal, me), as well as fainter echoes (sleeping, faithless, thoughtful). Auden later titled this poem "Lullaby," and its repetitions soothe the ear with continuity and connote stasis. But these repetitions also involve aural difference, thus change. There is, in other words, temporality in the very movement from one word to its echo, and the echoes often create ironic relations (e.g., lie/love).

Underlying all this, the meter—trochaic tetrameter catalectic—provides a rhythmic equivalent of perfect balance and enclosure in almost every line: stressed syllables at the beginning and the end cradle five syllables, alternating unstressed and stressed. But again, such a pattern only registers with repetition: the sense of static enclosure requires movement through each line and on to the next. Moreover, Auden tends to undercut the feeling of stasis as the meaning of one line is extended by another. "Lay your sleeping head, my love. . . ." *But* you are "Human" (i.e., *only* human?), and you lay it "on my faithless arm." "Time and fevers burn away. . . ." No, not *themselves,* but "Individual beauty from / Thoughtful children," etc. The stanza ends by naming the boy "entirely beautiful." The sentiment feels utterly simple and sincere in itself, but the words do not occur in isolation; they come after the qualifications of the previous line ("Mortal, guilty, but to me . . .")

and the earlier statement that "Individual beauty" is lost to "Time and fevers."

A universalizing reading of this poem might be said to underestimate space in favor of time. For Auden as for so many others writing about illicit love, space is an obsessive concern. His concern with time, however, seems conventional enough to invite universalizing responses in terms of the transitoriness of all love. The power of the poem—its beauty—comes from a sense that this blessed moment is precariously here and now: it happens only tonight and only in this bed and only because the boy is asleep. It can happen now, in other words, only because it can happen here. Outside of this poem, outside of this bed, it cannot continue any more than the individual beauty of individual verses or images can be absolutely isolated from others in the poem. What makes this poem feel different from Auden's sonnets to this boy is, first, that the self-enclosure of sonnet form strongly foregrounds social and spatial constraints on the relationship. Second, the Shakespearean wordplay of Auden's sonnets makes far more explicit the ethical and psychological crisis of the poet/lover.

To read "Lullaby" in the context of the same relationship is to see that it raises the very same ethical questions. For we are meant to see, I suggest, that the clear-sightedness of this speaker is rhetorically dishonest. The title "Lullaby" conjures the dramatic scenario of many of Auden's sonnets: the speaker poses as the mature lover addressing the sleeping boy; were the latter truly conscious, this message would hardly soothe. John Fuller has remarked, "One may object that the loved one is not convincingly present in the poem" (264), but this is exactly the point: the boy *cannot* be present in the poet's Vision of Eros. The confession of faithlessness is a lesson in disenchantment, but not for the implied auditor, since the boy is typically portrayed as not hearing it.

The lesson is instead for the reader, who may or may not wish to become conscious of the rhetorical contrivance of this soothing voice. Auden's comment on love poems a decade later, in "Squares and Oblongs," raises just this issue:

The girl whose boy-friend starts writing her love poems should be on her guard. Perhaps he really does love her, but one thing is certain:

while he was writing his poems he was not thinking of her but of [*sic*] his own feelings about her, and that is suspicious. Let her remember St. Augustine's confession of his feelings after the death of someone he loved very much: "I would rather have been deprived of my friend than of my grief."

("Squares" 175)

As a poem in which love is bound up proleptically with grief, "Lullaby" makes a confession akin to St. Augustine's: this is indeed a poem about the lover's own feelings, not the beloved. It bears a touch of the mercenary, even more so when we know that Auden wrote it out by hand for Benjamin Britten in January 1937, shortly before going to Spain. This gesture seems histrionic and calculated, especially since this confession of faithlessness seems literally so *attractive*. Ten months before, Auden had written to Britten, "now my dream of you cannot / Refer to you at all." If Auden was, not exactly kindly, telling Britten that this dream did not refer to him either, we might also see the poem as inviting Britten—and us—to become conscious of what the lover imagines telling the sleeping boy but doesn't. How Britten read the poem we cannot know, any more than we can be sure what Auden meant by giving it to him, or sure of how to judge the poem's speaker ethically. But to ask these questions is to see this love poem not as a lullaby but as a provocation to erotic self-knowledge.

II

In April 1939, a few months after arriving in the United States, Auden met Chester Kallman, an eighteen-year-old student at Brooklyn College. By May, Auden had written "The Prophets":

> Perhaps I always knew what they were saying:
> Even those earliest messengers who walked
> Into my life from books where they were staying,
> Those beautiful machines that never talked
> But let the small boy worship them and learn
> All their long names whose hardness made him proud;

Love was the word they never said aloud
As nothing that a picture can return.

And later when I hunted the Good Place,
Abandoned lead-mines let themselves be caught;
. . . .
And all the landscape round them pointed to
The calm with which they took complete desertion
As proof that you existed.   (CP 255–56)

These lines revisit Auden's poetic terrain of a decade before, now deciphering signs of a "face" and a "Place / Where all I touch is moved to an embrace." But where Auden had once found a land "Always afraid to say more than it meant" (EA 25), now its very "lack of answer" bespeaks the calm of certainty: "proof that you existed."

"The Prophets" shows the beginning of a transition in Auden's poetry, as issues of desire and unspeakability take on a religious cast. In the coming years, Alan Jacobs has noted, Auden's "thoughts about erotic love and the love of God would remain interwoven or, perhaps, entangled—so much so that it is impossible to intelligently discuss the one without invoking the other" (74). So although Auden's "queer theology" is dealt with more fully in chapter 6, religious issues inevitably arise here. From a sexual-political angle, the religious figures of "The Prophets" serve a closeting effect: if we read it as a meditation on time, memory, and love—in the mode of Eliot's "Burnt Norton"—there need be nothing especially erotic in its figures of hunting and catching, or those long hard "names." But read as a love poem, "The Prophets" figures the beloved as the messiah foretold to a worshipper who sought paradise and was given signs. Now at last, the lover knows "It was true": the beloved "asks for all my life." Here, the divine meaning of Kallman's love is a private cult: Auden is both proclaiming his new love and disguising it.[19]

With consequences for his life and work for decades to come, Auden was subsuming Kallman into just the Vision of Eros he had been so fatalistic about. Thus it is telling that he does not emulate Shakespeare's Sonnets, whose linguistic duplicity would undercut a sense that this Vision of Eros is for real. Images of gazing and language of knowledge do not occasion ironic wordplay here: the word "face" occurs twice, and Auden ends by affirming that "there is no such thing as a vain look." With much the same ecstatic tone, "Warm are the still and lucky miles" (October 1939) revisits the secret sharers, now resting safely in "the breathing wood / Where drowsy limbs a treasure keep," and sees an end to the erotic odyssey of "Through the Looking-Glass": "Restored! Returned! The lost are borne / On seas of shipwreck home at last. . ." (*CP* 267).

What had changed, apparently, was Auden's belief that love could be permanent. Writing to A. E. Dodds (whose husband had been a recipient of the 1928 *Poems*), Auden invoked marriage:

> Of course I know that Love as a fever does not last, but for some years now I've known that the one thing I really needed was marriage, and I think I have enough experience and judgement to know that this relationship is going to be marriage with all its boredoms and rewards.
>
> (Carpenter, *Auden* 259)

Auden took to wearing a gold wedding band, gave one to Kallman, and referred to a trip they took in the summer of 1939 as their honeymoon (262). What made this love different, Auden evidently felt, was its freedom from the narcissistic envy in his earlier relations.[20] His 1938 review of a biography of A. E. Housman had posed matters fatalistically:

> Does Life only offer two alternatives: "You shall be happy, healthy, attractive, a good mixer, a good lover and parent, but on condition that you are not overcurious about life. On the other hand you shall be attentive and sensitive, conscious of what is happening round you, but in that case you must not expect to be happy, or successful in love, or at home in any company."
>
> (*P* 437)

Auden was recapitulating the binary of mind and body that had governed his thinking about homosexuality for ten years. He saw himself, like Housman, as the second type, futilely in love with the first (a variant on The Truly Strong Man): " 'Socrates will always fall in love with Alcibiades; Alcibiades will only be a little flattered and rather puzzled.' "[21] Kallman may have been handsome and young, but Auden at last claimed to have outgrown *eros paidagogos*. In his letter to Dodds, he wrote, "I've spent years believing I could only love the world of the Alter Ego, but I was very foolish, because W. of the A. E. doesn't respond. Now I realize that I wanted someone rather like myself" (Mendelson, *Later* 35).

As Mendelson suggests, Auden's "Heavy Date" (October 1939) expressed this idea; more, it credited Kallman for the lesson. "Crying for the moon is / Naughtiness and envy," it comments, for "We can only love what- / -ever we possess":

> I believed for years that
> Love was the conjunction
> Of two oppositions;
>   That was all untrue;
> Every young man fears that
> He is not worth loving:
> Bless you, darling, I have
>   Found myself in you.   (*CP* 261–62)

The paradox here is that narcissism can be avoided only by proper self-love, versus ugly Socrates' envy of handsome Alcibiades. In Kallman, Auden was truly loving someone else, the poem implies, instead of a heroic Alter Ego to assuage self-doubt. In his earlier love poems, the lover's inadequacies had led to a will to power over the beloved, whom he made an image of innocence both childlike and superhuman; at its extreme, Auden put this as a sadomasochistic plea: "Be Lubbe, Be Hitler, but be my good / Daily, nightly" (*EA* 154). In "Like a Vocation" (May 1939), Auden enjoined Kallman to come "Not as that dream Napoleon," who arrives in erotic power, "dedicates a column and withdraws" (the ultimate "top," in gay slang), but as a figure of gentleness and charity (*CP* 256). For "the one who needs you" is "that terrified / Imaginative child," whose "weeping climbs towards your life like a vocation" (257).

The problem, to judge from all accounts, was that Auden was

counting on Kallman seeing their relationship similarly. For his part, Kallman seems to have sensed desperation in Auden's love. "Why this self-abasement?" he asked in a May 1939 letter. "Can you be assured? I love you" (Mendelson, *Later* 43–44). If Auden no longer thought himself seeking an Alter Ego, he still felt the Vision of Eros to be answering his most basic needs, and perhaps no more than anyone could Kallman sustain his idealization. Much has been written of their life together, and it seems undeniable that Kallman was hardly suited temperamentally to be the hero in Auden's Vision of Eros. Nor was he ready to be married. When Auden referred to their "honeymoon," Kallman assumed campy distance: "*Such* a romantic girl" (Davenport-Hines 194). Kallman evidently did not intend sexual fidelity, and in the summer of 1941 he told Auden that he had already had an affair; they never resumed sexual relations.

Looking back more than twenty years later, Auden indirectly described what had happened as a sin against the Vision of Eros. But he wavered on who was the sinner. It seems clear, for example, that in his Shakespeare essay of 1964, he was writing from personal experience:

> The story of the sonnets seems to me to be the story of an agonized struggle by Shakespeare to preserve the glory of the vision he had been granted in a relationship, lasting at least three years, with a person who seemed intent by his actions upon covering the vision with dirt.[22]

Similar language appears in "The Protestant Mystics"—also from 1964—when Auden cited Dante's "acts of infidelity" to a "vision of one human creature, Beatrice" (*FA* 68). His 1941 Christmas letter had told Kallman, "it is through you that God has chosen to show me my beatitude" (Farnan 66); his comment years later on Dante implied that his *own* infidelity to the vision "brought him near to perdition." Earlier in the essay, Auden explained why "the Vision of Eros cannot long survive if the parties enter into an actual sexual relation" or get married: "It is difficult to live day after day, year after year, with an ordinary human being, neither much better nor much worse than oneself, after one has seen her or him transfigured, without feeling that the fading of the vision is the other's fault" (64).

Such remarks indicate Auden's increasing explicitness about himself in his prose of the 1960s; as Mendelson says aptly, Auden would "leave his secrets hidden in plain sight," inviting readers to explicate his life in his work (*Later* 450). In the 1940s, he would be this open only in private, as in a 1948 letter to Alan Ansen, which listed a number of poems under the heading "L'affaire C," including "The Prophets" and "Like a Vocation." One can therefore reconstruct a narrative of this relationship through Auden's writing, as Mendelson has done in great detail in *Later Auden*. My specific concern here is with how his work dealt with anxieties about sex and its meanings in a long-term homosexual relationship. Ansen records Auden as remarking in 1947: "Sexual fidelity is more important in a homosexual relationship than in any other. In other relationships there are a variety of ties. But here, fidelity is the only bond" (81). This, one might object, would seem to underrate fidelity in heterosexual relationships or overrate it in homosexual ones; in fact, Auden's relationship with Kallman was sustained for years by shared domestic life and their collaborations on libretti.[23] But his comment reflects an ongoing concern with Kallman's infidelity and the question of how a long-term relationship can endure without sexual fidelity.

To judge from some of his poems of 1940–41, Auden was worried even before what he called, in his letter to Ansen, "The Crisis." The most elaborate of these is the epithalamion "In Sickness and in Health," from the fall of 1940, and it shows how badly Auden wanted marriage as a model for his relationship with Kallman. In spite of its dedication to two married friends, Auden wrote it originally for Kallman. The title, the repetition of the word "Rejoice," the references to wedding rings and vows: all this implies that these are Auden's own wedding vows.[24] But like the rings he had bought, the poem is a tendentious gesture. Its premise is that homosexual love can and should emulate heterosexual marriage. But the theology Auden musters is not traditional, and his major concern is with marriage as a bulwark against wandering eros.

The poem's structure and argument are indebted to Denis de Rougemont's *Love in the Western World*, which Auden reviewed in 1941. De Rougemont saw the tale of Tristan and Isolde as the defining western myth of eros; spawned from a heretical Manichaean dualism, this myth had abetted the modern decay of the institution of marriage, as well as totalitarianism and the passion for war. As different as de Rougemont was from Lawrence or Layard, his totalizing ambition appealed to Auden's love for linking psychosexual dysfunction and public disaster. Moreover, the book offered a theory to confirm Auden's sense of love's propensity for the will to power.

The opening stanzas of the poem focus on the war in Europe as a symptomatic eruption of twisted desire. The fifth stanza offers a general definition of perversion—"Nature by nature in unnature ends"—to make a transition from public crises to private dysfunction:

> Echoing each other like two waterfalls,
>   Tristan, Isolde, the great friends,
> Make passion out of passion's obstacles,
> Deliciously postponing their delight,
> Prolong frustration till it lasts all night,
> Then perish lest Brangaene's worldly cry
> Should sober their cerebral ecstasy.   (*CP* 318)

For de Rougemont, the major illusion of the Tristan-Isolde myth is that the two love each other: in fact, they embrace obstacles because *"What they love is love and being in love"* (31; emphasis in original). Their "self-imposed chastity," he argues, is "a way of purifying desire of the spontaneous, brutish, and active elements still encumbering it. 'Passion' triumphs over desire. Death triumphs over life" (36). For Auden, this theory would explain his earlier romantic fatalism as a way to authorize illicit desire—in his case, not adulterous but homosexual love: by making it spiritual, he made it impossible to realize for metaphysical reasons, not social ones, so all the more superlative. While Auden calls Tristan and Isolde "the great friends" terrified of passion, he elsewhere cited them as homosexual types and usually paired them (as here) with the antitype of Don Juan.[25] The compulsive promiscuity of Don Juan is (following de Rougemont) just an inversion of Tristan and Isolde: "so terrified of death he hears / Each moment recommending it / And knows no argument to counter theirs." In gay slang, Don Juan is the incurable cottager: "Unhappy spook, he haunts the urinals, / Existing solely by their miracles" (*CP* 318). Together, the three comprise the dark truth of the Vision of Eros, a "syllogistic nightmare," in Auden's words, that offers only radical idealism or radical materialism.

Cure comes only in rejecting the terms of eros entirely, Auden suggests in a stanza beginning, "Beloved, we are always in the wrong" (319). The phrasing, many have noted, comes from Kierkegaard's *Either/Or*, but the sentiment reflects Auden's perennial emphasis on faithlessness and the lover's will to power. What Kierkegaard offered was a conceptual and poetic escape from the double bind of eros. Through the "tohu-bohu" of our erotic "manias," Auden writes, "comes a voice / Which utters an absurd command—Rejoice." What we are to rejoice in with Kierkegaardian absurdity is "agape." Auden does not use the word here, but the second half of the poem (turning from sickness to health) offers de Rougemont's argument for agape as the basis of successful marriage. Eros embraces death to escape a corrupt world, but agape is "a reassertion of life . . . of our present life now repossessed by the Spirit" (de Rougemont 59). In his review of *Love in the Western World,* Auden's only caveat was that de Rougemont seems to imply "that there is a dualistic division between Agape and Eros rather than—what I am sure he believes—a dialectical relation"; agape, Auden wrote, is "Eros mutated by Grace" ("Eros" 757). Whether de Rougemont meant this, "In Sickness and in Health" works hard to argue it. Since "All chance, all love, all logic, you and I, / Exist by grace of the Absurd," love's salvation can come only absurdly:

> So, lest we manufacture in our flesh
> The lie of our divinity afresh,
> Describe round our chaotic malice now,
> The arbitrary circle of a vow.   (*CP* 319)

In de Rougemont's terms, vows of marital commitment are how agape tames the "chaotic malice" of eros, which wants romantic passion to be simply "divine." Without agape, that wish is only what Auden's love poems call a "lie."

As Jacobs perceptively argues, Auden's recourse to existentialism is bound up with two related issues: his worries about Kallman's fidelity, and his concern with the spiritual meaning of homosexual love

(76–81). This poem, after all, can invoke neither the primal marriage of Adam and Eve nor the doctrine that male-female marriage figures the relation between Christ and the Church. What Auden does instead is to offer a kind of existentialist antitypology:

> Force our desire, O Essence of creation,
> To seek Thee always in Thy substances,
> Till the performance of those offices
> Our bodies, Thine opaque enigmas, do,
> Configure Thy transparent justice too.

The sense of these lines, Jacobs notes, is that, cut off from direct knowledge of divine justice, "we may only 'configure' it opaquely and enigmatically" (80); only *negatively* can we manifest our status as children of God. In the standard view, God's creativity is manifest in human love not enigmatically but figuratively—in procreation; the biological absurdity of homosexual love would parallel its typological meaninglessness. But if, in the existentialist view, God is Wholly Other; if (as Auden puts it) "All chance, all love, all logic, you and I, / Exist by grace of the Absurd"; then homosexual lovers, performing "those offices / Our bodies, Thine opaque enigmas, do," become the perversely perfect sign of Absurd Love.

This theological justification is at the rhetorical service of Auden's argument for fidelity, directed to Kallman as the other half of "you and I." Rhetorically, the absurd logic of the argument may be less important than the sacramental aura with which Auden surrounds marriage. The last stanzas of the poem employ an interesting blend of registers. "That this round O of faithfulness we swear / May never wither to an empty nought / Nor petrify into a square," Auden prays, "Love, permit / Temptations always to endanger it" (320). This danger, I suggest, has haunted Auden all along, but now it is stated openly. The only safety— which is hardly safety—comes in the uncertain faith that agape trumps eros, that temptation affirms the free will God gives us for our own good: the "circle of a vow" is not so "arbitrary" after all. "That we, though lovers, may love soberly, / O fate, O *Felix Osculum,* to us / Remain nocturnal and mysterious. . . ." Auden tries to instigate a transformation of eros into agape. To love "soberly" is an injunction of the

Anglican marriage service utterly at odds with eros. But agape's "happy kiss" (expressed in the sexy *alienum eloquium* of Latin) draws its numinous trappings from the realm of eros, where love is "fatal" and (as in "Lullaby") something you do in the dark. To end the poem Auden abruptly switches back to a measured petition to sober agape: "Preserve us from presumption and delay, / And hold us to the voluntary way."[26]

As an argument for monandrous gay marriage, "In Sickness and in Health" takes two routes. One is to suggest that this is the "way" for homosexuals as for heterosexuals. The other is to suggest quite the opposite, that for homosexuals to undertake such a relationship is absurd but therefore sacred. If this tension reflects Auden's ongoing uncertainty whether differences between homosexuality and heterosexuality mean something, it also suggests his hope that marriage could circumscribe wayward homosexual eros but preserve its spiritual aura. The fact that Kallman did not want to be married hardly proves the fallaciousness of Auden's argument, but it does suggest that the poem was motivated more by Auden's own conceptual and emotional wish for stability than by a sense of what was possible for Kallman.

"In Sickness and in Health" is finally less an epithalamion than a persuasion poem, seeking rhetorically to lead Kallman to fidelity. By 1947, Auden could joke about hiring witch doctors to get Kallman to sleep with him (see Ansen 91). But he could joke, one assumes, because he knew his own mania on the subject. As usual, Shakespeare's *Sonnets* gave him occasion to indulge in displaced self-analysis. To Howard Griffin he remarked in the late 1940s:

> In the *Sonnets* [Shakespeare] desperately tries to do that which is forbidden: to create a human being. With the ardor of a Paracelsus . . . he mixes words as if they were chemicals that might bring forth [a] homonculus. Evidently he has selected someone at a stage of possibility. He wants to make an image so the person will not be a dream but rather someone he knows as he knows his own interest. He wishes the other to have free will yet his free will is to be the same as Shakespeare's. Of course great anxiety and bad behavior result when the poet's will is crossed as it is bound to be.
>
> (Griffin 98–99)

"In Sickness and in Health," like other poems Auden wrote in the months before and after Kallman's confession, is attempting verbal alchemy. The quasi-villanelle "Leap Before You Look" reiterates, in the idiom of Kierkegaard, Kallman's freedom to commit to the relationship or not, but it is clear what Auden wants: "A solitude ten thousand fathoms deep / Sustains the bed on which we lie, my dear: / Although I love you, you will have to leap . . ." (*CP* 314).

Perhaps not surprisingly, Auden's first poems to grapple with the *fact* of Kallman's infidelity, in the summer of 1941, are impressive mostly as evidence of his own pain. As expressed in "Though determined nature can," from the immediate aftermath of Kallman's confession, the truth about love is what Auden had always suspected: the lying Vision of Eros must be paid for:

> Aphrodite's garden is
>   A haunted region;
> For the very signs whereby
> Lovers register their vow,
>   With a look, with a sigh,
> Summon to their meetings One
>   Whose name is Legion.   (*CP* 271)

As with much of Auden's writing for the next few years, behind these lines is a sense that he himself had been guilty in his relationship with Kallman. Shortly after Kallman had confessed his infidelity, he awoke to find Auden's hands around his throat. As recounted by his stepmother, Dorothy Farnan, Kallman "pushed Wystan away and fled the room" (Farnan 57). In Auden's mind, his response to Kallman's betrayal became a crime of his own: his 1941 Christmas letter confessed, "On account of you, I have been, in intention, and almost in act, a murderer" (66). In a 1956 essay for a book of testimonials by Episcopalian converts, Auden alluded to this experience as one of those that led him back to the Church: "And then, providentially . . . I was forced to know in person what it is like to feel oneself the prey of demonic powers, in both the Greek and the Christian sense, stripped of self-control and self-respect, behaving like a ham actor in a Strindberg play" (Pike 41). This self-realization (as Auden saw it) is the subject of

"Canzone" (1942), which foreshadows his wording years later: "In my own person I am forced to know / How much must be forgotten out of love, / How much must be forgiven, even love" (*CP* 331). Like "Though determined nature can," with its ending plea "O my love, O my love . . . Save me from evil," "Canzone" seems at once deeply pained and subtly manipulative—confessing more than it knows in its pleas for forgiveness.

The dangers of such manipulation were the subject of a comment Auden made in 1966 in a letter to a friend whose marriage was breaking up. Returning to the "syllogistic nightmare" of eros, Auden now sees sexual waywardness as the lesser danger:

> The Tristan-Isolde myth is more dangerous to us than the myth of Don Giovanni. We have—at least I know I have—to beware in our relations with others of becoming emotional leeches—and in this sphere the one who appears to be *giving* the blood may well be the greater leech of the two.
>
> (Mendelson, *Later* 467)

These remarks resonate with one's sense that suffering and guilt became rhetorical weapons in some of Auden's poems to Kallman following "The Crisis." In "Amor Loci" (1965), long after he had stopped thinking of his relationship with Kallman as marriage, Auden returned to the landscape of "The Prophets." It was still a holy site, but no longer in the same way:

> How but with some real focus
> of desolation
> could I, by analogy,
> imagine a Love
> that, however often smeared,
> shrugged at, abandoned
> by a frivolous worldling,
> does not abandon?   (*CP* 780)

What Auden sensed in 1939 as the "calm" of "complete desertion" no longer seemed in 1965 the sign of presence in a Vision of Eros. By this time, Kallman had given up spending winters with Auden in New York, and Auden's idea of a divine love that "does not abandon," knowable only by "analogy" through its negative of "desolation," owed much to a sense of having lost Kallman. But not everything: the later Auden's greatest writing about love became possible only when he began to explore a far more fluid sense of "faithfulness."

III

"Being 'anders wie die Andern' has its troubles," Auden wrote to Elizabeth Mayer in 1943, alluding to the title of the classic 1919 German film on homosexuality (*Anders als die Andern*). "There are days," he went on,

> when the knowledge that there will never be a place which I can call home, that there will never be a person with whom I shall be one flesh, seems more than I can bear, and if it wasn't for you, and a few—how few—like you, I don't think I could.
>
> (Mendelson, *Later* 227)

This letter dates, Mendelson notes, from the time when Auden was writing one of the most beautiful lyrics in "The Sea and the Mirror": Miranda's song, a villanelle whose formal order figures the marriage from which Auden felt exiled. "My Dear One is mine as mirrors are lonely," she sings of Ferdinand, with the surety of a love that has done with self-regard (*CP* 421). But if Auden could not be "one flesh" with his Dear One, the reason he gives Mayer is not a matter of anyone's sins but an unalterable condition of queerness, the cost of being different from others. We can, I submit, stress this cost too much, reading Auden's later work entirely under the sign of loss, naturalizing it (as Auden often did) as the homosexual condition. This is one possible effect of Farnan and Clark's memoirs of Auden and Kallman, which unsparingly recount the conflicts and sordid moments of their later years together. Such knowledge can obscure how Auden, while never overcoming disappointment about this relationship, also explored other ways of configuring intimacy and homosexual love. "The Sea and the

Mirror" suggests that he saw himself as a Prospero who had to give up magically scripting the lives of others, above all Kallman's. It ends not with Ferdinand and Miranda but with Ariel and Caliban, who point, no less beautifully, to another kind of love. The "Postscript" offers a scripted expression of love, but it is not an act of emotional conjuring or rhetorical coercion. As the song of Ariel to Caliban, spirit to body, it pays tribute to love that goes on despite awareness of imperfections: "To your faults be true: / I can sing as you reply / . . . I" (445). The loving, echoing "I" is spoken by "the prompter," not Caliban himself. Inviting Caliban to reply, but not making him, Ariel renders the love lyric as an invitation to dialogue.[27]

Auden's letter to Mayer locates the homosexual in the world of marriage but never at home there, living out a sexual existentialism. But exile for later Auden is not only a condition to be endured. Robert Caserio has argued that "For the Time Being" (1941–42), which others have read in terms of Auden's relationship with Kallman, posits a notion of queer citizenship.[28] Negatively in the gay soldier George, who joins in state-sponsored murder (the Massacre of the Innocents); positively in "the gay Jewish couple Joseph and Mary," who have fled to Egypt, Auden suggests that the homosexual should not be at home in the world (103). "The better citizens," in Caserio's reading, "those more potentially the bearers of a redemptive public virtue, are migrating or in exile" (101).

Such a claim has implications both political and personal for Auden, who spent his last twenty-five years migrating annually from New York to Ischia and then Austria. My aim here is to link the condition of homosexual exile to Auden's later love poems and theories of poetry. For his abiding concern with personal relations—indeed his propositions about poetry as an intimate relation of I and Thou—show him entertaining poetry itself as a realm of erotic relation alternative to marriage. It becomes, I suggest, a way for Auden both to imagine the relationship he yearned for with Kallman and to be faithful to eros in its wandering, plural attachments.

"Few and Simple," as Auden put it in a 1944 poem, are the "facts" about love and sex, but they leave us in limbo. The poem reads like a rewriting of "To ask the hard question is simple" (1930), though Auden's concern is no longer with the enigmatic fact of homosexuality, but with the relation between love, sex, and the reality of his life with Kallman. "The mind," Auden writes, "Amazes me with all the kind / Old such-and-such it says about you. . ." (*CP* 326). It acts "As if I were the one that you / Attach unique importance to, / Not the one who would but didn't get you." Just as oblivious is "The flesh that mind insists is ours": it "Gets ready for no-matter-what / As if it had forgotten that / What happens is another matter." Both mind and body live in a state of "As if," where "I" am *still* "the one that you / Attach unique importance to." The "I" knows "you" don't, so what does it mean that mind and flesh continue as if you do?

"To ask the hard question" had ended by hoping that love might "recover" and "restore" a condition of "What has been dark and rich and warm all over" (*EA* 55). Now Auden seems resigned:

> Few as they are, these facts are all
> The richest moment can recall,
> However it may choose to group them,
> And, simple as they look, enough
> To make the most ingenious love
> Think twice of trying to escape them.   (*CP* 326)

There is no longer any question of what one can "recall" from the past (or "recover," as Auden put it in 1930): only bare "facts" remain for the I that observes mind and body. What makes these lines mysterious is that it is unclear which facts Auden means: the fact of past love, the fact of its pastness, or the facts of mind and body acting—contrary to fact, so to speak—as if things are still the same. Auden is groping at the edge of something here, and although Kallman is the implicit addressee, he is no longer the target of an argument on the virtue of fidelity or forgiveness. He is, to be sure, warned against "trying to escape" facts. But in being addressed as "you," as one of "us both" who are "startl[ed] . . . at certain hours" by arousal that does not acknowledge that the past is past, Kallman is also asked to construe the ambiguous "facts" of this love.

In its concern with the inescapable and the inscrutable, "Few and Simple" suggests that love was deeply bound up with Auden's later musings about freedom and necessity in life and in art. Like his theories of parable in the 1930s, his theories of poetry from the 1940s and after are entangled in his views of homosexual love. Although Auden reworked portions of it for various essays in *The Dyer's Hand,* his 1948 essay "Squares and Oblongs" shows more clearly than anything else that thinking about poetry meant thinking about guilt, crime, freedom and necessity in eros.

The essay begins with what Auden terms the "gratuitous" value of art, which appeals to people not only for social reasons (the pressure of modernity to be productive) but for psychological ones. St. Augustine, Auden says,

> was the first to see the basic fact about human nature, namely that the Natural Man hates nature, and that the only act which can really satisfy him is the *acte gratuite* (*sic*). His ego resents every desire of his natural self for food, sex, pleasure, logical coherence, because desires are given not chosen.
>
> (167)

Reading Augustine's theft from the pear tree as another parable of original sin, Auden argues that the appeal of the *acte gratuit* is that "what in its original form was felt as a given desire now seems to the actor a matter of free and arbitrary choice." The "chief satisfaction in the creative act is the feeling that it is quite gratuitous." Like St. Augustine's theft, "Nearly all crime is magic, an attempt to make free with necessities" (168).

In "Psychology and Art To-day" (1935) Auden had critiqued Gide's philosophy of the *acte gratuit;* in "Squares and Oblongs," he is no longer dismissive. The link between "crime" and "magic" returns in a later passage that recalls his autobiographical remarks to Howard Griffin on Shakespeare as poetic Paracelsus:

> Given the opportunity, a poet is perhaps more tempted than others to drop his old innocent game of playing God with words, and take up that much more exciting but forbidden game of creating a human being, that game which starts off with such terrific gusto but always ends sooner or later in white faces and a fatal accident.
>
> (179)

Such a game is really black magic—by analogy to Augustine's crime, theft of another's erotic freedom.[29] These comments reflect, I submit, Auden's sense of guilt not only for having misused his gifts in poems like "Spain" and "September 1, 1939," but for the crimes—poetic and otherwise—he had committed against the Vision of Eros experienced with Kallman.

Different from the forbidden game of magic is the "innocent game": "Games are *actes gratuites* in which necessity is obeyed because the necessity here consists of rules chosen by the players" (168). All of Auden's examples are verbal games: "crossword puzzles, spelling bees, quizzes, questionnaires," and when played properly, poetry:

> Two theories of poetry. Poetry as a magical means for inducing desirable emotions and repelling undesirable emotions in oneself and others, or Poetry as a game of knowledge, a bringing to consciousness, by naming them, of emotions and their hidden relationships.
>
> (173)

Auden ascribes the theory of poetry as magic to "the Greeks," "MGM, Agit-Prop, and the collective public of the world," flatly stating, "They are wrong." He says this not because poetry cannot be magic but precisely because it can, and while his targets are explicitly political, his logic is implicitly sexual-political. The opposition of "magic" and "game" recalls that of rhetoric and joking in *The Orators,* as well as Auden's coupling of totalitarianism in the state and in the heart. "Game of knowledge" becomes another way of defining poetry as a realm of intimate self-discovery and revelation. Like "parable," it is anticoercive and therapeutic, a way of allowing for particularity and free will.

The relation between the unique beloved and the plurality of desirable objects becomes a verbal and mathematical game in "Numbers and Faces" (1950). Faces, for Auden, imply unique particularity: "The Prophets" welcomed "the face / That never will go back into a book / But asks for all my life."[30] By contrast, numbers define the world of Don Juan (or John Rechy):

> The Kingdom of Number is all boundaries
> Which may be beautiful and must be true;

> To ask if it is big or small proclaims one
> The sort of lover who should stick to faces.   (*CP* 623)

In keeping with the allusion to Jesus' parables, critics have stressed religious aspects of this poem.[31] The "emotions" Auden is playing with, however, are as much erotic and sexual, and the verbal moves of this game are double entendres. The first two lines take on new meaning from the next two, with their joke about genital endowment. "To ask if it is big or small" is to identify with the Kingdom of Number, where all that matters is how much or (for Don Juan et al.) how many. But it is risky to ask about bodily "boundaries / Which may be beautiful and must be true": the body cannot lie, but the answerer can. Thus the believer in numbers is just "The sort of lover who should stick to faces," which cannot lie about themselves.

The middle two stanzas cleverly satirize lovers of small numbers and big ones. The former are harmless and childlike; the latter, controlling types who "empty bars, spoil parties, run for Congress": the joke is that lovers of big numbers are size-queens in life as in bed, seeking what they lack. The last stanza returns to faces:

> True, between faces almost any number
> Might come in handy, and One is always real;
> But which could any face call good, for calling
> Infinity a number does not make it one.   (624)

These lines explore the interplay of eros, the spiritual, and the directly sexual, all by way of mathematics. The first two lines might be read as saying that when between lovers—particular people valued for their uniqueness ("faces")—there is relief in just another body, big or small. There is sexual wit here ("come," "come in handy"), but Auden is also playing with various senses of truth (accuracy, perfection, fidelity) and with the differences between "any" and "One." The two words share an etymological root, but in the world of eros they are very different. Sexually, "any number" may be enough, and "One is always real." The mathematical pun is that "One" is a "real number" (i.e. divisible into integers), but the more serious suggestion is that One is the only real number that is "*always* real"—in erotic terms, therefore, "true."

Readers might pick up on allusions to Rudolf Kassner, a German philosopher and critic whose *Zahl und Gesichte* is paid tribute to in Auden's title. Kassner's view of the Incarnation as the Infinite God made flesh offers a way to read the statement that "One is always real." Thus Mendelson reads the obscure closing lines as responding to a question: "among all numbers, 'which could any face call good'? A possible answer—the infinity of the absolute—is dismissed in the final lines, and the personal godhead reaffirmed, 'for calling / Infinity a number does not make it one' " (*Later* 368). The sexual overtones of "number," however, suggest another reading as well: the One who is "always real" is the One True Love, the number that is also a face. If Auden was thinking of this One as Chester Kallman, he was also qualifying the idea. The One may instead be a Platonic beloved sought among all numbers. It would be "always real" only in a Platonic sense—therefore *ideal,* infinite like the boundless realm of Beauty for which Diotima enjoins Socrates to strive in *The Symposium.* In this reading, Auden's last line is quite dark: the search for the infinite among particular numbers is endless, for "calling / Infinity a number does not make it one," any more than telling the beloved he is "the Flower of the Ages / And the first love of the world" (*EA* 227) makes it true.

Kassner's ideas about the Incarnation inform this poem but do not conclude the game, neatly resolving numbers and faces, infinity and particularity. Among the hidden relationships Auden is bringing to consciousness here is that the Christian God does not supersede or eradicate the pagan Eros—the hope of finding the infinite in one beautiful body, the eternal good in the good lay. In this sense, the poem is a riddle with no finite solution in a "real" (i.e. indivisible) number. Rather, the poem works like an algebraic formula whose variables— true, beautiful, infinity, good, One—may be filled in by readers in different ways. This game of numbers comes down to faces—*ours*—and as such it offers poetry as a realm where numbers and faces may be played with innocently.

Poetry's capacity for reconciling differences had formal, political, and spiritual dimensions for the later Auden, but it also had sexual-political and erotic meaning. "In a successful poem," argues "The Virgin & The Dynamo," "society and community are one order and the system may love itself because the feelings which it embodies are all members of the same community, loving each other and it."[32] At moments like this, Auden portrays poetry as an order created from the chaos of one's own emotions. (He is also apt to see poetic form similarly—as a verbal and prosodic order that brings elements of linguistic and aural difference into meaningful relation.) In "Making, Knowing and Judging," he writes that since distinctions between the sacred and the profane have disappeared, poetry is no longer "esoteric" or "public" but "intimate" (*DH* 54). The poet writes about "sacred encounters," and these may be quite eccentric:

> Thanks to the language, he need not name them directly unless he wishes; he can describe one in terms of another and translate those that are private or irrational or socially unacceptable into such as are acceptable to reason and society.

> (59)

With its implication that poetry encodes unspeakable private experience, this passage recalls the concealments of Auden's early poetry. It also suggests the sexual politics at stake in his love poems. Shakespeare, Tristan and Isolde, messianic fable, mathematics: all serve as means of translating from private experience into "acceptable" public poetry.

Acceptability has further valences for the later Auden in the context of love. In "First Things First" (1956) and "Since" (1965), he returned to the beloved young man who had provoked most of his love poems in the 1930s. "First Things First," in fact, involves multiple "translations." The first of these has Auden awakening to hear "a storm enjoying its storminess in the winter dark," then mentally composing a poem—"Set[ting] to work to unscramble that interjectory uproar, / Construing its airy vowels and watery consonants / Into a love-speech indicative of a Proper Name" (*CP* 583). Into the present erupts a beloved "you" from the past, the storm now "Kenning you a god-child of the Moon and the West Wind / With power to tame both real and imaginary monsters. . . ." A past Vision of Eros recurs: "On a headland of lava beside you, the occasion as ageless / As the stare of any rose, your presence exactly / So once, so valuable, so there, so now" (584). The question motivating Auden is what this erotic memory means. "Grateful, I slept till a morning that would not say / How much it believed of what I said the storm had said," Auden writes, as if to leave things open. He ends by noting "So many cubic metres the more in my cistern," the storm sensibly "putting first things first: / Thousands have lived without love, not one without water."

In his very recording of this experience, Auden begs the question of this moral: the practical utility of the storm may outweigh its imaginative effect, but the latter has generated this poem. His dismissive last line is set up by a poem that reworks a venerable Petrarchan trope: the storminess of desire yielding a fructifying relief from dryness. "Since" records another apparition from the erotic past erupting in the present. While "other enchantments / have blazed and faded," Auden writes, "round your image / there is no fog . . ." (*CP* 778). "Of what, then, should I complain, / pottering about / a neat suburban kitchen?" Auden's answer is less than convincing:

> Solitude? Rubbish!
> It's social enough with real
> faces and landscapes
> for whose friendly countenance
> I at least can learn
> to live with obesity
> and a little fame.

There is, to be sure, something painfully lonely about both these poems, suggested above all by their avoidance of one implication of remembering: in coming into the present, the Vision of Eros reveals its pastness. Kallman perhaps and others would have known that the "you" addressed here is not Kallman but the young man Auden had written so many poems to in the 1930s (see Mendelson, *Later* 411–12). To realize this is to see Auden grappling not just with the pastness of a Vision of Eros but with the plurality of erotic experience and imagination. From one angle, Auden is writing to one person from his past—indeed, *in* his past. But their "sacred encounters" are here "translated" into "acceptable" terms—a poetry where one of Eros's many incarnations can be safely examined. Auden's dismissiveness suggests both guilt and a wish to accommodate Kallman's feelings. But in actually writing and publishing these poems he is also making a gesture of fidelity to someone else with whom he once had a sacred encounter, thus honoring the plurality of love.

Regarding "First Things First" Auden wrote at the time to Lincoln Kirstein that it concerned a "new little heart flutter" he had met (Mendelson, *Later* 412n). Rather than a false lead or a lie, his comment points to the interfusion of numbers and faces in erotic imagination—the psychological multiplicity of the singular "you." This is a subject to which Auden went on to devote his most elaborate later love poem. In "Dichtung und Wahrheit: An Unwritten Poem" (1959), he explored the relation of singularity and plurality as a poetic and linguistic problem: "Expecting your arrival tomorrow, I find myself thinking *I love You:* then comes the thought:—*I should like to write a poem which would express exactly what I mean when I think these words*" (CP 649; emphasis in original). The ensuing forty-nine numbered sections serve both as a prose confession of the impossibility of the poem and as the "Unwritten Poem" itself.

The heart of the problem, as it were, is that language is not self-verifying: "to satisfy me, the truth of this poem must be self-evident. It would have to be written, for example, in such a way that no reader could misread *I love You* as 'I love you.'" But both psychology and language work against this apparently simple three-word sentence. Neither *Who am I?* nor *Who are You?* can be answered definitively, he realizes. And as for the verb *love,* speech in poetry "lacks the Indicative Mood. All its statements are in the subjunctive and only possibly true until verified (which is not always possible) by non-verbal evidence" (650–51). The most "convincing" of love poems "written in the first person," Auden says, are "either the fa-la-la's of a good-natured sensuality which made no pretense at serious love," or lovers' complaints; "the least convincing were those in which the poet claimed to be in earnest, yet had no complaint to make" (661). But this is what Auden wishes to write. To write in the manner of Petrarch is no longer "to be a lover" but to be "an actor playing the role of the poet Petrarch"; clever comparisons may be fun, but Auden asks, "What do such comparisons provide? Certainly not a description by which *You* could be distinguished from a hundred possible rivals of a similar type" (662).

"Dichtung und Wahrheit" was occasioned by a twenty-five-year-old

Oxford student coming to visit Auden in Kirchstetten, Austria, where he spent his summers from 1958 to the end of his life. Auden's sexual interest was apparently unrequited, and he did not force the issue. After the visit, when Kallman realized who had inspired the poem, he fled to Portugal, writing to Thekla Clark that he was "running away from home"; he returned to Kirchstetten before long, however.[33] On one hand, Kallman's actions reflect an understandable jealousy that Auden was not writing about him, as if to point out that fancy philosophical demonstrations of the indeterminacy of *I love You* were beside the point. But one might also see Auden's "Unwritten Poem" as a way of negotiating the complex responsibilities of erotic truth-telling at a time when he and Kallman had long since ceased to be sexual lovers. "Dichtung und Wahrheit" is, from this angle, a gesture of erotic homage. But like "Since" and "First Things First," it also confesses its own impossibility, folding the personal reasons, as it were, into linguistic ones: the poem that says *I love You* cannot be a faithful one.

To put it this way, however, risks misrepresenting Auden's tone, for "Dichtung und Wahrheit" is amazingly untroubled by the varieties of unfaithfulness it acknowledges, both erotic and poetic, open and covert. The ideal of love he evokes is not a zero-sum game played by conventional rules of fidelity. For the indeterminacy of *You* brings about not a crisis of faithfulness but something quite different. In this regard, "Dichtung und Wahrheit" anticipates the ideal of poetry Auden extols in *Secondary Worlds* (1968). While "black magic" is "a way of securing domination over others and compelling them to do [one's] will" (112), the meaning of a poem "is the outcome of a dialogue between the words of the poem and the response of whoever is listening to them" (114). Auden's implicit metaphorical scenario, I suggest, is that of an intimate exchange between lovers: poetic meaning is the product of a virtual lovers' discourse. In such a relation, coercive generalization will not work:

> Not only is every poem unique, but its significance is unique for each person who responds to it. In so far as one can speak of poetry as conveying knowledge, it is the kind of knowledge implied by the biblical phrase "Then Adam knew Eve his wife"; knowing is inseparable from being known.

For all the sacramentalism of the wording, this amounts to a proposition that poetic knowledge is a virtual but primal erotic encounter, whose value consists in a relation free from the instrumentalism of magic or rhetoric. To read a poem is not to possess it or to be possessed by it (or by the poet) but to know someone and to be known to oneself. Poetry is a confidence game not in the sense of trickery but in the sense of an intimate, playful confiding. A corollary would be that all poetry that does not aim at magic is love poetry, a virtual lovers' discourse—for all poetic meaning involves intimate revelation and self-knowledge.

We would seem to be far from the world of the early Auden, with its terrain of secrecy and concealment. But Auden's later poems about love return persistently to the significance of what is unsaid. "That, dear me, how often / We kiss in order to tell," he writes in "Secrets" (1949), "Defines precisely what we mean by love:— / To share a secret" (*CP* 623). If this is what we mean, however, we are wrong, for "to share a secret" is not to keep it but to give it away. "The joke," Auden continues, "is on us; / For only true hearts know how little it matters / What the secret is they keep." To keep a secret is to honor the unspeakable, and in the realm of eros, the unspeakable can mean a number of things: what cannot be said, what ought not be said, and what goes without saying. A proper name, Auden writes in *Secondary Worlds*, "has male or female gender. But the first and second person pronouns, which we use when addressing each other as persons, have no gender" (107). From a sexual-political point of view, *I* and *You* in Auden's love poems hide a sexual truth, but they imagine a realm in which the sexual truth is unspoken because between lovers it is self-evident—it goes without saying. Auden's gender-free language of intimacy seems universalizing, but in fact it imagines a realm that is sacred precisely because it honors the particular and personal.

The intimacy of such a discourse is not that of marriage but that of erotic plurality, requiring plural fidelities. The failure of poetry to verify itself in saying *I love You* is also, therefore, a faithfulness to the multiple responsibilities entailed by erotic life. When Auden writes "You" or "Dear," it both is and is not Chester Kallman: it is you or me or even a composite beloved that includes everyone Auden has been in love with. And the relation of I and You that Auden projects is both the lovers' relation he wanted to have with Kallman in life but could not manage, and a relation that he sought in virtual terms in poetry.

"Love is responsibility of an *I* for a *Thou*," writes Martin Buber in *I and Thou*, a work that did much to shape Auden's later views of love (15). A *Thou* is not a *He* or a *She* or an *It*, for these are objects: "When *Thou* is spoken, the speaker has no *thing*; he has indeed nothing. But he takes his stand in relation" (4). In his later love poetry Auden is often exploring the implications of Buber's ideas in the realm of eros, and never far away is a sense of the risks involved in responsible love. To be responsible is, literally, to be answerable—to be obliged to give an answer if asked, and one hears Buber's words in Auden's statements about the dialogic basis of poetic meaning.

In "The Common Life" (1963), Auden adapts Buber's vocabulary to write about his relationship with Chester Kallman, and in a way that acknowledges the mutual responsibility of one I and one Thou. The last poem in Auden's sequence "Thanksgiving for a Habitat," it is dedicated to Kallman and focuses on the living room of their house in Kirchstetten. If the title concedes that this love is no longer lived out in the realm of Visionary Eros, the poem gestures quietly but defiantly at conventional notions of love and of commonality (i.e., both normality and sameness). This is "A living-room, the catholic area you / (Thou, rather) and I may enter / without knocking, leave without a bow. . ." (*CP* 714). But it enforces "no *We* at an instant, / only *Thou* and *I*, two regions / of protestant being which nowhere overlap" (emphasis in original).

Surveying the room, Auden asks what it indicates about the inhabitants, then moves to questions about love. "What draws / singular lives together in the first place," he writes, "is obvious," but why they remain together is not:

> how they create, though, a common world
> between them, like Bombelli's
>
> impossible yet useful numbers, no one
> has yet explained.   (715)

A relationship like Auden's and Kallman's, which is not a marital combination of two-in-one, involves "numbers" mathematically "impossible" yet somehow functional (like the square root of -1). With a casual-
ness contrived as the poetic equivalent of sane interior decoration, Auden moves to a conclusion that does not resolve the emotional and
domestic uncertainties of such a relationship but suggests that they can
be managed:

> Howbeit,
> fasting or feasting, we both know this: without
> the Spirit we die, but life
>
> without the Letter is in the worst of taste,
> and always, though truth and love
> can never really differ, when they seem to,
> the subaltern should be truth.

As a love poem to Kallman, this reads as an acknowledgment
and a confession of untruths on both sides. But while Auden pays
homage to truth, the poem suggests that love is not a matter of the
Letter of the Law. With regard to eros, I take this as his commitment
to the form of fidelity over the actuality. As a published—public—
declaration, it is rather astonishing. Auden praises "our common-room
small windows / through which no observed outsider can observe us"
(715), but he also opens this room to outsiders. In his tasteful obliquity, he poetically observes faithfulness to the Spirit over the Letter,
addressing Kallman but making every reader an intimate—a secret
sharer who keeps unspoken secrets.

Chapter 6

"JUST WHAT APPEARANCES HE SAVES": GOD AND THE UNSPEAKABLE

The title of this chapter invokes the closing stanzas of "Friday's Child" (1958), one of Auden's most powerful religious poems. Dedicated to the memory of Dietrich Bonhoeffer, the Lutheran theologian and resister executed by the Nazis in 1945, this elegy is in part about the impossibility of traditional elegy in the wake of the Holocaust. It also raises the challenge of theodicy in the Atomic Age, when God has left "the bigger bangs to us" (*CP* 675). All our instrumental power, Auden implies, is impotent before the reality of suffering like Bonhoeffer's, and the poem ends with a terrifying image of the inscrutability of Jesus' crucifixion:

> Meanwhile, a silence on the cross,
> As dead as we shall ever be,
> Speaks of some total gain or loss,
>   And you and I are free
>
> To guess from the insulted face
> Just what Appearances He saves
> By suffering in a public place
>   A death reserved for slaves.   (676)

We may no longer be confident of the promise of resurrection, but even "conscious unbelievers," as Auden writes earlier in this poem, "feel / Quite sure of Judgment Day": the fact of evil is all too real. The

crucifixion thus provokes our judgment in another sense, for any certainty about the redemptive meaning of this death is a casualty of
modernity. Our free will entails an interpretive freedom before an image of divinity that leaves us "free / To guess" the meaning of its utter
abjection and subjection.

"Friday's Child" might seem out of place in a study of Auden as a
homosexual poet. For while it is one thing to sense a link between homoeroticism and religious questioning in, say, Tennyson or Wilfred
Owen, Auden hardly eroticizes the "insulted face" of Jesus. Instead, he
sees the crucifixion as a radical provocation to sensibility: such suffering not only engenders a metaphysical crisis but registers as a symbolic
offense. If this is "total gain" for humanity, saving our souls, it comes
through a graphic degradation that does not "save appearances" in a
scientific sense or an aesthetic one: it is epistemologically and socially
rude. Implicit here, I submit, is a queer theodicy: divine love mirrors
the unspeakability of homosexual love, a *Ganz Andere* like all those
Anders als die Andern, flouting norms of public decency and conceptual coherence. Like the "country god" of "From the very first coming
down," the later Auden's God is disturbingly "reticent" (*EA* 25). Or, in
the words of "Control of the passes," we might ask of the crucifixion,
"Who would get it?" The *deus absconditus* leaves us adrift in an uncertainty like that of the secret agent or lonely lover.

Isherwood records Auden's best-known statement on religion and
homosexuality: he believed "it was sinful, though he fully intended to
go on sinning" (*Christopher* 335). While this rather Byronic attitude
would seem to imply that Auden acknowledged but felt untroubled by
Christian sexual dictates, its implication of moral duplicity is one he returned to often, as in his epigraph to *The Double Man* (1941), from
Montaigne: "We are, I know not how, double in ourselves, so that
what we believe we disbelieve, and cannot rid ourselves of what we
condemn."[1] One need not see Auden's epigraph as a coded confession
of original sexual sin in order to suspect that his concern with the contradictions of homosexual desire did not go away after he embraced
existentialist Protestantism.

The aim of this chapter is not primarily to make systematic sense of
Auden's religious views of homosexuality; still less is it to explain his

turn (or return, as he saw it) to Christian faith as a response to moral
anxiety about his homosexuality. That he felt such anxiety is clear from
his recorded comments, but it is also true that he began reading theology and attending church just as he was falling in love with Chester
Kallman. As for systematic analysis of Auden's thoughts on theology,
love, and sexuality, indispensable recent work by others makes such an
effort unnecessary.[2] Instead, this chapter takes as a directive one of Auden's "Marginalia" in *City Without Walls* (1969): "His thoughts pot-
tered / from verses to sex to God / without punctuation" (*CP* 797). To
punctuate Auden's potterings would be to seek conceptual order at the
cost of obscuring the subtle, oblique ways that his views of homosexual love and desire inform his religious poetry. That sex, for Auden,
has something to do with God (and poetry with both) might serve as
a thesis for this chapter, but it will quickly become clear that he was
not consistent on the spiritual meaning of homosexual desire or of
eros more generally.

Crucial to the poetry examined here is Auden's ongoing proclivity
for poetic figures of crookedness, with all the sexual overtones they
have in his earlier work. At the same time, crookedness—or
angularity—also signifies his sense of the relationship between the
fallen human and the divine. In early Auden, such tropes typically
bring together sexual deviance with psychic, social, or linguistic duplicity. In his later work, crookedness suggests sin and guilt, and in
this Auden is very much in the Augustinian tradition, understanding
evil as perversion.[3] But crookedness also serves, contrarily, as a key
figure for the contingency that necessarily conditions the human
search for divine truth. Broadly speaking, Auden's earlier social concerns with secrecy, duplicity, and unspeakability become in his religious writing metaphysical conditions. God cannot be seen face to face
but can be configured through angular poetic imaginings, rendered
inevitably from positions of particularity: historical, geographical, and
also sexual.

This chapter's second half considers together two longer poems that
illustrate the intricate angularities of Auden's potterings: "Pleasure Island" and "In Praise of Limestone," both from 1948. The former is a
dark ode to Fire Island, where Auden owned a cabin in the 1940s; "In

Praise of Limestone" was inspired by Ischia, where he and Kallman spent summers from 1948 to 1957. As meditations on homosexual desire and salvation, these poems form, as it were, complementary angles: while "Pleasure Island" is unmasked as Golgotha, a site of naked power relations and humiliation, "In Praise of Limestone" celebrates homoerotic fantasy as an analogy to paradise. "In Praise of Limestone" is also one of Auden's most ambitious meditations on public and private, on the psychological roots of homosexual desire, and on the capacity of art for modeling paradisal reconciliations of sameness and difference. But reconciliation is not, for Auden, elision or erasure. His imagining of the divine is intensely homoerotic, and his final message really a riddle: as children of God, we are all queer.

I

Much has been written, both sympathetic and hostile, on Auden's religious "conversion" of the early 1940s.[4] Auden himself pointed to a number of experiences in which he believed he had had direct, traumatic experience of evil. In his 1956 essay for *Modern Canterbury Pilgrims,* he instanced his shock at seeing churches closed in Spain in 1937, and without offering details, he referred to his own violent reaction to Kallman's infidelity (see Pike 32–43). Such experiences, he claimed, forced him to confront evil as a moral reality beyond the explanatory power of Marx or Freud.

Considered philosophically, Auden's turn to Christianity suggests an evolution of his thinking. Kierkegaard, Niebuhr, Tillich, and the other theologians Auden began reading and using in his work in the early 1940s represented not so much a rejection of Marx and Freud as a way of explaining their limits. As Replogle has argued, Auden's turn to existentialism may be seen as a lateral movement within the post-Hegelian tradition broadly conceived.[5] For Kierkegaard as for Marx and Freud, freedom involves consciousness of necessity in the empirical world. But Kierkegaard posits also a further, higher reality determined by God, and a higher form of necessity. Consciousness of *this* necessity is, in Replogle's words, "synonymous with religious faith:

faith in the blessedness of God's design," for it is an "indiscernible design made by an unknowable designer" (55). Kierkegaard's is "an empirical philosophy insisting, contrary to empirical evidence, that God exists" (53).

In Mendelson's view, existentialism gave Auden something Freud and Marx could not: "It perceived its relation to an absolute value; and it understood that it could never claim to know or embody that value" (*Later* 130). As Auden later commented to Oliver Sacks, Kierkegaard "knocked the conceit" out of him (Carpenter, *Auden* 285), helping him to reject the roles of political redeemer and cultural diagnostician, with their aspiration to a transcendent analytical position. Such roles were ones that Auden had long been skeptical of, and we have seen how his worries about political complicity involved the epistemological entanglement of observer and observed. With his turn to existentialism, he began to see this double bind as an effect of metaphysical necessity. To believe in an unknowable divine reality is to experience the double consciousness Kierkegaard described in *Unscientific Postscript:* "The reflection of inwardness gives to the subjective thinker a double reflection," for "in thinking, he thinks the universal; but as existing in this thought and as assimilating it in his inwardness, he becomes more and more subjectively isolated" (quoted Replogle 58). From an existentialist view, the crisis of Auden's Airman or John Nower is the metaphysical problem of every human being. "Freedom" lies not in cure, in revolution, or in the effort to resolve this double bind, but in accepting it—recognizing a divine necessity that transcends the empirically knowable world.

This schematic picture of Auden's existentialism is complicated by his poems. But it is worth considering in the abstract what it might imply for his sense of homosexuality as a nexus for psychological and political double binds. It seems likely that in raising such double binds to a metaphysical level, existentialism suggested to Auden that his homosexuality was a sign not of radical difference but of a universal human condition—we are *all* double in ourselves, as Montaigne puts it. From a moral point of view, homosexuality would be one sin among many, but not exceptional, for all sin reflects the gulf between divine truth and human contingency. At the same time, Auden's continuing emphasis on the duplicity and self-contradictions of the subject suggests that he found in existentialism a universalizing view congenial to a preoccupation with his own sexual eccentricity.

Within the terms of existentialism, these two possibilities are perhaps inevitable: Auden may have been thinking the universal, but we see him becoming more and more subjectively isolated in the very process of doing so. If this is how Auden was thinking about thinking, so to speak, an effort to derive from his writing a philosophical account of his later views of homosexuality is fraught. This critical and historical problem arises not because we must accept existentialist terms but because Auden seems to have done so. Thus we can never be sure how deeply his "thinking the universal" is haunted by his self-consciousness about the impossibility of doing so except from a position of isolation and particularity.

We cannot escape this hermeneutical circle, any more than Auden could. But it is telling that his articulations of existentialism entailed distinctly sexual valences. An exemplary instance is "The Rewards for Patience," a 1942 review of Louise Bogan's poetry. Auden tells his usual story of modernity as the collapse of community into a "public," but his concern is now with the poet's solitary status as a moral and metaphysical problem, rather than a social one.[6] He starts by quoting Kierkegaard on "Genius," which "does not define itself teleologically in relation to other men" but "immanently relates itself to itself" ("Rewards" 336). Auden then elaborates on the dangers of narcissism in the development of the poet: without community to offer "a source of value outside himself," the poet must fall back on "The Interesting," "which in practice means his childhood and his sex-life" (337). Auden's comments about Bogan in this regard are autobiographically suggestive:

> In the early sections [of her work] Miss Bogan employs her gift in the way in which, as a rule, it should at first be employed, to understand her weakness to which it is dialectically related, for wherever there is a gift, of whatever kind, there is also a guilty secret, a thorn in the flesh[,] and the first successful poems of young poets are usually a catharsis of resentment.
>
> (337)

Mendelson observes that readers might have discerned Auden's own "thorn in the flesh" as "some variety of sexual and intellectual loneliness" (*Later* 195). Homosexuality seems, in fact, like the paradigmatic "thorn in the flesh." For the first danger Auden notes is that of arrested artistic development: "Some excellent poets," he says, "never get beyond this stage"—e.g., Housman and Dickinson. Whether this anticipates more recent interest in Dickinson as a lesbian poet, certainly Auden had seen the closet as a driving force in Housman's life and poetry.[7] That Auden was thinking about himself is hard to deny, especially as he goes on to describe the danger for a poet who outgrows the narcissism of "believing that the relation of his life to his work is a direct one": "escape from the Self" through "a convenient Myth" like Yeats's, or "the Id or Miss History" of Yeats's "younger and less-talented colleagues" (338). To any reader familiar with Auden, these comments campily imply that Freud and Marx were his own cheap escapes, for Myth "is not a religion" and "does not have to be believed in real life."

The value of Auden's review of Bogan here is its implication that he saw his homosexuality as crystallizing the philosophical situation of the poet, in whom the gift and the guilty secret are bound together dialectically. In "The Waters," from his 1940 sonnet sequence *The Quest,* Auden offers a parable of this predicament and its attendant dangers. Its logic is existentialist, but the semantic and figurative elements laid out in the first stanza suggest a queer reading of Kierkegaard:

> Poet, oracle, and wit
> Like unsuccessful anglers by
> The ponds of apperception sit,
> Baiting with the wrong request
> The vectors of their interest,
> At nightfall tell the angler's lie.   (*CP* 295)

Like *The Quest* as a whole, this poem concerns true and false paths in an archetypal search, but to put it this way is to lose something. For part of the point of "The Waters" is that the search for impersonal truth inevitably folds back on its own contingency. Fuller observes that the metaphor of angling implies that "poet, oracle, and wit" take the wrong way to the truth. They lie "because they cannot bear to think that the fish got away"; "the right question would produce Icthus" (343). Be that as it may, these are "ponds of *ap*perception," in which the mind should be (but isn't) conscious of itself as perceiving: their antecedent is as much the pool of Narcissus as the Sea of Galilee. "Poet, oracle, and wit" are, in effect, stuck in the first phase of development Auden describes in his Bogan review, their truths really lies that are indices to their own self-interest. But the situation is virtually the same for everyone, as the second stanza suggests: "With time in tempest everywhere, / To rafts of frail assumption cling / The saintly and the insincere . . ." (CP 295). Auden's ingenious couplet, with its echo of Humpty Dumpty, concludes by not concluding: "The waters long to hear our question put / Which would release their longed-for answer, but." While the "longed-for answer" does not come, its absence tells us something about our angling—that we never, in fact, ask real questions at all, questions to which we do not have an answer in mind. "Narcissus," as Auden writes in "Alone" (1941), "disbelieves in the unknown" (CP 312). In "baiting with the wrong request, / The vectors of our interest," we merely want our own desires confirmed. So in another sense, the lack of answer is itself the answer: "but"—the negation of our narcissism.

The gift and the guilty secret, according to Auden's review of Bogan, are dialectically related. So it is telling that this parable of philosophical uncertainty recalls the scenarios of erotic self-consciousness in Auden's early poetry of the closet. Employing their respective gifts, poet, oracle, and wit are cruising the waters on the "ponds of apperception," but to no avail. For as "anglers," they offer only crooked questions serving as "vectors of their interest."[8] It is not (or not only) that Auden was encoding his own guilty secret here, for the anxiety about narcissism that haunts his writings about homosexual love and desire registers in this poem's semantic and figurative operations. Homosexuality is the model of deviance by which he constructs a poetic parable of angularity. One message of the poem is that things could not be otherwise: knowledge must be sought at the angle of a vector determined by the seeker. At the same time, by ending with "but," the poem implies that in becoming aware of our angularity, we can posit an answer that does not merely reflect back a self-interested

image. Formal and grammatical completeness would be, in effect, narcissistic circularities, into which a real answer can appear only as a disruptive angularity.

It makes sense, therefore, that some of Auden's most anxious lyrics
in his existentialist vein of the early 1940s are also love poems addressed to Chester Kallman: this relationship was the vector of Auden's own interest. Two poems mentioned briefly in chapter 5 deserve
further comment: "Leap Before You Look" and "If I Could Tell You,"
dating from late 1940. Each projects an unknowable future, at once
confessing a lover's uncertainty and raising it to a cosmic condition the
beloved is enjoined to confront. "Leap Before You Look," a modified
villanelle, describes a journey in which "The sense of danger must not
disappear": "The way is certainly both short and steep, / However
gradual it looks from here; / Look if you like, but you will have to
leap" (*CP* 313). Succeeding stanzas describe all that does not help on
this journey, which clearly asks to be read in spiritual terms. But the
poem concludes with a stanza that locates the starting point for this
quest in the bed of eros:

> A solitude ten thousand fathoms deep
> Sustains the bed on which we lie, my dear:
> Although I love you, you will have to leap;
> Our dream of safety has to disappear.   (314)

Opening with Auden's favorite Kierkegaardian image, this stanza obviously suggests the existentialist leap of faith. "In Sickness and In
Health," as we saw, reads the absurdity of homosexual love as a sign of
the divine, and I argued that much of Auden's purpose there is to harness marriage as a bulwark against fear of infidelity. His tone here is
much darker; the absurd leap is not a cause for rejoicing.

Existential uncertainty is also the philosophical point of "If I Could
Tell You," but Auden's strict adherence to villanelle form lends a peculiar quality to the repeated lines: "Time will say nothing but I told you
so"; "If I could tell you I would let you know" (314). The claim that
there is "a price we have to pay" looks forward to Auden's certainty in
"Friday's Child" about Judgment Day. But just as "Our dream of
safety" recalls the illusions Auden associates with the Vision of Eros in

his love poems of the 1930s, so this "price" echoes "Lay your sleeping head, my love": "Every farthing of the cost, / All the dreaded cards foretell, / Shall be paid. . ." (*EA* 207). The structure of villanelle form offers a nice prosodic illustration of the existentialist relation between freedom and necessity. The echoing effect also provides an aural parallel to the reflective unresponsiveness Auden portrays in "The Waters": the meanings of the repeated lines are elaborated with each successive stanza, but the uncertainty becomes only more acute. Intentionally or not, however, the repetitions also become almost hectoring, especially since Auden's ingenious wordplay begs the question of his own motives. "If I could tell you I would let you know" suggests pathos and compassion; "Time will say nothing but I told you so," gives voice to the unspeakable with a certainty (and cleverness) not quite compensated for by the line's fatalism.

"If I Could Tell You" and "Leap Before You Look" seem like persuasion poems designed to subdue either Auden's or Kallman's uncertainty about their relationship. As such, they suggest that much of the power of existentialism for Auden in the early 1940s was that it spoke to anxieties about fidelity and permanence in homosexual love. But if these poems seem rhetorically calculated, they can also be taken as earnestly deliberate. For a recurrent theme in Auden's writing at the time is the need for becoming self-conscious of our desires so as to recognize our own contingency—an idea well suited to a theory of poetry as parable or game of knowledge. Writing on Kierkegaard in 1944, Auden cited the existentialist emphasis on "man's immediate experience as a *subject,* i.e. as a being in *need,* an *interested* being whose existence is at stake." One must abandon the myth of the "timeless disinterested I who stands outside my finite temporal self and serenely knows what there is to know; cognition is always a specific historical act accompanied by hope and fear." The search for "common truth," Auden says, means that "the individual" must "begin by learning to be objective about his subjectivity" ("Preface" 683). Paul Tillich's *The Interpretation of History* makes a similar point in a passage Auden quoted in the notes to "New Year Letter" in *The Double Man:*

> The fundamental Protestant attitude is to stand in nature, taking upon
> oneself the inevitable reality; not to flee from it, either into the world

of ideal forms or into the related world of super-nature, but to make
decisions in concrete reality. Here the subject has no absolute position.

(*Double* 132)

Or, as Tillich puts it in the context of discussing Marx and Kierkegaard's repudiation of idealism and essence, "truth is bound to the
situation of the knower, to the individual situation in Kierkegaard and
to the social situation in Marx" (Tillich 63). If existentialism denies
all pretension to a transcendent subject position, therefore, the con-
verse of despair at uncertainty is an acceptance of epistemological limits: one cannot seek the truth except by way of the vectors of one's
own interest.

In "Law Like Love" (1939), Auden's explication of these limitations
shows existentialism offering him a new idiom for poetry as a game of
knowledge about human difference, including differences of sexuality.
The first part of the poem tabulates various definitions of "Law":

> Law, say the gardeners, is the sun. . . .
> Law is the wisdom of the old,
> The impotent grandfathers feebly scold;
> The grandchildren put out a treble tongue,
> Law is the senses of the young.   (*CP* 262)

Like all the voices that follow (judge, priest, scholars, etc.), these define the Law—transcendent necessity—in self-interested terms. Each,
that is, falsely assumes what Tillich calls the impossible "absolute position." Having exposed their delusion, Auden concedes in the second
part of the poem that "No more than they can we suppress / The universal wish to guess / Or slip out of our own position / Into an unconcerned condition" (263). Like all others, we are "being[s] in need," as
Auden puts it in his 1944 Kierkegaard review. What we can do, however, is to be aware of "our own position," and in this case, "we" are
beings in love: the second part of the poem is addressed to "dear." The
conclusion confesses the contingency of the poet, who speaks as a
lover:

> Although I can at least confine
> Your vanity and mine
> To stating timidly
> A timid similarity,
> We shall boast anyway:
> Like love, I say.
>
> Like love we don't know where or why,
> Like love we can't compel or fly,
> Like love we often weep,
> Like love we seldom keep.

Where the others make equations to define Law by identity ("Law is"), Auden offers similes, whose provisionality foregrounds the contingency of the subject. The fatalism is characteristic of his 1930s love poems, but the power of these lines is also a function of his concern with the inscrutability of homosexual love, which "we can't compel or fly." And if "the Law" that is "Like love" is existential necessity, it metonymically calls up worldly laws that occasion weeping and lawbreaking for those whose desires they seek to control. To read this poem in relation to homosexual love is therefore to add another dimension to its lesson about "the universal wish to guess," the aspiration to "an unconcerned condition." For lurking here is another simile never expressed openly, never "boasted," to be sure—only posited to be questioned: homosexual love is like heterosexual love. But is it? The implication of the poem is that one cannot know, precisely because the question can be posed only from the position of one kind of love or the other.

As psychological and political concerns, the cruces of sameness and difference motivated Auden's theory of parable in the mid-1930s. In tone and poetic form, a passage like the following, from "New Year Letter," seems far removed from "Letter to Lord Byron." But it echoes Auden's earlier concerns with eccentricity, neurosis, and political coercion:

> In this alone are all the same,
> All are so weak that none dare claim

"I have the right to govern," or
"Behold in me the Moral Law,"
And all real unity commences
In consciousness of differences,
That all have wants to satisfy
And each a power to supply.
We need to love all since we are
Each a unique particular
That is no giant, god, or dwarf,
But one odd human isomorph.   (*CP* 241)

We are accustomed to reading such lines in religious or political terms. But their sacramental tone may obscure what we tend to think of as a postmodern insight into the priority of difference. And while Auden's neo-Augustan couplets have seemed to some a sign of appalling regression on the part of a poet who had written *The Orators*, his use of this form here is something of a joke, since his point is precisely *not* that poetry can yield Johnsonian general truth.

The existential Auden, in other words, is not far from the theorist of joking contradiction who devised the trickster Airman of *The Orators*. Auden's dedication of his 1945 *Collected Poetry* to Isherwood and Kallman is followed by these lines:

Whether conditioned by God or their neural structure, still
All men have this common creed, account for it as you will:
The Truth is one and incapable of contradiction;
All knowledge that conflicts with itself is Poetic Fiction.
                                               (*CP* 296)

The truth value of poetry, from this point of view, is negative, consisting in the awareness poetry fosters of the gap between its conflicted "knowledge" and singular "Truth." One can gloss these lines by way of existentialism (or Freud or Marx), but one might also note that Auden's view of art has an important precursor in Wilde's comment in "The Truth of Masks": "In art there is no such thing as a universal truth. A Truth in art is that whose contradictory is also true" (432). For Auden as a queer nephew of Wilde, contradiction is bound up with an

epistemology conditioned by the duplicitous significations of homosexuality. Like Wilde, the later Auden enjoyed playing with paradoxes
about the truth of lying, and one hears Wilde behind a passage like the
following, from *The Age of Anxiety* (1947):

> Human beings are, necessarily, actors who cannot become something
> before they have first pretended to be it; and they can be divided, not
> into the hypocritical and the sincere, but into the sane who know they
> are acting and the mad who do not.
>
> (CP 518)

Such a view seems at something of a remove from Auden's comments
in his 1942 Bogan review: there Auden derided the adherence of some
poets to a Myth like "the Id or Miss History" which does not demand
the commitment of belief outside of art. But rather than "belief," Auden's target here is the pretension to metaphysical certainty.

This distinction between sanity and madness would apply to poetry
as well: the sane poem foregrounds its aspirations to truth as pretenses
contradicted by its own contingency. In "Law Like Love," simile does
not forget its aesthetic garb; it is "out" as Poetic Fiction, while
metaphor is not. Metaphor is madly given to taking itself as identity,
while Poetic Fiction knows its own tendentious angularity.[9] In " 'The
Truest Poetry Is the Most Feigning' " (1953), Auden proposes an aesthetic of artifice that updates his early poetic of coding by way of
Shakespeare and Wilde. (Auden's title comes from *As You Like It.*) As
Alan Sinfield has noted, the poem seems to present a "closeted gay
aesthetic" (*Cultural* 60). But the rhetorical contradiction of doing so
publicly is implicit in the poem, which is a performance that depends
on Auden's reputation by 1953 as an older, establishment poet—a public figure.

Auden's prescription to the aspiring love poet is for unashamed
Petrarchism—"ingenious fibs" (CP 620). "The living girl's your business," Auden writes, "but some odd sorts / Have been an inspiration to
men's thoughts," he adds parenthetically. "Odd" sorts indeed, we can
bitchily reply, but in doing so we simply accept his invitation to see
this poem as itself an ingenious fib, right down to the calculated
prosodic slovenliness of rhyming "sorts" and "thoughts." As it pro-

ceeds, the performance gestures to Auden's youthful role as a political
poet. Should a time come when "Poets are suspect with the New
Regime," Auden advises a modern inversion of the 16th-century practice of dressing the political poem in amatory drag:

> Stick at your desk and hold your panic in,
> What you are writing may still save your skin:
> Re-sex the pronouns, add a few details,
> And, lo, a panegyric ode which hails
> (How is the Censor, bless his heart, to know?)
> The new pot-bellied Generalissimo.

Such tactics are not even dishonest, since the original love poem was
made of "ingenious fibs." Or rather, the truth about human discourse
lies in its artifice, since for the human being—"The only creature ever
made who fakes"—there is "no more nature in his loving smile / Than
in his theories of a natural style." (621).

From a sexual-political point of view, Auden's condoning of duplicity is a prescription for survival. But the poem's conclusion complicates
matters in a way that should challenge the reader who would see here
the coded confession of a gay Auden:

> What but tall tales, the luck of verbal playing,
> Can trick [Man's] lying nature into saying
> That love, or truth in any serious sense,
> Like orthodoxy, is a reticence?

Resexing the pronouns is a way of dealing with the political unspeakability of personal love, but this question raises unspeakability to a
metaphysical condition entailing "reticence" as a spiritual duty. A tall
tale is not meant to be taken literally, and in this sense the poem is an
invitation to recognize Auden's entire career as a sexual performance.
(As Sinfield observes, Auden uses the phrase "tall story" to praise
Cavafy's openness about his homosexuality in his work: "In the arts,
one must distinguish, of course, between the lie and the tall story that
the audience is not expected to believe.")[10] The poet who resexes the
pronouns will be attacked, but "True hearts, clear heads will hear the

note of glory / And put inverted commas round the story." They will
see through but honor his reticence with their own inversions. Such
an ethic surely marks Auden as a pre-Stonewall poet, but his invocation of "orthodoxy" here is not simple conservatism. This argument
for artifice in love, after all, implies a critique of essentialist identity in
the lover and of essentialism's rhetorical equivalent—sincerity. Meta-
physically, lying is commendable reticence because the unspeakability
of "truth" is a matter not only of safety and propriety but of impossibility for our "lying nature." Real "orthodoxy," in other words, means
not speaking straight but speaking crookedly.

In giving the lie to neat distinctions between closeted and out, honesty and hypocrisy, " 'The Truest Poetry Is the Most Feigning' " shows
Auden tracing once more the trajectory of his ancestry in Wilde, Byron, and Shakespeare. Yet it is also about "Man" as liar, "Imago Dei
who forgot his station." Through his angularity, in other words, Auden
is also pursuing a game of knowledge about sameness and difference,
universal and particular. Metaphysics, for the later Auden, has to be a
self-consciously ridiculous enterprise—a performance art that never
forgets its station, its particular "human position."

To call this queer metaphysics or queer theology might seem like
bowing to a later critical fashion that, had he lived to see it, Auden
would probably have deplored as grotesquely indiscreet. But it is hard
to know how better to describe his deconstruction of norms, sexual
and otherwise, in these poems or in his 1965 "Epithalamium." After a
quarter-century with Kallman, Auden addresses Rita Auden, his niece,
and her husband, Peter Mudford, to call marriage "a diffy undertaking" (*CP* 760). "All [that] folk-tales mean by ending / with a State
Marriage," Auden begins, "we wish you," but his levity comments as
much on the absurdity of this institution in the modern age as on the
joy of the occasion. Bride and groom are "two idiosyncrasies / who
opt in this hawthorn month / to common your lives." Perverting
"common" from noun to verb, Auden echoes his 1963 poem to Kallman, "The Common Life," suggesting that the model here for heterosexual marriage is a long-term homosexual love.

After proceeding through generically conventional but linguistically
idiosyncratic invocations of Venus and Hymen, Auden starts queering
science. The wedding is cause for celebration, he writes, because it ex-

emplifies the absurdity that humans exist at all: the "uncanny" fact that
our species evolved from a genetic liar—"a gangrel / Paleocene pseudo-
rat" (761). Descendants of a mutant "Ur-Papa," we too are bent:

> As genders, married or not,
> who share with all flesh
> a left-handed twist, your choice
> reminds us to thank
> Mrs. Nature for doing
> (our ugly looks are our own)
> the handsome by us.

A grammatically dangling opening cagily finesses the commonality of
speaker and addressees: "married" (like Peter Mudford and Rita Auden) "or not" (like Wystan and Chester), "all flesh" and "genders" have
deviance in common. As the metaphorical vehicle for deviance, the
"left-handed twist" suggests "we" are all queer: the particular abnormality of the homosexual signifies the universally human precisely because not all humans are homosexual.

Auden ends by turning from deviance and difference as genetic facts
to considering them as theological signs:

> as Adams, Eves, commanded
> to nonesuch being,
> [we] answer the One for Whom all
> enantiomorphs
> are super-posable, yet
> Who numbers each particle
> by its Proper Name.

Divinity, these lines suggest, can reconcile human sameness and difference without effacing either. "Enantiomorphs" are two compounds
whose molecular structures are mirror-images. Auden posits a definition of God: "the One" who can "super-pose" them (in geometric
terms, setting one above another so that they occupy precisely the
same space), while at the same time recognizing the differences between them that warrant a "Proper Name" for "each particle." Only at

a superhuman level, in other words, can commonality and particularity be reconciled.

Adam and Eve—male and female—comprise one pair of enan-tiomorphs for this poem, but Auden's figures of mirroring suggest others: right-handed and left-handed, heterosexual and homosexual. These too, by his logic, are singular and super-posable only by God, and the brilliance of the poem is to make us feel as if we know what this might mean. But Auden's cleverness actually testifies to ultimate uncertainty. For if reticence forms one response to the unspeakability of truth, its contrary is garrulity. "Epithalamium" suggests that un-ashamed contrivance—here, an absurdly rapacious allusiveness to clas-sical myth, geology, evolutionary biology, anthropology, biochemistry, and mathematics—can approach truth. But it cannot express truth. Rhetorically speaking, Auden is contriving to superpose openness and secrecy, seriousness and joking. The frivolity of "Epithalamium" is a suitably oblique angle not only for the queer uncle addressing bride and groom at the start of their "diffy undertaking," but for the queer human addressing an apparently queer God.

II

Shortly before his death, Yeats wrote that all his work came down to one realization: "Man can embody truth but he cannot know it" (Ell-mann 285). Auden's ambivalence about Yeats is famous, and he proba-bly would have agreed with Yeats on the second proposition but pro-nounced him wrong on the first.[11] The poems considered so far sug-gest that Auden thought divine truth impossible to know except as an absent synthesis implied by the self-conflicting knowledge of "Poetic Fiction." As for embodying truth, he would surely have denied that this can occur either in the self or in art.

Auden's distance from the Symbolist poetic of Yeats can be seen in "The Virgin & The Dynamo," with its comment that "Every poem . . . is an attempt to present an analogy to that paradisal state in which Freedom and Law, System and Order are united in harmony. Every poem is very nearly a Utopia. Again, an analogy, not an imitation; the harmony is possible and verbal only" (DH 71). "Analogy" is Auden's key term, as against "imitation," for analogy is provisional and approximate, a sane comparison that knows that it is acting, not embodying the truth. Like joking and parable (as opposed to rhetoric), like games of knowledge (as opposed to magic), analogy allows Auden to indicate poetry's truth claims without claiming too much:

> The effect of beauty . . . is good to the degree that, through its analogies, the goodness of created existence, the historical fall into unfreedom and disorder, and the possibility of regaining paradise through repentance and forgiveness are recognized. Its effect is evil to the degree that beauty is taken, not as analogous to, but [as] identical with goodness, so that the artist regards himself or is regarded by others as God, the pleasure of beauty taken for the joy of Paradise, and the conclusion drawn that, since all is well in the work of art, all is well in history. But all is not well there.

This passage owes much to a conviction that the evil coercions of history are the social manifestation of an aesthetic rage for order. But in Auden's poetry, the temptation to identify beauty with goodness arises with perhaps greatest intensity in the realm of love. His early love poems are obsessed by the allure of feeling that truth is embodied—*literally* embodied—in the beloved. Auden's characteristic erotic hope is that Plato is right—that the beautiful body is a vehicle for a beautiful soul. His typical anxiety is a Shakespearean one—that the identity of bodily and spiritual beauty is a lie. As Auden saw it at least, life with Chester meant learning once more that the "pleasure of beauty" is not "the joy of Paradise," that "all is not well" in the history of eros.

This realm of personal history forms a crucial context for the two poems with which I conclude this chapter and the main part of this book: "Pleasure Island" and "In Praise of Limestone." Written in 1948, they are about the effects, both good and evil, of bodily pleasure and beauty. It is more than a coincidence that Auden also wrote "The Platonic Blow" in 1948, a poem that bears pornographic witness to the sacredness of bodily pleasure: in a meter adapted from the poetry of Charles Williams, whom he admired as a religious thinker and as a friend, Auden celebrates the sublime joys of giving a blow job (see Mendelson, *Later* 298). In forms more suitable for public consumption, "Pleasure Island" and "In Praise of Limestone" use homosexual desire as a crucial analogy for exploring knowledge of divine truth and the nature of paradise. Although Auden was only 41 years old in 1948, these read like poems of an older—even an old—man. As everyone knows, Auden aged very quickly in the 1940s and 50s, both physically and temperamentally. One implication of these poems is that his sense of his own aging body was reinforced by the worship of youth that permeates gay male subculture. But in exploring the relation between "paradise" and worldly life, Auden was also writing about his relationship—by this time non-sexual—with Kallman, who was 27 in 1948.

"Pleasure Island" must rank among the grimmer poems written about gay subculture by an insider, but its tone is not simply condemnatory. Auden writes as an observer peripheral to the scene but qualified as an anthropologist because he is a member of the tribe. The poem's setting is Fire Island, where he had bought a rundown cabin in the mid-1940s, when it was already something of the gay mecca it has since become.[12] The appeal of this place is that it is hardly a place at all—a strip of sand before an ocean that "Stares right past us," beneath "dazzling miles" of the indifferent "eye, true / Blue all summer, of the sky . . ." (CP 343). Nature plainly, unapologetically does not care. It bears the nonchalant, impervious look of the stranger to whom we aren't worth eye contact. But just because we are free to look, this place has spawned a frontier culture celebrating pleasure:

> The coast is a blur and without meaning
>   The churches and routines
> Which stopped there and never cared or dared to
>   Cross over to interfere
> With this outpost where nothing is wicked
>   But to be sorry or sick,
> But one thing unneighbourly, work.

The lassitude of these verses makes them oddly pleasurable to read. They are casual and conversational, with few end-stopped lines, but they slightly unsettle the ear by rhyming penultimate and final syllables in lines of quite different length. This place, one feels, is peopled by outcasts going nowhere and not particularly fast, but neither are they ever quite at rest.

Although less elaborately (and affectionately) than "In Praise of Limestone," "Pleasure Island" analyzes gay male sexual culture as a paradisal fantasy of pagan bodily freedom. But the fantasy becomes edgier as Auden proceeds. This is less an isle of the blest than a land of lotus-eaters, where drink and leisure overcome all plans of the "visitor" for self-improvement:

> soon he gives in, stops stopping
>   To think, lets his book drop
> And lies, like us, on his stomach watching
>   As bosom, backside, crotch
> Or other sacred trophy is borne in triumph
>   Past his adoring by
> Souls he does not try to like; then, getting
>   Up, gives all to the wet
> Clasps of the sea. . . .

The pleasure of this place is, properly speaking, not erotic but sexual, an ersatz Greek Love in which body parts express strength to dominate and virility to be worshipped, not "souls" to "like," much less love. The "waves reject / Sympathy," groping the body with impersonal "wet / Clasps"—crude knockoffs of the delighted caresses that Neptune once bestowed on naked Leander swimming the Hellespont in Marlowe's famously homoerotic poem. For all the rites of indulgence enacted here, this is a landscape of the sublime, not the beautiful, where the elements of ocean and sky enforce a modern inversion of the pagan. Instead of worshiping gods of sun and sea who magnify human qualities, the denizens of this place embody the pure physicality of uncaring nature.

The timeless fantasy of bodily pleasure, free from messy entanglements of soul, conceals a deathly transitoriness that, in Auden's analysis, gives the lie to dreams of naked beauty and free love:

>   for our
> Lenient amusing shore

> Knows in fact about all the dyings, is in
>   Fact our place, namely this
> Place of a skull, a place where the rose of
>   Self-punishment will grow.

The shock of this passage comes in its abrupt shift from casual satire of pagan fantasy to unironized Christian mythos, in which life devoted to "all the dyings" of sexual bliss is not paradise but hell. In terms of worldly, historical geography, this is Golgotha—that site where the embodiment of the divine is killed. By calling it "our place," Auden reads it as an emblem of universal human guilt but also as the particular, self-chosen damnation of his own tribe, whose rites involve not just worship of the body but humiliation. In his 1950 review of a book on Wilde, Auden wrote, "The tough and pessimistic Greek who identified pleasure and happiness knew that pleasure depends upon power; accordingly his Happy Place is inhabited only by the beautiful, the strong and the wise; the weak, the ugly, the poor, the old, the stupid are excluded" ("Playboy" 394). "Pleasure Island" portrays the price of these exclusions: the pagan Happy Place cannot seem, in the wake of Christianity, a Garden of Eden except in the ironic sense that this is "where the rose of / Self-punishment will grow."

The poem ends with night coming to those who haven't worked all day. "The bar is copious / With fervent life that hopes / To make sense," but Auden attends instead to "some decaying / Spirit," walking the beach, "excusing itself / To itself with evangelical gestures / For having failed the test." The cult of pure pleasure is unmasked as a zero-sum game of pure power, in which there is no reciprocity of pleasure or forgiveness for failure to score. And even the winner can have sudden doubts:

> A little before dawn,
> Miss Lovely, life and soul of the party,
>   Wakes with a dreadful start,
> Sure that whatever—O God!—she is in for
>   Is about to begin,
> Or hearing, beyond the hushabye noises
>   Of sea and Me, just a voice

> Ask, as one might the time or a trifle
> Extra, her money and her life.

The tone here has a weird, uncanny urgency: as Davenport-Hines observes, "The exclamation 'O God' has a doubleness—theological gravity as well as camp silliness—and reflects a Kierkegaardian existentialism" (251). This can be read as the tone of hungover regret at the price of hedonism, or as the tone of spiritual dread. Similarly, the demand of the closing lines can sound like the entangling request of a trick, or a radically serious challenge to the soul.

The disturbing campiness of Auden's conclusion suggests the complexity of his thinking about the spiritual meanings of bodily desire. On one hand, the body's boundedness by time and space obscures the realm of higher necessity that Karl Barth calls "Wholly Other," although it may wring an "O God!" at the empirical world's shabby inadequacy and thus give "a dreadful start" to the true religious life. If the puritanical strain of "Pleasure Island" owes something to existentialism, it also reflects Auden's bitterness about his relationship with Kallman. A letter Auden wrote from Fire Island in 1947 suggests that he tried to see Kallman's affairs as his own purgatory: "The triple situation, of being sexually jealous, like a wife, anxious like a momma, and competitive like a brother, is not easy for my kind of temperament. Still, it is my bed, and I must lie on it" (quoted Davenport-Hines 248). In early 1949, Auden wrote rather bitterly to Kallman that God might demand a "chaste fidelity to the Divine Miss K," but he just did not have "the strength" (Farnan 158). Such mixed feelings shape "Pleasure Island," where Kallman may well be the antecedent for "Miss Lovely, life and soul of the party," waking "with a dreadful start" amid "the hushabye noises / Of sea and Me."

Much later, in 1972, Auden criticized existentialism as "a form of gnosticism. It doesn't pay proper attention to the body" (Mendelson, *Later* 277). Written the same year as "Pleasure Island," "In Praise of Limestone" suggests that even in the 1940s, he was of two minds about the spiritual meaning of the body and sex—that he was quite able to conceive of homosexual eros as sacred. One way to explain this is to note that along with existentialism, Auden's work reflects the Catholic tradition of natural theology, with its Platonic view of human love as figuring the divine.[13] If existentialism gave grounds for skepticism about the value of bodily life, it was the tradition of natural theology that explained why the Vision of Eros could happen at all and why it meant more than transitory physical intoxication.

But "In Praise of Limestone" also illustrates how a sense of the sacredness of the body and its desires could follow from existentialism itself. As we have seen, a corollary for Auden of the contingency of the subject was the need to accept contingency as the ground of all knowledge. The search for "common truth," he wrote in 1944, compels the subject to "begin by learning to be objective about his subjectivity" ("Preface" 683). If "Pleasure Island" tries to be objective about homosexual fantasies of bodily pleasure, "In Praise of Limestone" accepts the desiring and desirable body as ground zero for the contingent subject in search of paradise. Eros, as the vector of Auden's interest, becomes a model for agape; homoerotic fantasy becomes an analogy for "a faultless love / Or the life to come" (*SP* 187)

Contingency governs this poem from the very start via grammatical mood and pronoun choice: "If it form the one landscape that we the inconstant ones / Are consistently homesick for, this is chiefly / Because it dissolves in water. Mark these rounded slopes . . ." (184). The conditionality of Auden's fastidious subjunctive locates the landscape not in actuality (where verbs are indicative) but in potentiality. Formulations like "this is chiefly" and "Mark these rounded slopes" evoke the dispassionate lecturer standing above all contingency, but in following "we" with "the inconstant ones," Auden complicates this posture. Set off by commas, as in Auden's revised text, this appositive might be construed as non-restrictive—denoting the inconstancy common to all.[14] But the emphatic "one" in "the one landscape" and the evocative, unexplained specificity of "the inconstant ones" pull against a commonality between poet and reader, particularly in Auden's earlier text, which lacks a comma after "we." Critics have asked just whom Auden is referring to in "we the inconstant ones," and among their answers are tourists, northerners, all mortals, artists, Wystan and Chester, and homosexuals.[15] All these answers respond to something important in this poem. But it is the way in which the phrase calls up different specific answers—one of which is "all of us"—that gives this opening its angular effect. This is, as Michael Wood puts it, "a poem about differences, and about shifts in the perception of difference" (Auden, *"In Solitude"* 250). We may all be homesick exiles, but not together: the limestone landscape is offered to us from one contingent perspective.

As critics have often observed, this Mediterranean landscape is geologically kin to the limestone cliffs of northern England.[16] Its meanings, as Edna Longley has commented, involve the meanings of landscape in Auden's early work, making the poem itself a " 'secret system' which encodes personal and literary history," including "a homosexual narrative" (Auden, *In Solitude* 255). Like his lyrics of the closet, this poem estranges in the act of including us as insiders—"we, the inconstant ones." But this is an early Auden terrain transfigured, and the estrangement is not antagonistic but playful. All the fear and anxiety once acted out amid angular escarpments and cold waters have given way to their un-English contraries: "springs / That spurt out everywhere with a chuckle," the "little ravine whose cliffs entertain / The butterfly and the lizard" (*SP* 184–85). "Beneath" all this is a "secret system of caves and conduits": both a transformed version of the dark, alluring mine-shafts in early Auden, and an emblem for semiotic and psychic links between that terrain and this one.

Revisiting that northern landscape in "New Year Letter," Auden wrote that there he had first known "The deep *Urmutterfurcht* that drives / Us into knowledge all our lives": "Adits were entrances which led / Down to the Outlawed, to the Others, / The Terrible, the Merciful, the Mothers" (*CP* 228). In the southern climate of Ischia, Auden wears his Freudianism more lightly. It is not a discourse for diagnosing his own psychosexual disorder—or if it is, he is at ease doing so. Homosexual desire no longer means going underground to dark places, symbolically or rhetorically:

> What could be more like Mother or a fitter background
>   For her son, for the nude young male who lounges
> Against a rock displaying his dildo, never doubting
>   That for all his faults he is loved, whose works are but
> Extensions of his power to charm?   (*SP* 185)

A Freudian diagnosis would be that this *genius loci* suffers from arrested development, except that he does not suffer: mother-fixation is a trope for the comfortable fit between body, soul, and world. This is camp Freudianism, in the spirit of Auden's habit of referring to himself among friends as "Mother." These lines offer, of course, only an analogy for paradisal contentment: this is a landscape that "we, the inconstant ones, / Are consistently homesick for"—a paradise lost. Given Auden's conviction that homosexual men are congenitally promiscuous, this line in part confesses his sexuality by admitting his own infidelities.[17] But if Auden is punning on his mother's name— Constance—his portrayal of the "nude young male" imagines forgiveness for filial as well as sexual inconstancy, through an image of absolute certainty of maternal love. Ultimately, as an analogy for a condition of being at home, these lines testify to homosexuality less as arrested development—the inability to leave one's psychic home—than as permanent but livable exile.

The unashamed eroticism of Auden's "nude young male" evokes classical beauty in high art and low: this figure descends from both Michelangelo's "David" and Wilhelm von Gloeden's homoerotic photos. His dildo, however unself-consciously displayed, is an artificial erection: to be au naturel, the word implies, requires artifice. This is a standard later Auden conceit about sincerity in art and in identity, but it also invites the reader to feel innocent homoerotic pleasure both in and at the nude young male.[18] It takes art—statues, dildos, poetry—to awaken us to the tactile beauty of the body as a good in itself. This body is a "modification of matter" (as Auden puts it near the end of the poem) that is "made solely for pleasure": thus enjoyed, it has no more productive purpose than a dildo. There is, therefore, an amoral theory of art and sexuality here, very much in the spirit of Wilde's aestheticism.

Where "Pleasure Island" finds the ethic of Greek Love belied by the alienations of gay sexual subculture on Fire Island, "In Praise of Limestone" discovers in Ischia a place where it seems to be true:

> Watch, then, the band of rivals as they climb up and down
>   Their steep stone gennels in twos and threes, sometimes
> Arm in arm, but never, thank God, in step; or engaged
>   On the shady side of a square at midday in
> Voluble discourse, knowing each other too well to think

> There are any important secrets, unable
> To conceive a god whose temper-tantrums are moral
>   And not to be pacified by a clever line
> Or a good lay.

These are at once the real young men of Ischia and the mythic "band of rivals" for Mother Nature's affection, of which the statuesque young male is one. Auden is playing here, not unself-consciously, with the fantasies of bodily pleasure and beauty long projected onto the Mediterranean by northerners, particularly male homosexual writers and artists (including erotic photographers like von Gloeden). Behind these lines, in other words, is Greek Love not in Platonic form but as reimagined by writers from Byron to Pater to Forster.[19]

For Auden, the modern homoerotic cult of the Mediterranean crystallized a certain moral insight. Discussing this poem in 1971, he commented that "the limestone landscape was important to me as a connecting link between . . . the northern protestant guilt culture I grew up in, and the shame culture of the Mediterranean countries, to which I was now exposed for the first time."[20] If "In Praise of Limestone" indulges an element of sexual tourism, this poem reveals the tendentiousness of its fantasies about culture and the body, both at a psychological level and at a metaphysical one. In 1949, Auden reviewed a reissue of five novels by Ronald Firbank, and his comments about how we imagine paradise speak to this poem. Firbank always had something of a gay cult following, with his exotic settings, insane plotting, and campy style. Auden had already come out as a fan of Firbank in "Letter to Lord Byron," but in his review he made grand claims for works like *The Flower Beneath the Foot* (1923) and *Concerning the Eccentricities of Cardinal Pirelli* (1926):

Firbank's extraordinary achievement was to draw a picture, the finest, I believe, ever drawn by anyone, of the Earthly Paradise, not, of course, as it really is, but as, in our fallen state, we imagine it to be, as the place, that is, where, without having to change our desires and behavior in any way, we suffer neither frustration nor guilt.

(Auden, "Firbank" 5)

"In Praise of Limestone" imagines the Earthly Paradise as a place where there are "no important secrets" in "the band of rivals," each of them a Mother's boy whose gods are appeased "by a clever line / Or a good lay." This is, in other words, a gay fantasy of the Earthly Paradise as a realm of free sex—which is to say, free *love,* for here they mean the same thing.

Difficulties and problems there may be, but not guilt, for the flesh-and-blood inhabitants of this place have no more interiority than classical and neoclassical statues. As in Firbank, "what people are and what they want or ought to become are identical." Auden both honors and judges this fantasy, laying bare the contrary spiritual implications of homosexual desire. "The fact that Firbank's novels are so funny," he wrote, "is proof that he never lets us forget the contradiction of life as it is and life as we should like it to be, for it is the impossibility of that contradiction which makes us laugh."[21] The statuesque inhabitants of the limestone landscape are "accustomed to a stone that responds"—Nature as Mother Nature—because they have never gone where "life as it is" takes place: sites of inhuman sublimity like a "crater['s] blazing fury," the "infinite space" seen by desert nomads, or "the jungle," with all its "monstrous forms and lives" (*SP* 185). Dwellers in a "region / Of short distances and definite places," these sons of natural artifice can only "go to the bad" by purveying fraudulent beauty: they can "become a pimp / Or deal in fake jewelry or ruin a fine tenor voice / For effects that bring down the house." They never, in other words, stray beyond the comfortable bounds of Firbankian disaster, and as stereotypically Italian demises, their comic bad ends point to the "contradiction" between Auden's fantasy paradise and "life as it is."

In shifting, at this point, to the "best and worst" who sought something more, Auden is exploring what it means to face the contradiction between life as we should like it to be and life as it is. The latter he figures as happening not in a limestone landscape but in "Immoderate soils" where "the meaning of life" is "Something more than a mad camp" (186). These are sites of the sublime, whose voices summon "Intendant Caesars" to shape history from people and places, and "Saints-to-be" to invent morality by embracing asceticism. The most disturbing lines in the poem, however, resonate powerfully with Auden's darker views on eros:

> But the really reckless were fetched
> By an older colder voice, the oceanic whisper:
> "I am the solitude that asks and promises nothing;
> That is how I shall set you free. There is no love;
> There are only the various envies, all of them sad."

These last words come from nature demythologized, voicing what the ocean in "Pleasure Island" never says but Auden does when he names "our place" "this place of a skull." In conversation in the fall of 1947, he commented that "it's wrong to be queer," in part because "all homosexual acts are acts of envy" (Ansen 80). Here, to be sure, the "oceanic whisper" implies it is so for all love. But this is the claim insinuated in so many of Auden's more anxious love poems—that homosexual love always risks narcissism, the lover's selfish desire for what he lacks, be it strength, youth, innocence, or anything else the beautiful beloved is seen to embody. The heart of love is envy in this view: a pathetic emotional theft which is not gay at all, but "sad" like all the various envies.

From this angle, the limestone landscape "is not the sweet home that it looks," Auden concedes, casting off the pseudodetachment of the lecturer: "They were right, my dear, all those voices were right. . . ." But as in "Law Like Love," apostrophe signals that this has been a love poem all along: its questions about life as it is and life as we should like it to be are posed by a homosexual lover. To a disenchanted eye, the homosexual Earthly Paradise is a "backward / And dilapidated province"—regressive, degenerate, as fraudulent as Aschenbach's Venice. Even so, it serves a "worldly duty" that Mann's story does not portray: it "calls into question / All the Great Powers assume; it disturbs our rights." Twenty years later, in "The Garrison" (1969), Auden commemorated the "personal song and language" that defined his life with Kallman in Kirchstetten (CP 844). "We, Chester, / and the choir we sort with," he wrote, have a "duty to the City" in a "Present, / so self-righteous in its assumptions": "to serve as a paradigm / now of what a plausible Future might be." It is easy to sneer at the image of a gay utopia embodied in Wystan and Chester—besotted with martinis and wine, smoking themselves to death, resenting each other's infidelities. But Auden is aware of the absurdity and invites the sneer. And this absurdity resonates with "In Praise of Limestone," which is also about the meanings of backward, dilapidated desires in a world ruled by righteous Great Powers.

The poem's movement at this point could be reduced to an abstract question: what, then, is the relation between pleasure, desire, and truth? Auden's response is not an intellectual answer but an affirmation of the power of the physical to provoke moral knowledge of his earth-bound contingency. This landscape "disturbs our rights" with insistent appeals to the attractions and reality of the sensual body, distracting the poet and the scientist in their attentions to higher things. By including himself in their category, Auden uses the poem for confession, gesturing toward truths unspoken but known to the one he addresses:

> I, too, am reproached, for what
> And how much you know. Not to lose time, not to get caught,
> Not to be left behind, not, please! to resemble
> The beasts who repeat themselves, or a thing like water
> Or stone whose conduct can be predicted, these
> Are our Common Prayer. . . .   (*SP* 186–87)

Universal though the reader may try to make them, Auden's anxieties are tendered here as no more than his own eccentricities. The explicitly Anglican wording is a characteristic gesture, wrapping his quirks in the garb of orthodoxy. Kallman is surely, as Fuller observes, addressed in this "domestic version of Common Prayer" (409). This is "*our* Common Prayer" in the sense that Fire Island is "our place" and Auden and Kallman's living room in Kirchstetten reveals their "Common Life." The fears Auden admits to would seem to involve aging, shame, and unspoken guilts, but as for exactly "what / And how much," Kallman knew him (and them) well enough that here they can go unsaid.

"In so far as we have to look forward / To death as a fact," Auden writes, "no doubt we are right": to recognize that the fantasy of home, free of frustrated desire and guilt, is only a fantasy, is to know that there is no real consolation in "life as it is" for real, historical sadnesses. The limestone landscape is a paradise lost. But in a subtle, crucial shift, Auden turns "life as it is" into a matter of conditionality: "In so far," but no farther. Recognition of contingency, that death is the final "fact" of life, can license fantasy, giving it potential truth value:

> But if
> Sins can be forgiven, if bodies rise from the dead,
>   These modifications of matter into
> Innocent athletes and gesticulating fountains,
>   Made solely for pleasure, make a further point:
> The blessed will not care what angle they are regarded from,
>   Having nothing to hide. Dear, I know nothing of
> Either, but when I try to imagine a faultless love
>   Or the life to come, what I hear is the murmur
> Of underground streams, what I see is a limestone landscape.

This is an analogy, reinforced as such by grammatical markers of contingency: "But if," "but when." Yet conditionality allows Auden to use the limestone landscape to imagine a plausible future for the embodied soul: "a faultless love / Or the life to come." Whether we name this utopia or paradise, it is a hope rendered along the vector of Auden's erotic interest, which imagines an end to guilt and frustration, prophesied by "these modifications of matter into / Innocent athletes and gesticulating fountains, / Made solely for pleasure."

As modifications of the material of Auden's own life, these lines make his guilty secrets into something that both matters and does not matter—a reality intensely present in his poetry, but fashioned by language into occasions of innocent pleasure. He posits a state beyond contingency, in which "The blest will not care what angle they are regarded from, / Having nothing to hide." This is also another angler's lie, an ingratiating joke about bodily vanity and what we hide from others in life as it is. But it is equally an angler's truth—which is to say, the only kind of truth possible in life as it is. Those we love will get it, as Kallman surely did, and as a love poem addressed to him, "In Praise of Limestone" proffers unspeakability not as the price of inconstancy but as the sign of faultless love: faithlessness that is no longer cynicism but certainty.[22]

"In Praise of Limestone" invites all readers, as Lipking comments, to imagine themselves as Auden's addressee—as his beloved (Auden, *In Solitude* 271). It therefore imagines poetry as a working analogy for a homosexual utopia or paradise: a condition in which the poet's subterfuge and artifice are no longer necessary, in which any angle shows his best side. To be in paradise would be, in the words of the Anglican *Book of Common Prayer,* to dwell where all hearts are open, all desires known, and no secrets are hid. About "a faultless love / Or the life to come," of course, Auden says, "Dear, I know nothing of / Either": God remains unspeakable. Written from the angle of life as it is, not everything can have its "Proper Name"; some things are of necessity hidden. By the same token, the limestone landscape is a utopia, not only because it is where different desires are freely lived, out in the open, but also because it is precisely nowhere. Yet even as Auden admits he knows nothing of such matters, we are free to hear him being true to his faults.

The artist's maxim: "Whoso generalises, is lost."
The politician's maxim: "Hard cases make bad law."
—"The Prolific and the Devourer" (*EA* 404)

Afterword

AUDEN'S BIASES—AND OURS

Why read Auden as a homosexual poet? One answer—for some readers the most important one—is set out in the introduction of this
book and shapes its argument throughout: critical and historical understanding of Auden has been impoverished to the degree that the
relevance of homosexuality to his writing has been overlooked, under-
estimated, ignored, or suppressed. This book, then, constitutes an exercise in literary history that makes a certain truth claim: Auden's
homosexuality is as much an "aspect" of his work as his class, his politics, his religious beliefs, or his Freudianism, and to think adequately
about these things requires that we think about his homosexuality
more than casually. From another angle, however, such a claim indicates only the cost of *not* reading Auden as a homosexual poet. Here I
explore a proposition consciously deferred in unfolding this book's argument: Auden's work has important things to say to queer studies.
More precisely, it can serve as a useful lens for considering the aims,
results, and risks of pursuing lesbian/gay literary criticism as an exercise in historical study.

In largely suppressing parallels between Auden's engagements with
sexual politics and the concerns of academic queer studies, I have
sought to let them emerge as much as possible from his own writing
and in his own terms. But however convincing, the very proposition
that such parallels exist calls up a rather cumbersome hermeneutical
circle. I have ignored this problem, since drawing attention to it at
every turn would have overloaded my analysis with unending qualifi-

cations. In addressing these issues here—which is to say, in addressing the truth status of my historical claims about Auden—I am using him as a writer whose work provokes, in an exemplary way, questions that ought to arise about what we are finding when we read an earlier queer writer: Who are "we"? What does it mean to "find" something in "reading" a queer writer? What, exactly, do we mean by "queer"? For queer studies, I submit, there is something of value in Auden's work, not simply because it prefigures later sexual-political and intellectual concerns, but because he uses literary forms and modes to address them. It is not that Auden offers solutions that have eluded those working in queer theory or lesbian/gay studies. Rather, his poetry can provoke us to know the value of uncertainty in queer studies—a value that consists, perhaps, in its very unproductivity.

If, as this book implies, Auden's poetic explorations of the contradictions that fracture the homosexual subject *do* foreshadow the concerns of Eve Sedgwick and others, a number of conclusions might follow. One of them—an odd one, at first glance—might be that queer studies predates gay and lesbian liberation. From this point of view, the period in which lesbian and gay people embraced essentialist notions of identity and turned them to intellectual account was actually a fairly brief interlude in a longer history of homosexual self-interrogation that might better be termed "queer." It is not simply that Auden was being circumspect and writing in code—although he often was. His manifold exploitations and performances of duplicity constitute something far more interesting and important than mere self-closeting, for they suggest a lifelong performance as queer poetic sage. (In sheer length, the best analogue is not the career of Byron or Wilde, but the ongoing self-refashionings of Yeats.) Although Auden's performance took place in conversations, public readings and lectures, libretti, and a vast quantity of reviews and essays, its major locus is his poetry. To look at writers like Stein, Forster, Crane, and Bishop similarly would be to see modern homosexual literature not merely as writing that includes essential gay or lesbian content to be outed by the critic, but as a way of practicing queer identity in all its contradictions between public and private, universality and marginality.

At the same time, this book has argued that Auden's poetry engages in a variety of theoretical and analytical pursuits in which the psychological and political meanings of homosexuality are very much at issue. Seen thus, much of his work might be considered as a form of queer theory *avant la lettre,* suggesting that literary form itself, historically speaking, has served many of the purposes that theory has come to fulfill since the mid-1980s. If this is so, one implication for the practice of queer literary-historical study is that literary texts should be approached as more than objects to be explained by critical recourse to sexual-political and discursive context, or by a privileged theoretical apparatus brought to bear by the critic. It is worth considering the cost to queer studies—culturally and intellectually—of neglecting the historical functions of the aesthetic in modern lesbian/gay culture, even if we ourselves are healthily skeptical of the ideology of the aesthetic. Auden was fond of asserting the political inconsequentiality of art—sometimes because he believed it, sometimes because he saw in politics the coercive practice of art as black magic, but often (one suspects) because he liked to annoy critics and academics. And while his claims about the political impotence of art seem questionable in the categorical terms he liked to use, it also seems hard to argue that poetry in its high-art forms has had large political effects in modern or postmodern Britain and America. Its cultural marginality, however, would in another sense make it an ideal mode for inquiry into sexuality and sexual politics in decades before sexual liberation made them available for popular, public discourse.

But it is risky to make such claims, for they beg a host of questions. Christopher Lane puts it this way: "Can we 'queer' our relationship to history without also defining the past as a record of contemporary conflicts?"[1] If it is a truism that literary history responds to the needs of those who write it, consciously revisionist literary history can find in this truism at least as much anxiety as comfort. We need not apologize for having motivations for rereading the past, since it could not be otherwise. But the anxiety comes in suspecting that we project ourselves onto the past in the very process of thinking we recover someone or something else. It is, as Lane implies, all too easy to find what we want in history—be it an object lesson in self-closeting complicity, a hero of queer subversion, or a champion of universal human values. While Auden at different moments seems to perform each of these roles, often he seems to be playing them off against each other. It would be foolish, therefore, to confine him to one. But like any other, this book's construction of Auden reflects my own needs and desires. The claim that he anticipates key concerns in contemporary queer studies is, after all, just the sort of case that someone working in queer studies would make.

While no more than anyone else can I escape this hermeneutical circle, confronting its peculiar inevitability in the realm of queer literary studies can make possible a different kind of knowledge. It is not merely encouraging but culturally significant, in this regard, that both Auden and Wilde recognized this crux, in the sense that both addressed the dangers for the queer reader confronting past writers. Wilde's "The Portrait of Mr. W. H." can be read as a parable of fatally uncritical attraction, whereby the hermeneutical circle forms the exact dimensions of the pool of Narcissus. In Wilde's story, the desire to prove a hypothesis—that the Young Man of Shakespeare's *Sonnets* was Willie Hughes—is strong enough to kill two of its adherents, Cyril Graham and Erskine. This is, one might say, a lesson in the infectious risks of critical narcissism, in which desire for the beautiful face of a boy takes the form of desire for a beautiful theory about poetry. For his part, Auden reworks the point in his essay on the *Sonnets* as a catty gibe at the "homosexual reader" who would recruit Shakespeare as a member of "the Homintern" (*FA* 99). Since this reader ignores the "unequivocally sexual" sonnets to the Dark Lady, the only casualty (Auden implies) is clear thinking. Still, it is intellectual death by watery mirror.

But for Auden as for Wilde, Shakespeare's *Sonnets* are not just the paradigmatic locus of anti-historical blindness in the queer reader. In Wilde's story, the narrator models a relation to the Willie Hughes theory different from that of Erskine and Cyril, both of whom die from commitment to its objective truth. The narrator goes through phases of attraction, belief, and skepticism, but he ends the story alive and well, content with the beauty of the theory but not believing it. This is, of course, one way to describe the trajectory of love—of what Auden calls the Vision of Eros—in which idealization of the other cannot last forever, and the wish to make it permanent is fatal. (I take it that Wilde is, consciously or not, suggesting that the aesthetic beauty of remembered infatuation is the only kind one can live with for long.)

The value of "The Portrait of Mr. W. H.," like that of the theory of Willie Hughes, is that it offers not truth but pleasure in entertaining our desires. So too, Auden in private was happy to take the *Sonnets* as expressing homosexual love for the Young Man, and in fact, his essay never quite says that they don't. As we have seen, Auden's conjectures in print and in conversation about Shakespeare's love for the Young Man owe much to his own relationship with Chester Kallman. Whatever the dangers to historical "truth," in other words, Auden treated the *Sonnets* privately and publicly (if discreetly) as a mirror for self-reflection.[2]

Well aware of the intractability of the hermeneutical circle, Wilde and Auden imply that art should be used as a mirror not to see the world, but to look at oneself in an act of, as it were, enlightened narcissism. This is the positive, non-cautionary aspect of what Wilde means when he says, "It is the spectator, and not life, that art really mirrors." The "peril" lies in forgetting this, seeking like Narcissus to "go beneath the surface" (236). Such perils destroy the Airman in *The Orators,* who is undone by discovering his complicity with the Enemy—which is to say, by realizing that his every gesture of opposition inscribes himself in the image of the hated other. His solution is "the sacrifice of all resistance" (*EA* 93). In implying that Auden realized he could never master critical distance on homosexuality and its political meaning in English culture, the Airman's demise also implies the futility of queer epistemology as an oppositional weapon: it will always backfire. But as Auden's self-projection, the Airman also suggests art's power as a mirror for political self-knowledge, and no less for Auden's readers. From this angle, it only makes sense that the politics of *The Orators* have been interpreted so variously. As Auden writes in "Letter to Lord Byron"—where Byron serves as his mirror—"What we see depends on who's observing," and to realize this is to make possible a measure of self-knowledge (*P* 335). The lesson for the queer reader, then, is not to abandon reading because of the intractability of the hermeneutical circle, but to turn it back on oneself.

Of course, to realize that Auden, like Wilde, was fascinated by the problem of the hermeneutical circle, and himself linked it with homosexual desire, is not to escape its sway in queer literary history. But as a critical mirror for historical queer studies, Auden's work suggests something about the impulses that motivate such endeavors. In "The Prolific and the Devourer" (1939; published posthumously), he tried once again to sort out in prose the relation between politics and art that had so vexed him in the 1930s. The title itself, taken from *The Marriage of Heaven and Hell*, defines this relation as one of Blakean contraries:

> The Prolific and the Devourer: the Artist and the Politician. Let them realise that they are enemies, i.e., that each has a vision of the world which must remain incomprehensible to the other. But let them also realise that they are both necessary and complementary.
>
> (*EA* 404)

Auden proceeds to elaborate the distinction between artist and politician through a series of assertions about the relative value for each of general ideas and particular phenomena. "To be useful to an artist," he writes, "a general idea must be capable of including the most contradictory experiences, and of the most subtle variations and ironic interpretations." Contrarily, "The politician also finds a general idea useful, but for this purpose, which is to secure unanimity in action, subtlety and irony are drawbacks." (In his use of discourse, the politician acts as an orator, and Auden quotes Hitler at this point.)

The challenge for a historicist queer literary criticism is that it functions as both politician and artist. As politician, it seeks to recover homosexual/gay/lesbian/queer experience and meanings in writers of the past on the principle that such things matter because they matter to us today. But as artist, queer studies finds variation, difference, and contradiction more "useful," for they aid in complicating and revising inherited views of the past. In Auden's terms, this is a problem of the relation between the general and the particular. To recover the truth about Shakespeare, Wilde, Dickinson, and so forth, is to believe that the sexual particularities of their work have been lost in the coercive generalizations of earlier critics' blindness or homophobia. But perception of the particularities to be recovered would seem to depend on a sense of sameness between Shakespeare—or Sappho, for that matter—and the gay/lesbian/queer critic. This hermeneutical circle might be understood as the effect of an unconscious but no less coercive form of political generalization, based on the critic's conceptual projection. As Christopher Lane writes, "The irony is that queer theory increasingly *assists*—rather than avoiding—this eclipse of historical difference by substituting terms such as 'deviance' and 'perversion' for the dissimilarities, aporias, and discontinuities they only partially represent" (227). It is an irony because queer theory has sought to avoid the dangers of essentializing, yet such avoidance in the name of acknowledging historical difference seems to be haunted by a latent ahistorical essentialism. The major practical implication of all this for queer literary history is that only persistent self-questioning can prevent a blind reinscription of coercive, narcissistic generalizations. Thus, as Lane argues, queer studies must "relinquish the attraction of critical certainty" about the past (244). In Auden's terms, this would be to follow at once the irreconcilable maxims of artist and politician, Prolific and Devourer: "Whoso generalises, is lost," and "Hard cases make bad law" (*EA* 404).

At the same time, Auden's work, like Wilde's, suggests that the hermeneutical circle can also be an occasion for pleasure, as any but the most humorless reader of "Journal of an Airman" or "Letter to Lord Byron" will likely see. In her introduction to *Novel Gazing*, Sedgwick distinguishes two primary modes of queer studies: those energized by what Silvan Tomkins calls "strong theory" and its paranoic hermeneutics of suspicion, and those driven by pleasure-based, "reparative" motives (see *Novel* 4–24). At its best, Sedgwick opines, queer studies has allowed these motives to coexist. So, I would argue, does Auden's work as a homosexual poet, for his most elaborate stagings of the hermeneutics of suspicion are also his most entertaining, as when he responds to his homophobic political accusers in "Letter to Lord Byron":

> "No, I am that I am, and those that level
>   At my abuses reckon up their own.
>   I may be straight though they, themselves, are bevel."
>   So Shakespeare said, but Shakespeare must have known.
>
> (*P* 328)

As with the Airman, the hermeneutics of suspicion are practiced here quite self-consciously. These lines therefore constitute gestures of self-reflection on Auden's part, and invitations to the reader for something similar, via reflection on Auden and on Shakespeare. Such moments serve, I suggest, both to illustrate and to invite a different mode of reading, and a different kind of knowledge, from those blindly sought by the hermeneutics of suspicion, puritanically obsessed with certainty about the queer past. What do we "know" when we say, with Auden, that "Shakespeare must have known," or when we say ourselves that Auden must have known? Nothing about them that passes the test of falsifiability, to be sure, but something about ourselves in our very desire to make such statements.

In a passage that (to my ear) sounds uncharacteristically earnest, Wilde puts it this way in "The Portrait of Mr. W. H.":

> All that [art] shows us is our own soul, the one world of which we
> have any real cognizance. And the soul itself, the soul of each one of
> us, is to each one of us a mystery. It hides in the dark and broods, and
> consciousness cannot tell us of its workings. Consciousness, indeed, is
> quite inadequate to explain the contents of personality. It is Art, and
> Art only, that reveals us to ourselves.
>
> (209)

The "soul," one infers, hides in the closet, beyond the reach of policing. But it can be "revealed" by "Art" if consciousness attends to what happens when we look in Art's mirror. I submit (for I can hardly prove it) that as much as Freud, it is Wilde at a moment like this who inspires Auden's definition of poetry as a "game of knowledge": "a bringing to consciousness, by naming them, of emotions and their hidden relationships" ("Squares" 173). It provokes a desire for knowledge on the part of the reader, pursued in the effort to infer, through language, the poet's emotions and intentionality. But in refusing to satisfy such desire—ever—poetry can unsettle certainties of self and of other, in the poet and in the reader. Poetry can do so, first, because neither poet nor reader is self-identical. The "soul," in Wilde's words, "hides in the dark"; the "hidden relationships" of our emotions, as Auden puts it, are not automatically available to consciousness.[3] And poetic games of knowledge, for Auden, are possible also because words are not self-identical either, but subject to endlessly promiscuous, suggestive slippages.[4]

Considered in their own terms as games of knowledge, Auden's poems do not reveal him as essentially homosexual; nor, I think, do they seek to reveal the reader as anything but queer. For in "bringing to consciousness" the reader's "emotions and their hidden relationships," Auden's poems call into question the inevitably biased, desire-driven identifications, disavowals, and projections by which his identity and the reader's come to life in acts of writing and reading. Or so his poems should, if treated as games of knowledge rather than as containers of certainties. The distinction between same and other in such games is no longer stable, since the relation between poet and reader, as imagined by each, is implicated in narcissism. One intellectual consequence of such a process is that sexual-political distinctions between universal and minoritizing models of identity seem hopelessly crude for describing what happens epistemologically and psychologically in particular acts of reading. For a straight reader (to grant the term for the moment) to construe at all meaningfully the duplicitous propositions of so many Auden poems, the poem would seem to require, whether the reader knows it or not, a narcissistic identification with Auden as a homosexual poet. But if such identifications enable the construction of the reader's identity, to bring them to consciousness in reading is to destabilize that identity. And if such identifications are at all possible, they must also destabilize Auden's perceived identity as other. Both reader and poet, it seems, are engaged in queer relations by way of the poem.

A second implication of Auden's games of knowledge would be that it ceases to be philosophically meaningful to distinguish "canonical" and "minority" poets or poems. It is pedagogically and socially valuable to do so, of course—above all because the alternative is routinely a thoughtless assertion of universal commonality that effaces material, historical differences. And as I have argued through much of this book, Auden was deeply preoccupied with poetry as an anti-coercive, anti-generalizing mode, not least because it could model for him the freedom of particularity that he saw as the ethical charge of love. To think, then, of poetry as both a game of knowledge and a virtual lovers' discourse is to see it as always on the verge of intimacy, forever proposing but never ratifying the commonality of poet and reader. For it is to see poetry as instigating knowledge of the contingency and fractures of our own identities, the self-interestedness of our self-constructions, and thus begging the question of the adequacy of those we project onto others. But at this point, narcissism, in folding back on itself, can imagine getting beyond itself.

What is the outcome of such relations between poet and reader? Constrained by the circularity of narcissism, they would seem epistemologically bent on the sterility—biological and spiritual—that is traditionally ascribed to "unnatural love." The point is as old as Chaucer's emasculated Pardoner—older, even, since perversion is how St. Augustine defines evil: desire whose end is not God but oneself (see Dollimore 131–47). In Auden's model of poetry as a game of knowledge, the reader never generates poetic meaning as an object distinct from its pleasurable entanglements. And in this game, reader and poet always construct each other—at least provisionally—in same-sex terms, for interpretation inevitably involves suspect gestures of narcissistic projection and identification, whether positive or reactively negative. Thus the closest thing to certainty the reader can attain, it would seem, is a recognition of the desire that the poem mean one thing and not another, or one thing and not many, or many things and not one—in short, that it be faithful to something. At the same time, such recognitions do change the reader, precisely because the reader's knowledge now includes recognition of its own contingency, and of poetry's refusal to consummate our desires with the certainty of an embrace.

That such knowledge would not be productive or useful only recalls, of course, Wilde's proposition that all art is quite useless. Auden makes much the same point in calling art an *acte gratuit,* and its gratuity is where the political and the sexual political meet in his later thinking. In a world run by "Managers," he argues in "The Poet & The City," the political value of art is solely that it does not serve The City, that it is a form of unproductive play reminding Management that "*Homo Laborans* is also *Homo Ludens*" (*DH* 88). However enlightened it may be, narcissism is not a useful encounter, for it leads nowhere (which is perhaps another way of saying that the hermeneutical circle is endless). As in sex, so in art, the value of productivity entails a puritanical view of desire. But to posit the useless value of uselessness is to allow for desire as fruitless pleasure, and poetry as an endlessly fluid entertaining of unfixed identities and identifications.

We are accustomed to tracing the ancestry of such notions and their utopian hopes to Paris in 1968 and to writers like Roland Barthes (see Beaver 119). But the queer overtones of such an aesthetic—or better yet, such an aestheticist ethic—seem to me distilled with brilliant intricacy in Auden's 1939 sonnet "Our Bias":

> The hour-glass whispers to the lion's roar,
> The clock-towers tell the gardens day and night
> How many errors Time has patience for,
> How wrong they are in always being right.
>
> Yet Time, however loud its chimes or deep,
> However fast its falling torrent flows,
> Has never put one lion off his leap
> Nor shaken the assurance of the rose.
>
> For they, it seems, care only for success:
> While we choose words according to their sound
> And judge a problem by its awkwardness;
>
> And Time with us was always popular.
> When have we not preferred some going round
> To going straight to where we are?   (CP 277)

Like "Our Hunting Fathers" and many other Auden poems, this sonnet is built on a contrast between human self-consciousness and natural instinct. The emblematic hour-glass and clock-tower also convey one of his other pet ideas, that only humans perceive time and keep track of it. But as Julian Patrick has noted in a subtle reading of this poem, Auden's distinctions rely on deceptive pronouns: in line four, "they"—those who are so "wrong . . . in always being right"—can refer to human time-pieces or to lion and rose, who are unconscious of time (293–94). What does it mean, in either case, to "be right"? One might respond that to be right in the way of the natural world is "wrong" for us, and vice versa. But such a paradox depends on identifying "us" as a coherent, self-identical unity, and the poem at every turn works against such a move. The blessed unity of being we ascribe to lion and rose, after all, is something we posit but cannot know, in any sense of "know": it is a coherence only projected from a condition of its felt absence in us.

As the sonnet continues, "we" are further defined in ways that beg the question of whether nature or humans are "wrong" in "always being right." If nature is wrong, it seems, that is because it is never capable of "error" anyway—of wandering from those ends that define it—attack (for the lion) and blossom (for the rose). If human time-pieces are "wrong," that is because the very notion of telling time, correctly or not, entails an arbitrary, righteous parsing of a continuum into artificial intervals. But then, who are "we," anyway? The third stanza makes explicit another definition, implicit in the images of lion and rose as being unself-conscious in their gestures of aggression and desire: because "we choose words according to their sound," we are language-users. Lion and rose "care only for success" (or so "it seems")—that is, the meaning of their expression is simply what they desire, be it food or reproduction. But "we" are concerned with manner of expression and "judge a problem by its awkwardness": its aesthetic "feel," so to speak, its elegance or crudity rather than its solution. (We don't just want things: we want them and want to get them in certain ways.) By the final stanza, "we" seem to be poets. Poets are, of course, obsessed with time and timing, and the final question offers a definition of poetry that is parabolic in every sense: "When have we not preferred some going round / To going straight to where we are?"

The tropes of bias in this poem include, of course, manifold sexual overtones as well. The most obvious one involves the distinction between "going round" and "going straight." But the distinction between being "wrong" and "being right" has a similar semantic charge, suggesting as it does an opposition between being natural and being artificial. So, for that matter, do Auden's seemingly transparent but decidedly Shakespearean images of lion and rose, as well as his association of desire with bias. The rose needs little commentary, I suspect, but the lion alludes to Shakespeare's sonnet 19: "Devouring time, blunt thou the lion's paw" (see Patrick 293). The association of same-sex desire with bias informs not only sonnet 121, with its line "I may be straight, though they themselves be bevel," but also sonnet 20, notoriously concerned with the natural artifice of the young man's beauty:

"A woman's face, with nature's own hand painted, / Hast thou, the master-mistress of my passion."[5]

To treat the sexual overtones of this sonnet as codes is to read it as a poem whose oblique message involves a paradox of homosexual desire and identity: "we" are queer, for it is "our bias" not to go "straight." Thus to deviate from the sexually "right," i.e. to be "wrong," is in fact "right," since to be human at all is to be "wrong." Such a reading is, in the terms of this poem, by definition a *biased* reading, reflective of how we want to see ourselves when we read "we." Any reading would be equally biased, however. To read it in terms of Auden's 1930s theory of parable is to see it as an account of deviance to be interpreted in particular ways according to the reader's own needs: it is about human nature, or about poetry, or about being queer, depending on how the reader identifies words and what the reader wishes to conclude from them. What seems impossible—tautological—is a universalizing reading that, having recognized the sexual and other overtones that evoke alternative readings, fails to acknowledge its own contingency. Such a reading would be no more or less biased than others, but blindly so. The only universal truth the poem tells is a self-contradictory one: that "we" are all biased—deviant, perverted, queer.

A universalizing reading of "Our Bias," in other words, would be one of countless readings rendered according to what we "prefer": its meaning depends on how we identify Auden and thus ourselves through his words—an inevitably circular but playfully roundabout process. To the extent that this is an innocent game in which differences are reconciled in one plural pronoun—"we"—this process would, as Auden writes in "The Virgin & The Dynamo," bear witness to "Utopia" or "Paradise" or "the forgiveness of sins" (*DH* 71). Such a feeling might, in sexual-political terms, be described as the sense that the reader, however self-identified, has identified with Auden as a queer poet, or that the differences do not matter.

At the same time, "Our Bias" also illustrates the willful aesthetic contrivance that sustains such feelings of paradisal or utopian reconciliation of difference. The "effect [of beauty] is evil," as Auden has written, "to the degree that beauty is taken, not as analogous to, but [as] identical with goodness . . . and the conclusion drawn that, since all is well in the work of art, all is well in history. But all is not well there" (71). So it is fitting that "Our Bias" is fashioned to be, metrically speaking, imperfect. "When have we not preferred some going round / To going straight to where we are?" Not only does Auden end with a question, the last line has only four feet (see Patrick 296). The finished poem, its contradictions resolved, does not exist in this world, in the measured time of history or of poetry. Here and now, we do not "go straight to where we are" but "choose" artificial modes of expression that beg questions at every turn. The answer to Auden's final question, and the end of the poem, are left for us to supply. And that answer depends on how we prefer to go about identifying ourselves.

NOTES

INTRODUCTION

1. On these events, see Carpenter, *Auden* 368–70, and Davenport-Hines 275–76.

2. Prominent among these are gay or lesbian poets for whom Auden was a powerful example: John Ashbery, Elizabeth Bishop, Robert Duncan, Allen Ginsberg, Thom Gunn, Richard Howard, James Merrill, Frank O'Hara, Adrienne Rich, James Schuyler. On Auden's influence on later American poets, see Wasley; Spiegelman 3–24.

3. Although Auden freely acknowledged the influence of *The Waste Land* (1922) on his early work and was polite toward Eliot in print, his politics remained substantially to the left of Eliot's, even after the 1930s. On differences between Auden and Eliot, theological and otherwise, see Mendelson, *Later* 150, 301–2. In ascribing to Auden a "poetics of indeterminacy," I adopt Perloff's term but disagree with the view that he was a Baudelairean Symbolist in the Eliot line, rather than an inheritor of Rimbaud (see Perloff 23–28). Even so, works like James Merrill's *The Changing Light at Sandover* (1980) suggest that Auden also mediates the Symbolist tradition for later gay poets.

4. For the text of Auden's reply, which neither confirms nor denies his homosexuality, see Woods 247.

5. For further examples of Auden's views on the relation of the artist's life to his or her work, see "Making, Knowing and Judging" (*DH* 49); "A Poet of the Actual" (*FA* 262); "An Improbable Life" (302–3); and "One of the Family" (368).

6. See Davenport-Hines 78–80 on Auden's reading as an undergraduate of Richards's work, including *Science and Poetry*, where Richards develops his term "pseudo-statement."

7. See "Papa Was a Wise Old Sly-Boots," *FA* 450–58.

8. 135–36. This essay went, to my knowledge, uncited by any Auden critic until Firchow's important 1977 study of *The Orators* (see Firchow 268). See also Woods (175–80) for comments on Southworth's essay. Woods also cites Clive James's perceptive and moving 1973 memorial essay on Auden in *Commentary*.

9. I am indebted for this term to Thomas E. Yingling's study of Hart Crane (see 1–23, 59–60).

10. In his review of *Look, Stranger!* (1936), Leavis suggested that Auden's association with so many writers who shared a public school background caused harm to "serious critical standards" (Haffenden 225). Q. D. Leavis saw a homosexual conspiracy at work in literary politics:

> We who are in the habit of asking how such evidently unqualified reviewers as fill the literary weeklies ever got into the profession need ask no longer. They turn out to have been "the most fashionable boy in the school," or to have had a feline charm or a sensual mouth and long eye-lashes. . . . It is no use looking for growth or development or any addition to literature in such an adolescent hot-house.

This passage is quoted in Valentine Cunningham's 1988 *British Writers of the Thirties* (149–50). While this encyclopedic study offers valuable evidence of homosexuality's role in the writing and the literary politics of the decade, it also recapitulates the attitude of commentators like the Leavises in sentences like the following: "Much of the period's writing about the proletariat is vitiated by the bourgeois bugger's specialist regard" (150).

11. Influential arguments for the historical and critical value of this methodology may be found in Jerome J. McGann's work; see especially "The Monks and the Giants: Textual and Bibliographical Studies and the Interpretation of Literary Works" (*Beauty* 69–89) and "Shall These Bones Live?" (90–110).

12. Unless otherwise indicated, dates following book titles refer to year of first publication, while dates for poems and other works refer to year or years of composition.

13. For an outline of the development of queer theory and its revisionary aims, see Jagose 72–93. An influential early articulation of the philosophical and social motivations of queer theory may be found in de Lauretis.

14. For Foucault's comments on the contrary effects of the medicalization of homosexuality, see *History* 1, 53–73.

15. See Bersani, "Is" and *Homos* 48–52.

16. Wayne Koestenbaum's work on the homoerotics of literary collabora-

tion (*Double Talk*) and on opera and gay culture (*The Queen's Throat*) suggests that much may be written on Auden in this regard, since nearly all of his plays and operas are collaborative efforts—with Isherwood on the plays and with Kallman (and various composers) on the libretti.

17. For an important analysis of Auden's concerns with citizenship and exile (both sexual and cultural) in *For the Time Being* and *The Age of Anxiety,* see Caserio.

I. "BUT WHO WOULD GET IT?": SEXUAL POLITICS AND COTERIE POETRY

1. While few of these writers (except for Byron and Wilde) were as self-consciously concerned with secrecy and coding as Auden, they foreshadow many of his techniques of coding. For important analyses of coding in these writers, see Bennett, Collecott, Crompton, Dowling, Moon, Martha Nell Smith, and Stimpson, "Mind" and "Somagrams."

2. For analogous treatments of Byron that have helped shape my argument, see McGann, "Byron" and "Hero." On Wilde, see Christopher Craft.

3. For an outline of the philosophical and cultural implications of the phrase, see Sedgwick, *Epistemology* 1–12.

4. *Bringing* 18. In *Early Auden,* Mendelson argues that the "central subject" of Auden's early poems is "their own failure to be part of any larger interpretive frame" (10). While this view points up the self-referential quality of Auden's writing, it sidesteps questions about the material or social conditions that provoked such a mode of poetry. In critiquing Stimpson's encodement arguments about Stein's writing, Roof points up the dangers of "assum[ing] a very certain and monolithic lesbian identity that correlates with the lesbian meaning of the text" and thus "inadvertently limiting textual interplay and contradiction in favor of a correct translation" (165). My argument requires neither an essentialist identity for Auden (or "the homosexual") nor unitary meanings for his encoded poems. Rather, the "textual interplay" of his work attests to the fluidity of identity under the pressures of the closet, and the interfusion of sexual politics with a variety of other concerns in his writing.

5. For a more developed consideration of the problem of the hermeneutical circle in queer literary-historical study, see the "Afterword."

6. See Isherwood, *Christopher* 125–27.

7. Since Auden's early poems often portray an incompatibility between homosexual desire and Romantic Nature, the Wordsworthian associations of the Wye may further ironize Paul's erotic failure with his friend Marston. See part III of this chapter.

8. On the French and German connections for English homosexuals in the 1920s, see Annan 116–17. Isherwood lived for a time in Berlin at Hirschfeld's scientific and political Institut für Sexual-Wissenschaft. See *Christopher* 14–21 for Isherwood's account, and Page 42–44.

9. It could be argued that Germany represented a displaced Mediterranean homoeroticism for Auden et al. In his study of the homosexual cult of the Mediterranean, Aldrich sees the pseudoclassical homoerotic photography of Wilhelm von Gloeden, dating back to the 1880s, as the ancestor of the "Bauhaus-like simplicity" of Herbert List, who began work in the 1920s (158). Isherwood and Spender knew List, and he is portrayed as the photographer Joachim in *The Temple*, whose title alludes to Paul's impression of one of Joachim's photos of a nude male torso (69). Beginning in 1948, when Auden began visiting Ischia, his work invoked a more direct Mediterranean homoeroticism in poems like "In Praise of Limestone" and "Good-Bye to the Mezzogiorno."

10. On the relations between sexual politics and the politics of left and right in the Auden group and Oxford more generally, see David 99–105.

11. See "The German Auden: Six Early Poems," trans. David Constantine, in Auden, *Map* 1–15.

12. For the 1946 publication of "The Railway Accident," Upward adopted the name "Allen Chalmers," from Isherwood's *Lions and Shadows*. There, Auden is called "Bernard Weston" and Spender "Stephen Savage." In *The Last of Mr. Norris*, the narrator is "William Bradshaw," Isherwood's two middle names.

13. Auden revisited this poetic landscape periodically in later years, most importantly in "The Prophets" (1939) and "Amor Loci" (1965), both of which draw out the erotic forces at work in this fantasy world (see chapter 5). See also Part III of "New Year Letter" (1941) and "In Praise of Limestone" (1948), both discussed in chapter 6.

14. For a brief history of Mortmere, see Bucknell's introduction to Isherwood and Upward, *Mortmere Stories* 9–21. Replogle offers a useful overview of the figurative and thematic elements of Mortmere in Auden's poetry and other works by Isherwood, Spender, C. Day-Lewis, and Rex Warner (16–30).

15. Mizejewski analyzes the blankness of "Chris," the narrator of "Sally Bowles" and the rest of *Goodbye to Berlin*, in terms of male fear of female sexuality (37–84). For an extended study of Isherwood's reticences and obliquities about sex in his Berlin fiction, see Page 181–204.

16. See Carpenter, *Auden* 119. Auden claimed that the original version of the story (still unpublished) suffered from Upward's ignorance, as a heterosexual, of homosexual experience.

17. *EA* 25. Aside from adding the title, Auden's only other revisions involved punctuation and minor changes in wording for the 1966 *Collected Shorter Poems, 1927–1957*. In line four, "seduced with the old tricks" was revised

to "seduced by," and line fourteen became "Parting easily two that were never joined" (*CP* 32).

18. For details on the production of *Poems* (1928), see Carpenter, *Auden* 82–83; Bloomfield, "First"; Tolley, "Printing"; Spender's foreword to Auden, *Poems* (1928); and *J* lxi–lxiv.

19. Spears uses it solely to illuminate Auden's early style and form (19–31). Relegating it to a footnote, Mendelson calls it a "pamphlet" (*Early* 32). For a brief reference to this poem in the context of Mitchell's *Another Country*, see Morris 15.

20. I rely here generally on Carpenter's account of Auden's time at Oxford, *Auden* 42–84. On Auden and McElwee, see esp. 68–69; on Carritt, see 75–79.

21. Mendelson, *Early* 36; emphasis in original. Carpenter connects the poem to Auden's relationship with Carritt, who is alluded to in other poems from late 1927, but he urges a similar reading: "If Auden's unsatisfied love for Carritt was the immediate cause of some of these poems, it was no more than a pretext for them" (*Auden* 77). Davenport-Hines reads the poem in terms of adolescent warfare against the adult world (84–85).

22. See Spears 26; Replogle 23; Callan 51. Mendelson emphasizes the psychic (*Early* 36); Fuller reads the poem in terms of undefined sexual desire (15).

23. In "Letter to Lord Byron" (1936) and "The Cave of Nakedness" (1963), Auden employs "greens" as a noun derived from the Scots dialect verb "to green," meaning "to desire intensely" (Mendelson, *Later* 463).

24. "I chose this lean country," discussed below, refers to several friends of Auden, including Isherwood (*EA* 439).

25. "Pass" is a Middle English and Renaissance form for "pace" or "passus": "A passage (in a narrative or writing); a canto of a poem, a chapter, section, or division of a book" (*OED* I.2).

26. For an extended study of Auden's early poetic development, see Bucknell's introduction to *J*; on Wordsworthian Nature in Auden's juvenilia, see also Mackinnon 49–51.

27. For the classic study of the Greater Romantic Lyric, see Abrams. Although Auden would not, of course, have been familiar with Abrams's term, he certainly understood the psychological, formal, and ideological workings of the Greater Romantic Lyric, as can be seen in his critiques of Wordsworthian Nature in his 1929 Berlin journal (*EA* 298), discussed in detail in chapter 2.

28. *J* 127–28. See also "The Engine House" (72). For Auden's own comments on his youthful infatuation with such machinery, see "Making, Knowing and Judging" (*DH* 34).

29. *EA* 440. This text incorporates Auden's autograph changes in Spender's copy of the 1928 *Poems*. The typeset text concludes with verses less explicitly sexual:

Talked feverishly to one
Professional listener
I know old boy, I know,
And reached his hand for mine.

(*Poems* 10)

30. *EA* 28. The ellipsis marks lines unchanged from the first stanza of "I chose this lean country."

31. Riffaterre outlines the concept in *Semiotics of Poetry*. See Collecott 104.

32. See Mendelson, *Early* 33; Boly, *Reading* 87.

33. Auden's suppression of the poem for more than thirty years may indicate a sense of this game's diminishing returns. Apart from a printing in *Cambridge Left*, Summer 1933, under the ironic title "Interview," the poem was unpublished until his 1966 *Collected Shorter Poems, 1928–1957*.

2. "THE QUESTION IS WHAT DO WE MEAN BY SEX": DIAGNOSIS AND DISORDER

1. Quoted Carpenter, *Auden* 96. Parts of the 1929 Berlin journal are quoted in Carpenter and Mendelson, and several entries are printed in *EA*. Except as noted, quotations are from unpublished portions of the journal, located in the Berg Collection, at the New York Public Library.

2. On Auden's life with Layard, see Carpenter, *Auden* 99–102; Gardiner 9–12.

3. See Isherwood, *Lions* 238–42; "Some Notes" 20–21; Mendelson, *Early* 55–57; Carpenter, *Auden* 86–88.

4. Mendelson's remarks make it hard to separate Auden's attitudes from his critic's. Auden "amused himself by *posing* as an example" of the Pure-in-Heart but privately "*knew* himself to be the opposite." He "analyzed his homosexuality as an inner disorder whose cure *he could never hope* to find," and "His sexuality *had nothing to do with* the real impulses whose release, in Lane's view, produced happiness and virtue" (*Early* 59; my emphasis).

5. See Groddeck 130–35 for a summary of his ideas about disease as the expression of "the It."

6. For Freud's classic connection of homosexuality with narcissism, see "On Narcissism," *SE* 14, 88. Rieff offers a valuable comparison of Freud and Lawrence (189–231).

7. Presumably, a poetry of the body's "community thinking" once existed as what Schiller called "naïve" art, but a modern poet could no more write such poetry than Wordsworth could. In *The Orators,* Auden locates homoerotic "community thinking" in fascistic rhetoric. See chapter 3.

8. For further doubts about how fully Auden believed in this art of self-consciousness, see Mendelson, *Early* 66–67.

9. Auden may have been influenced by a passage in Gide's *Si le grain ne meurt:*

> Exotic beauty can best be compared to the Queen of Sheba, who came to Solomon "to prove him with hard questions." There is nothing for it. Some people fall in love with what is like them; others with what is different. I am among the latter.
>
> (273)

Of course, Auden's point is not, "There is nothing for it."

10. Auden's earliest use of the coded trope of left-handedness occurs in his undergraduate poetry. See "Narcissus" (*J* 185–86). He may have read of the sexual implications of left and right in *The Interpretation of Dreams* (*SE* 5, 357–58).

11. Quoted Mendelson, *Early* 40, except for the unpublished passage "Death [is] that which precedes life."

12. The sense of repetition in this "backward love" recalls the neurotic's "compulsion to repeat," the clinical problem Freud sought to solve with the death instinct in *Beyond the Pleasure Principle* (see *SE* 18, 18–19).

13. The sources in Freud for this model are too numerous to know which Auden read, but many had been translated by the late 1920s. See "Three Essays on Sexuality" (1905), *SE* 7, 231–37; "Five Lectures on Psychoanalysis" (1910), *SE* 11, 43–46; "Group Psychology and the Analysis of the Ego" (1921), *SE* 18, 108–9.

14. Quoted Mendelson, *Early* 59. The previous two entries are unpublished.

15. In his interest in psychoanalysis, a discourse that served the cause of bourgeois health, Auden may reflect an emerging cultural sense of middle-class gay identity. In *Christopher and His Kind,* Isherwood emphasizes his relations with his own mother. By contrast, the homosexual coterie of Brian Howard and Harold Acton echoed Wilde's aristocratic dandyism; they had little interest in psychoanalysis or political ideals of liberation. Of course, much of Auden's aesthetic theory has resemblances to Wilde's. But the sheer anxiety about desire in early Auden, and the way he figures authority as parental, suggest he reflects an early stage in the fusion of one type of modern, bourgeois, Anglo-American gay male identity. See chapter 3, which reads *Paid on Both Sides* as partly a coded parable about coming out to family.

16. Although degeneration theory in Victorian culture has been much studied, the only extended application of such work to later periods is found in Mosse. English wartime rhetoric—when Auden was in school—played a great

deal on prejudices about German racial inferiority and fears about the decline of the English race. A 1918 revival of Wilde's *Salome* in London was attacked at a time of hysteria about the dangers sexual deviants presented for England at war. See Hynes, *War* 14–17, 225–29; Kettle.

17. On Freud's relation to degeneration theory, see Greenberg 423–24; Sulloway 318; Gilman, "Sexology, Psychoanalysis, and Degeneration: From a Theory of Race to a Race of Theory," Chamberlin and Gilman 72–96. The concept of degeneration was not consistently or clearly defined by theorists. For overviews, see Chamberlin and Gilman, "Degeneration: An Introduction," ix–xiv; Nancy Stepan, "Biological Degeneration: Races and Proper Places," Chamberlin and Gilman 97–120.

18. On sexology and Victorian anxieties about the decline of the state, see Weeks 81–93, 105–8.

19. Unpublished entry. A later unpublished entry, however—"The segregation of maleness and femaleness"—glosses "Buggery" as "an attempt to complete oneself" by taking "the female form, because [sensual] feelings have been called feminine." Auden seems to have held his theory of sex as sympathetic magic virtually to the end of his life, using it in his 1969 review of Ackerley's *My Father and Myself* (see "Papa was a Wise Old Sly-Boots," *FA* 453).

20. Isherwood, *Lions* 57–58. For a broader argument about the meaning of the War for the Auden group, see Hynes, *Auden* chapter 1.

21. On these terms, see Mendelson, *Early* 135–36. Auden uses them in a 1934 review of Liddell Hart's biography of T. E. Lawrence (see *P* 61–62).

22. Stockinger discusses this view in relation to both the French Revolution and Stalin's reinstatement of the pre-1917 sodomy laws abolished by Lenin. See "Homosexuality and the French Enlightenment," Stambolian 174–75.

23. Auden's tone here recalls Lawrence's *Fantasia:*

> There will *have* to come an end. Every race which has become self-conscious and idea-bound in the past has perished. And then it has all started afresh, in a different way, with another race. . . . Our day is pretty short, and closing fast. We can pass, and another race can follow later.
>
> (115)

24. Buell 66–67. He critiques Jarrell's view that Auden assumes the *enfant terrible* role unconsciously, in reaction to his guilt in rebelling against Authority. See Jarrell, "Freud" 162–69.

25. Another entry runs: "Freud says it is better to recollect infantile experience than to repeat this [experience]. This is wrong. Recollection does nothing. If the fool would persist in his folly he would become wise" (Mendelson, *Early* 50).

26. My analysis of "1929" here and below is much indebted to Mendelson's treatment of the poem in *Early* 69–79.

27. See Nunokawa, *"In Memoriam"* and "All."

3. "HAVE YOU HEARD THIS ONE?": QUEER REVOLUTION IN *PAID ON BOTH SIDES* and *THE ORATORS*

1. The quotation is from Alain Robbe-Grillet, "Order and Disorder in Film and Fiction," Beaver 115.

2. For a concise explanation of the antidefinitional agenda of queer theory, see de Lauretis iii-v; see also Warner xxvi-xxviii. Morton offers an important materialist critique of queer theory's postmodernist assumptions in *Material* (273–76) and "Politics"; see also Bersani, *Homos* 1–6.

3. For a more detailed analysis of the reception of *The Orators*, see part III of this chapter.

4. For the composition history of *Paid on Both Sides*, see *PDW* 525–27.

5. See Mendelson, *Early* 54. Auden wrote to his friend David Ayerst that Spa was "quite an amusing place, full of Lesbians weighing 110 kilos"; he also said, "I find I am quite ambidextrous now," referring in code to his new bisexuality (Carpenter, *Auden* 82).

6. Mendelson, *Early* 52. In fact, Freud does entertain this notion but discounts it for lack of any external "environment" by which to define "normality" for a society. See *Civilization and Its Discontents, SE* 21, 144, and *The Future of an Illusion, SE* 21, 43.

7. See editorial note on "Preliminary Statement" (*PDW* 459) for comments on the manuscript and possible links to *The Enemies of a Bishop*, an abortive collaboration with Isherwood.

8. *SE* 12, 63 (emphasis in original). Also relevant to John's hatred is Freud's claim that "paranoics *endeavor to protect themselves against any . . . sexualization of their social instinctual cathexes*" (62; emphasis in original).

9. Groddeck, whose work influenced Layard, argued that physical disorders are the purposive language of the "It," a childish force controlling our bodies and behaviors (14–15). Diseases will disappear once recognized as manifesting immature desires of the It. To the It, he argues, the tooth is a child, and a mother's toothache expresses an unconscious desire to abort a fetus (see 27–28). In a letter to William McElwee dating from the month he completed the second version of *Paid on Both Sides*, Auden glossed homosexuality as an identification with the mother reflecting "the wish to have a child" (Mendelson, *Early* 59). Thus, the tooth extraction in the dream might be read as either a birth or the extraction of the homosexual wish to bear a child. In *The Interpretation of Dreams*, however, Freud interprets "dreams 'with a dental

stimulus' " in "a young man with strong homosexual leanings" as expressing fantasies of mutual masturbation (*SE* 5, 385, 387). Thus one could read the tooth extraction in the dream not so much as a cure of homosexuality but as a symbolic expression of a homosexual act or of identification with the mother as child-bearer.

10. See Bucknell's speculations on the poem's links to Emile Coué's therapeutic techniques of autosuggestion, which Auden may have been acquainted with (*J* 247).

11. Given Auden's coded use of left and right elsewhere, it is possible that he is picturing bisexuality as a viable route for himself and John Nower (which would imply that the dream-cure was ineffective).

12. See *Jokes and Their Relation to the Unconscious, SE* 8, 125.

13. All except the comment about Proust's Man-Woman are unpublished entries.

14. John Hayward (Haffenden 115).

15. Graham Greene wrote in a 1932 review, "The subject of this book is political, though it is hard to tell whether the author's sympathies are Communist or Fascist" (Haffenden 115). For a critique of *The Orators* as fascist, see Tolley 99–101.

16. See, for example, Firchow 267–69; Mendelson, *Early* 110–11; Spears 51; Woods 173.

17. On the homosexual as the hybrid that contradicts the binary logic of Judeo-Christian moral systems, see Beaver 111.

18. For a study of *The Orators* in relation to Auden's work as a schoolmaster, see Stan Smith, "Loyalty."

19. The movement combines Freud's two main examples in *Group Psychology* of libidinally based groups—the Church and the army. See *SE* 18, 93–99.

20. *EA* 68–69. This passage adapts lines from a lyric in Auden's 1928 *Poems,* "Because sap fell away," which tropes the failure of homosexual desire as a loss on the playing field (*EA* 441). Cf. Freud on those pursuing exclusive sexual bonds: "The rejection of the group's influence is expressed in . . . a sense of shame" (*Group Psychology, SE* 18, 140).

21. In *The Poetics of Indeterminacy,* Perloff quotes Auden's introduction to *Some Trees* in order to distinguish Ashbery's "indeterminacy" from the later Auden's Eliotic Symbolist poetics of resolution (249–50). But the stylistic affinities between Rimbaud, the early Auden, and Ashbery suggest otherwise. As suggested in the "Introduction," one can draw a genealogy of gay poetic indeterminacy from Rimbaud through Auden to Ashbery and Frank O'Hara. For the influence of *The Orators* on O'Hara, see Gooch 365, 400; on Ashbery's "Europe," see Shoptaw 62.

22. In his 1933 review of *The Orators,* Parkes wrote: "[It] has obvious signs

of immaturity. . . . There are passages which need a drastic pruning and others which show a schoolboyish crudity" (Haffenden 124).

23. My reading of the journal is much indebted to Firchow's essay, as well as to Mendelson's treatment in *Early Auden*. See also Layard's essays on the Bwili, "Malekula" and "Shamanism."

24. The Airman refers periodically to his lover, E; in the 1932 edition E is female, while in later editions E is male.

25. For the first view, see Replogle 105–6, Beach 84–92; on Auden's political uncertainty, see Mendelson, *Early* 111.

4. "WHAT WE SEE DEPENDS ON WHO'S OBSERVING": POLITICS AND AUTHORITY IN THE 1930S

1. *EA* 237. These lines combine allusion to Verlaine's "Art Poétique" and to Auden's personal life: Isherwood recalls a radiator bursting in the Brussels hotel room where Auden was writing the poem (*Christopher* 329). In "New Year Letter" (1940), Auden imagines Rimbaud on a tribunal of poetic conscience: "The adolescent with red hands, / Skilful, intolerant and quick, / Who strangled an old rhetoric" (*CP* 204).

2. "Visions of Violence: Rimbaud and Verlaine," in Stambolian, 235; emphasis in original.

3. Auden uses the word "declination"—an allusion to Rimbaud's "Adieu"—for the Airman's end in a 1932 letter to Henry Bamford Parkes; see Mendelson, *Early* 110.

4. In 1965 Auden said of his decision to emigrate: "I felt the situation for me in England was becoming impossible. I couldn't grow up. English life is for me a family life, and I love my family but I don't want to live with them" (Carpenter, *Auden* 243). Isherwood recalls telling Auden on the boat to the United States, " 'You know, it just doesn't mean anything to me any more—the Popular Front, the party line, the anti-Fascist struggle. . . . I simply can't swallow another mouthful.' To which Wystan answered, 'Neither can I' " (*Christopher* 333).

5. For useful comments on Auden's attitudes toward communism in the 1930s, see Mendelson, *Early* 137–38, 305–8; see also Cunningham 221–24. Hynes's *The Auden Generation* provides a valuable overview of how the "thirties myth"—and Auden's role in it—was constructed (378–94).

6. Most critics refer to this volume by its Faber title, which was not chosen by Auden (see Carpenter, *Auden* 204). His title for the Random House edition (1937)—*On This Island*—more clearly shows a preoccupation with isolation and identification.

7. *EA* 156. The lesson about escapism prefigures not only "September 1, 1939" but "Pleasure Island," Auden's 1948 ode to Fire Island, and "In Praise of Limestone," about Ischia. Hecht's comments (53) about the "unembarrassed fantasy" element of this stanza seem belied by Auden's subsequent dismissal of "every flabby fancy."

8. The fourth poem Auden contributed to *New Country*, "A Happy New Year," is only indirectly about politics. Its first part—a dream vision modeled on *Piers Plowman*—portrays "blurring images / Of the dingy difficult life of our generation" (*EA* 451); Auden never reprinted it. The second, "Now from my window-sill I watch the night," describes the "Lords of Limit" to whose "discipline the heart / Submits when we have fallen apart / Into the isolated personal life" (116).

9. *EA* 116. The *New Country* text begins with lines in which the rhythm and alliteration of Whitman and Hopkins convey a kind of bodily arousal at nature's own leftist movement:

> Me, March, you do with your movements master and rock
> With wing-whirl, whale-wallow, silent budding of cell;
> Like a sea-god the communist orator lands at the pier.   (421)

10. The full stanza reads:

> For our hour of unity makes us aware of two worlds:
> That one was revealed to us then in our double shadow,
> Which for the masters of harbours, the colliers, and us,
>> For our calculating star,
>> Where the divided feel
>> Tears in their eyes
>> And time and doctors heal,
>> Eternally sighs.

These lines raise a host of troubling problems. Can an "hour of unity" expose "two worlds" and still be an hour of unity? How can "one" (i.e. "one *world*"?) be "revealed in our double shadow"? Of the "two worlds" we became aware of, which is "That one"? What is the antecedent of "Which"? For an effort to make sense of this stanza, see Mendelson, *Early* 139–40.

11. This confusion arises because to "choose the crooked" might mean to embrace homosexual desire or identity, or to choose a certain method of expressing homosexual desire or identity (which are otherwise not open to choice). The ambiguity does not seem to affect the larger point of the stanza, but it suggests that Auden is still unsure whether the problem is the closet or

homosexuality itself. These convolutions of "choice" foreshadow his later existentialist concern with necessity and freedom, discussed in chapters 5 and 6.

12. Smith makes this point in the symposium on "A Communist to Others" in Auden, *Map* 187. At least as much as Burns, however, Skelton may have been Auden's model.

13. On pronouns, see also Stan Smith's commentary (Auden, *Map* 189–90) and Mick Imlah's (192–93).

14. In *Early Auden*, Mendelson argues that the voice of the poem is not Auden's but that of "a Communist telling Auden what he needs to learn" (143). But it is unclear whether Auden was trying to teach himself something specifically communist or putting a fashionable label on what he needed to learn, whatever its actual content. Stan Smith's earlier comments treat the poem as evidence of Auden's ongoing concern with his insider/outsider status towards the bourgeoisie (see *Auden* 79, *Inviolable* 139); more recently he has stressed its "ideological confusion" and uncertainty about audience (see Auden, *Map* 186–91).

15. Auden, *Map* 185; see also Cunningham 221–24.

16. See Mendelson, *Early* 144; Heard 311.

17. For an informative analysis of the politics and contents of *New Country*, see Hynes, *Auden* 102–15.

18. *EA* 212. *Letters from Iceland*, as Hynes remarks, makes for "a very eccentric travel book indeed" (*Auden* 288). It contains verse and prose in varying degrees of seriousness; maps, charts, and photos by Auden; letters to the dead and the living; extracts from earlier travelers' accounts of Iceland; and a mass of information about Icelandic culture, much of it misconstrued (see *P* 773–74). Among its contents is MacNeice's letter from "Hetty to Nancy," a long narrative of a camping trip in Iceland, written for Isherwood, in which "Maisie Reynolds" delivers herself of Audenesque pronouncements about (among other things) the value of neurosis.

19. Frederic Prokosch, who also had several of Auden's love poems published by Cambridge University Press in the 1930s, was the correspondent in question. On the revelatory effect of Auden's early poems on Prokosch, see Davenport-Hines 149.

20. These lines bear elaboration. As "angels," the Auden group are spoiled, childlike, and effeminate, minions of their sissy-god editor Michael Roberts, who put together the *New Signatures* and *New Country* anthologies, which helped advance the Auden group. They are "bhoyos"—as opposed to real men like MacDiarmid; "yellow"—i.e. "chicken," so not real Red meat; and "twicers"—probably, liars about their "work" as activists ("twicer" is printers' slang for those who claim to work at both typesetting and press).

21. Auden's revisions and eventual rejection of "Spain" focused on the line

that bothered Orwell, but he began changing it before Orwell's essay appeared. For a description of variants in "Spain," see *EA* 424–25; for Auden's comments on these issues, see his "Foreword" to Bloomfield, *Bibliography* (viii). A valuable, sympathetic elucidation of the sexual politics of Auden's reputation may be found in Fenton, "Auden's Enchantment."

22. In his 1966 Byron introduction, Auden cites "political despair among liberal-minded people" as a reason for the popularity of Byron's Childe Harold, "that rebel without a cause" (Byron, *Selected*, xvi); Auden's comments on disappointment with Napoleon among liberals and on the "concentration-camp-like horror" of English mines and factories imply a parallel to the 1930s. On the cynicism and disillusion of *Don Juan*, see McGann, *Beauty* 268–71.

23. *P* 332. Of prep school, Auden states with overt obliquity, "Surnames I must not write—O Reginald, / You at least taught us that which fadeth not," remarking, "Your moral character was all at sea" (330–31). The passage refers to a master who (Carpenter argues) may have been dismissed from St Edmund's for "moral" reasons (*Auden* 17); Auden emended the text in proof to prevent libel (*P* 770). The "friend" who suggested Auden write poetry (332–33) was Robert Medley, who inspired his earliest love poems (780; see Carpenter, *Auden* 28, 30–33).

24. On "cant" as the target of *Don Juan*, see Auden's introduction to Byron, *Selected*, xxiii and McGann, *Beauty* 284.

25. See especially "The Virgin & The Dynamo" (*DH* 70–71) and "The Poet & The City" (82–84).

26. In Hynes's words, parable-art as Auden conceived it "is functional— that is, message-bearing, clarifying, instructive—but it is not didactic. . . . It is moral, not aesthetic, in its primary intention; it offers models of the problem of action (*Auden* 15). The clearest examples of Auden's parable-art in this sense are his plays from the 1930s, which Mendelson treats in *Early Auden* in chapters titled "Parables of Action," and Auden's documentary film work for the G.P.O. For an important analysis of masculinity and homoeroticism in the latter, see Bryant.

27. In this regard, it is important that "Letter to Lord Byron" appeared in *Letters From Iceland*, which presents Iceland as a place where traditional community is as strong as it was in England before the Industrial Revolution, and the disjunction between traditional and modern art is absent. "Letter to Lord Byron" critiques those who would forcibly recover such social uniformity. Elsewhere in *Letters from Iceland*, Auden notes: "The Nazis have a theory that Iceland is the cradle of the Germanic culture. Well, if they want a community like that of the sagas they are welcome to it. I love the sagas, but what a rotten society they describe, a society with only the gangster virtues" (265).

28. In "Epitaph on a Tyrant" (1938), Auden sees dictatorship as a coercive art: "Perfection, of a kind, was what he was after, / And the poetry he invented

was easy to understand." All individuals are absorbed into the expressivist art of the leader: "When he laughed, respectable senators burst with laughter, / And when he cried the little children died in the streets" (*EA* 239).

29. Auden's attribution of these words to Lenin was a mistake; in fact, the phrase comes from a memoir by Lenin's widow, Nadezhda K. Krupskaya (see Jenkins 13–14).

5. "TELL ME THE TRUTH ABOUT LOVE": CONFESSIONAL LYRIC AND LOVER'S DISCOURSE

1. On the Auden-Kallman relationship, see Dorothy Farnan's *Auden in Love* (1982) and Thekla Clark's *Wystan and Chester* (1995). Along with Mendelson's *Later Auden,* see also Jacobs and Caserio.

2. See Britten 1093–95. Besides Britten's various settings of Auden lyrics, they collaborated on three song cycles—*Our Hunting Fathers* (1936), *On This Island* (1938), and *Hymn to St. Cecilia* (1942)—incidental music for *The Ascent of F6* (1937), and the opera *Paul Bunyan* (1940–41).

3. Carpenter, *Britten* 107. Auden was free with advice on how to pick up men, and their efforts seem to have had effect after Britten's mother died in 1937. Donald Mitchell describes this period in his introduction to Britten's letters and diaries (Britten 16–23).

4. Spender, Isherwood, and Peter Pears (Britten's lover) all expressed skepticism, but it is telling that the question of whether Auden and Britten ever slept together seems to have been one they all entertained (see Carpenter, *Britten* 82, 107–8).

5. See, for example, "Quique Amavit," which Auden included in a 1927 letter to W. L. McElwee, with the inscription "To the onlie begetter Mr. W. L." (*J* 181–82).

6. Auden takes the distinction from Dag Hammarskjöld's diary, which he quotes in his essay. His 1964 introduction to Hammarskjöld's *Markings,* he believed, cost him the Nobel Prize (see Carpenter, *Auden* 404–5). In terms with a strong autobiographical and sexual subtext, he suggests that Hammarskjöld had "an exceptionally aggressive superego" and

> an ego weakened by a "thorn in the flesh" which convinces him that he can never hope to experience what, for most people, are the two greatest joys earthly life has to offer, either a passionate devotion returned, or a lifelong happy marriage.

"Consequently," Auden continues, Hammarskjöld had "a narcissistic fascination with himself" (*EA* 442).

7. On the conversation in question, see Robert Craft 256–58. See Fenton, "Auden's Shakespeare," for a thoughtful elucidation of homosexuality and Auden's views on Shakespeare.

8. In conversation with Howard Griffin in the late 1940s, Auden drew a parallel between the Shakespeare-Mr. W. H. relationship, and Socrates and Alcibiades (Griffin 98).

9. Five were published in *New Verse* in 1934. See *EA* 423–24 for textual notes on these poems' orderings. Academic commentary on homosexuality and Shakespeare seems to have been on the rise since the 1920s; in *The Sonnets of William Shakespeare and Henry Wriothesley* (1938), Walter Thomson complained about efforts of "the perverse" to use the sonnets "as a defence of their perversities" (Stallybrass 101). A useful overview of commentary on homosexuality and the *Sonnets* up through the 1930s may be found in Rollings's 1944 *Variorum* edition (232–39).

10. Foucault, *History* I, 63; see Bruce Smith 228–70.

11. Smith's comments (239–45) about orthography in Thorpe's 1609 quarto of the *Sonnets,* and about coterie manuscript culture among Elizabethan gentlemen, suggest a Renaissance prototype for the sociology of insider knowledge and secrecy in early Auden. Cyril Connolly remarked in 1975: "I always felt that the influence of Shakespeare's sonnets . . . was extremely stimulating to the younger poet seeking to revive a convention in which it was possible to celebrate homosexual love" ("Some Memories," Spender, *Tribute* 71).

12. Auden probably was influenced here by A. E. Housman's retelling of the Narcissus myth in poem XV of *A Shropshire Lad,* which begins:

> Look not in my eyes, for fear
> > They mirror true the sight I see,
> And there you find your face too clear
> > And love it and be lost like me.
>
> > > > > (Housman 23)

13. *History* 2, 202; Bruce Smith 257.

14. Richard Lanham's contrast in *The Motives of Eloquence* between "rhetoric" and "seriousness" is suggestive here (111–15). He shows that Shakespeare's insistence on both rhetorical surface and depth intensifies the Petrarchan tension between "a sublime goal and a game procedure" (127). He argues that while the Petrarchism of the sonnets "could . . . find a home" in an actual "[homo]sexual relationship," Shakespeare's vagueness about the relationship with the young man makes things more interesting. This is odd, since Lanham also finds a productive tension between seriousness and rhetoric in *The Symposium,* where sex certainly *is* part of the equation. Auden's sonnets suggest that

consciously homosexual love, far from resolving all tension between rhetoric and seriousness, can exacerbate a crisis that turns on a sense of narcissism as a profound but deeply attractive ethical error.

15. Cancer, in Auden's psychosomatic imaginary, represents a refusal to love, as in "Miss Gee" (*EA* 214–16). Unlike his equation of *caritas* and *eros paidagogos* in "The Good Life," this stanza places homosexuality and Christianity in opposition.

16. See Mendelson, *Early* 225–26. Fuller argues that the choice in this stanza is "a straightforwardly ethical antinomy," and "it should be stressed that 'crooked' and 'straight' here should have no sexual connotations." (170).

17. Tennyson 195. For an analysis of homosexuality in *In Memoriam* as a stage on the way to heterosexuality, see Nunokawa, *"In Memoriam."*

18. Cunningham 150. See also Carpenter, *Auden* 208.

19. Farnan was the earliest commentator to connect the poem with Auden's relationship with Kallman. Christian interest in the mutual suffusion of human and divine love goes back, of course, to the Middle Ages, and as we shall see below, Auden drew parallels with Dante and Beatrice. Even in the modern history of homoeroticism, Auden's conflation of beloved and savior is hardly original, Tennyson's apotheosis of Arthur Hallam in *In Memoriam* being one major precedent.

20. Both Mendelson (*Later* 35) and Carpenter (*Auden* 260) make this point in connection with Auden's letter to Dodds.

21. *P* 438. The reference to Socrates and Alcibiades recalls Auden's quotation from Hölderlin in "Letter to Lord Byron"; see chapter 4, above. My argument about the early poems to Kallman relies on Carpenter, *Auden* 259–63, and Mendelson, *Later* 44–53.

22. *FA* 103. Mendelson discusses this passage in relation to "Ascension Day, 1964," in which Auden, knowing that Kallman was no longer to spend winters in New York with him, "records the end of the vision [of Eros]" (see *Later* 466–68).

23. Auden's 1964 comment in his journal anticipates Wayne Koestenbaum's work in *Double Talk* on the homoerotics of collaboration. Auden writes:

> The marriage of true minds. Between two collaborators, whatever their sex, age, or appearance, there is always an erotic bond. Queers, to whom normal marriage and parenthood are forbidden, are fools if they do not deliberately look for tasks which require collaboration, and the right person with whom to collaborate—again, the sex does not matter. In my own case, collaboration has brought me greater erotic joy—as distinct from sexual pleasure— than any sexual relation I have had.
>
> (Mendelson, *Later* 470–71)

24. See Carpenter, *Auden* 263. Carpenter wonders whether Auden and Kallman literally exchanged vows (313); Davenport-Hines writes that "there seems to have been a proposal, or the exchange of marriage vows" (194). In the absence of evidence, my suspicion is that there were no actual vows—only Auden's poetic attempt to conjure them in "In Sickness and in Health."

25. Mendelson argues that Tristan and Isolde are not homosexual types in this poem (*Later* 154). They need not be *only* that, as the dynamic that Auden describes can certainly obtain in heterosexual relations. But his judgment on their "spirituality" about love suggests he is being critical of a perversion of Greek Love into a puritanical Platonism. Auden cites Tristan and Isolde as homosexual types along with Don Juan in "The Greeks and Us" (*FA* 25); to Ansen he remarked, "Neither extreme, Tristan or Don Giovanni, is compatible with heterosexual love" (Ansen 17). In the context of discussing "In Sickness and in Health," Hecht offers numerous examples of this pairing in Auden's work (178–80); see also Fuller 392.

26. Auden changed the last phrase from "the voluntary way" (*Collected 1945*, 33) to "the ordinary way" for the 1966 *Collected Shorter Poems, 1927–1957* and later editions. The earlier version makes the question of individual agency in fidelity more urgent, but it seems contradictory to ask a higher power to "hold us to the voluntary way." The later version avoids this problem, suggests the rectitude of normality, and implies commonality between heterosexual and homosexual love.

27. Auden's letters suggest the fluid way that his relationship with Kallman informed "The Sea and the Mirror." To Theodore Spencer he wrote that Caliban is "The Prick"; to Isherwood he implied that Ariel and Caliban both embody Kallman: "It's OK to say that Ariel is Chester, but Chester is also Caliban . . . Ariel is Caliban seen in the mirror" (Mendelson, *Later* 231).

28. See Mendelson, *Later* 182–84; Auden's 1941 Christmas letter to Kallman reads every figure of the nativity story in terms of his relationship with Kallman.

29. Auden's use of "theft" in this context recalls the Airman's problem with his hands in *The Orators,* which implies both masturbation and kleptomania; the early Auden also read theft as "that attempt to recover the lost or stolen treasure, love" (*P* 12). Mendelson argues that "in his darkest imaginings," Auden saw his homosexuality as a crime that was his own punishment, "through a Dantesque *contrapasso* of the original act," for having "caused" his mother's miscarriage before he was conceived (*Later* 220). Auden's 1944 review of *Either/Or* focuses on theft as viewed according to Kierkegaard's stages of the aesthetic, ethical, and religious ("Preface" 683–84); Jacobs argues that Auden was trying here to make sense of his love for Kallman (85–86).

30. *CP* 256. On the uniqueness of beautiful faces, see Auden's comments in

"The Protestant Mystics" (*FA* 65–66) and "Dichtung und Wahrheit" XXVIII (*CP* 657).

31. See, for instance, Fuller 424, Mendelson, *Later* 367–68.

32. *DH* 69. Auden consistently makes the point that in the historical world, however, the reconciliation of multiplicity and individuality comes about only through totalitarianism. See "Squares and Oblongs" (178–79) and the corresponding passage in "The Poet & The City" (*DH* 84–85).

33. See Mendelson, *Later* 433 for details on these events.

6. "JUST WHAT APPEARANCES HE SAVES": GOD AND THE UNSPEAKABLE

1. *Double* [3]. Auden apparently found the Montaigne passage in Charles Williams's *Descent of the Dove* (see Fuller 318). On Williams's role in Auden's religious thinking, see Jacobs 82–83, 142–43n.

2. See Mendelson, *Later* 148–204, and Jacobs 73–95.

3. The most important work in queer studies to explore Augustine's role in theorizing evil as perversion is Dollimore's *Sexual Dissidence;* see esp. 131–47.

4. Almost every book-length analysis of Auden might be cited here, and many shorter essays. Influential critiques of the later Auden may be found in Beach and in Jarrell, "Freud"; positive critical treatments include Johnson and Replogle. More recent defenses of the later Auden include Lucy McDiarmid's *Auden's Apologies for Poetry* (1990) and Jacobs (1998). Stan Smith's *W. H. Auden* (1985) uses poststructuralist approaches to argue against distinctions between earlier and later Auden.

5. See Replogle 50–57. As Replogle notes (52), Auden himself aligned Kierkegaard with "what is most valuable in Marx and Freud" in his 1944 "Preface to Kierkegaard" ("Preface" 683).

6. For earlier versions of this "story," see the discussion of "Letter to Lord Byron" in part III of chapter 4, and Auden's introduction to *The Oxford Book of Light Verse.*

7. See the sonnet "A. E. Housman" (*EA* 238) and the review essay "Jehovah Housman and Satan Housman" (*P* 437–39). For a reading of Auden that explores this same tension, see Clive James's essay in *Commentary.*

8. Along with the mathematical meaning of "vectors" may be the suggestion of phallic erection and, perhaps less plausibly, the epidemiological usage for routes of infection.

9. These issues form the nub of Auden's analysis of Romanticism near the end of Part II of "New Year Letter":

> O how the devil who controls
> The moral asymmetric souls,
> The either-ors, the mongrel halves
> Who find truth in a mirror, laughs.

(CP 220)

In a note to these lines from the poem's first printing in *The Double Man* (1941), Auden glosses "The either-ors, the mongrel halves" as "the impatient romantics" (*Double* 115). He then defines Romanticism as "Unawareness of the dialectic." Romantics narcissistically "find truth in a mirror." The "lazy romantic," Auden continues, "is too woolly-minded to recognize a paradox when he meets one"; the "impatient romantic sees more clearly, but sees only one side of the paradox; the other he ignores or denies." But while "the Devil" encourages Romanticism, he is also, Auden writes, "the father of Poetry" rightly understood, "for poetry might be defined as the clear expression of mixed feelings. The poetic mood is never indicative" (116). These comments, in turn, gloss the closing lines of Part II of "New Year Letter," where Auden writes that the Devil "may never tell us lies, / Just half-truths we can synthesise." The Devil is the agency by which Poetry as Magic becomes, *felix culpa*, Poetry as Game of Knowledge: "So, hidden in his hocus-pocus, / There lies the gift of double focus . . ." (*CP* 220).

10. *FA* 336; the passage is quoted in Sinfield, *Cultural* 63.

11. To Yeats's earlier declaration that "the intellect of man is forced to choose, / Perfection of the life, or of the work," Auden dismissively responded, "This is untrue; perfection is possible in neither" ("Writing," *DH* 19).

12. Esther Newton touches briefly on Auden and Kallman's visits to Fire Island in *Cherry Grove, Fire Island* (46–48); see also Farnan 116–17.

13. For an extended discussion of these issues, see Jacobs 81–85. In his *Modern Canterbury Pilgrims* essay, Auden comments: "A planetary visitor might read through the whole of [Kierkegaard's] voluminous works without discovering that human beings are not ghosts but have bodies of flesh and blood" (Pike 42).

14. The text used here, from *Selected Poems* (1979), is based on that of *Nones* (1951). Auden's revised text for the *Collected Shorter Poems* (1966), used also in the posthumous *Collected Poems* (1976; 1991), includes other changes in accidentals, as well as a crucial change in lines 11–12 (see note 18, below).

15. Among recent commentators, Hecht, Jacobs, and Fuller address this issue most directly. Hecht offers three possibilities: "homosexuals, who are often thought compulsively promiscuous, as Auden noted"; "tourists, northerners, come south to bask in this temperate, gentle climate"; and "all mortals, exiled since Adam's Fall from the ideal Eden" (306–7). Jacobs grants these possibilities but argues that "inconstancy in this poem is primarily a matter of

spiritual temperament," as opposed to sexual behavior (145n). Fuller adds several other ways to read "the inconstant ones" in light of the imagery of the poem: artists, the English, valley-dwellers (406). For a reading that emphasizes the homoerotic aspects of the poem, see Longley's commentary in Auden, *In Solitude* 254–59.

16. On Auden's fusion of northern and southern landscapes, see Mendelson, *Later* 293n, and commentary by Lipking in Auden, *In Solitude* 265.

17. See Hecht 305. See also Auden's comments on homosexual promiscuity and its causes in his 1969 review of J. R. Ackerley's *My Father and Myself* (*FA* 451–52).

18. Auden's revision of these lines for later collections tone down their homoeroticism: "the flirtatious male who lounges / Against a rock in the sunlight" (*CP* 540).

19. See Aldrich 69–100 on English writers in this vein; on von Gloeden, see 140–52.

20. "Phantasy and Reality in Poetry" (*In Solitude* 193). This passage is quoted in Fuller (406). See also "Good-Bye to the Mezzogiorno" (*CP* 642–45), which Auden wrote in 1958, after he and Kallman had moved north to Kirchstetten for their summers.

21. On paganism, Christianity, and the moral meanings of frivolity, see also "Postscript: The Frivolous & The Earnest" (*DH* 429–32); Johnson brings Auden's comments usefully to bear on questions of perspectivism in "In Praise of Limestone" (64).

22. As Lipking observes (Auden, *In Solitude* 263), Auden made a Freudian slip in reading "In Praise of Limestone" for the Caedmon recording (TC 1019): "when I try to imagine a faith—a faultless—love. . . ." In his 1944 review of *Either/Or*, Auden quotes Kierkegaard on the difference between the faithlessness of Don Juan and the moral quality of "Greek Love," which assumed a multiplicity of erotic attachments. In Kierkegaard's words:

> When one considers Greek love, it is, according to its own ideas, essentially faithful. . . . It is accidental in the certain individual that he loves many, and with regard to the many he loves, it is again accidental every time he loves a new one.
>
> ("Preface" 684)

Auden's quotation of this passage suggests that existentialism provided a way to articulate, in terms amenable to Christian theology, a pagan sense of the holiness of erotic life: rather than being redeemed by its continuity with agape, Eros in Greek Love is divine in its own right.

AFTERWORD: AUDEN'S BIASES—AND OURS

1. Christopher Lane 224; Lane's "Afterword" deals at length and quite persuasively with many of the issues raised here.

2. Like his essay on Shakespeare, Auden's poems about and addressed to Byron, Rimbaud, Housman, and Lear might be read as exercises in queer self-reflection; so might his various reviews of books by or on Wilde and Ackerley. Regarding Auden's sonnets on Rimbaud, Housman, and Lear, see chapter 3, which also discusses "Letter to Lord Byron." For his essays on Wilde, see "An Improbable Life" (*FA* 302–24) and "Playboy."

3. Behind this view of the self, for Auden, are Freud and (in later years) the I-Thou terminology of Buber. Together, they helped him to argue the dialogic nature of self-disclosure:

> There are other social animals who have signal codes, e.g., bees have signals for informing each other about the whereabouts and distance of flowers, but only man has a language by means of which he can disclose himself to his neighbor, which he could not do and could not want to do if he did not first possess the capacity and the need to disclose himself to himself. The communication of mere objective fact only requires monologue and for monologue a language is not necessary, only a code. But subjective communication demands dialogue and dialogue demands a real language.
>
> ("Balaam and His Ass," *DH* 109)

This passage is quoted in Boly, *Reading* (3–5), which offers a penetrating analysis of Auden's theories of language and communication in poetry.

4. A passage from "Writing" suggests Auden's sense of the productive promiscuity of language:

> *My language is the universal whore whom I have to make into a virgin.* (Karl Kraus.) It is both the glory and the shame of poetry that its medium is not its private property, that a poet cannot invent his words and that words are products, not of nature, but of a human society which uses them for a thousand different purposes.
>
> (*DH* 23)

5. According to Booth's commentary in his edition of Shakespeare's sonnets, "master" and "mistress" were both names for the target ball in bowling, reached only by casting balls that rolled on a bias (see Shakespeare 163).

WORKS CITED

Abrams, M. H. "Structure and Style in the Greater Romantic Lyric." *From Sensibility to Romanticism*. Ed. Gordon Haight and Harold Bloom. New Haven: Yale UP, 1965. 527–60.

Aldrich, Robert. *The Seduction of the Mediterranean: Writing, Art, and Homosexual Fantasy*. London: Routledge, 1993.

Annan, Noel. *Our Age: English Intellectuals Between the World Wars—A Group Portrait*. New York: Random House, 1991.

Ansen, Alan. *The Table Talk of W. H. Auden*. Ed. Nicholas Jenkins. London: Faber, 1990.

Ashbery, John. *Some Trees*. Yale Series of Younger Poets. New Haven: Yale UP, 1956.

Auden, W. H. *Collected Poems*. Ed. Edward Mendelson. New York: Random House, 1976, 1991.

—— Ms. Journal. 1929. Henry W. and Albert A. Berg Collection of English and American Literature, The New York Public Library, Astor, Lenox, and Tilden Foundations.

—— *The Collected Poetry of W. H. Auden*. New York: Random House, 1945.

—— *The Double Man*. New York: Random House, 1941.

—— *The Dyer's Hand*. New York: Vintage, 1990.

—— *The English Auden: Poems, Essays and Dramatic Writings, 1927–1939*. Ed. Edward Mendelson. London: Faber, 1977.

—— "Eros and Agape." Rev. of *Love in the Western World*, by Denis de Rougemont. *Nation* 28 June 1941: 756–58.

—— "Firbank Revisited." Rev. of *Five Novels of Ronald Firbank*. *New York Times* 20 November 1949, sec. 7: 5.

—— *Juvenilia: Poems, 1922–1928*. Ed. Katherine Bucknell. Princeton: Princeton UP, 1994.

Auden, W. H. *"In Solitude, for Company": W. H. Auden After 1940*. Auden Studies 3. Ed. Katherine Bucknell and Nicholas Jenkins. Oxford: Clarendon, 1995.

—— *"The Language of Learning and the Language of Love": Uncollected Writings; New Interpretations*. Auden Studies 2. Ed. Katherine Bucknell and Nicholas Jenkins. Oxford: Clarendon, 1994.

—— *"The Map of All My Youth": Early Works, Friends, and Influences*. Auden Studies 1. Ed. Katherine Bucknell and Nicholas Jenkins. Oxford: Clarendon, 1990.

—— *The Orators: An English Study*. 3d ed. New York: Random House, 1967.

—— "A Playboy of the Western World: St. Oscar, The Homintern Martyr." Rev. of *The Paradox of Oscar Wilde*, by George Woodcock. *Partisan Review* 17 (1950): 390–94.

—— *Poems*. 1928. A Facsimile of the Copy in the George Elliston Poetry Collection of Twentieth-Century Poetry. Cincinnati: Elliston Poetry Foundation, U of Cincinnati, 1964.

—— "A Preface to Kierkegaard." Rev. of *Either/Or*, by Soren Kierkegaard. *New Republic* 15 May 1944: 683–84, 686.

—— *Prose and Travel Books in Prose and Verse, 1926–1938*. Princeton: Princeton UP, 1996. *The Complete Works of W. H. Auden*. Ed. Edward Mendelson. 3 vols. to date. 1988– .

—— "The Rewards of Patience." Rev. of *Poems and New Poems*, by Louise Bogan. *Partisan Review* 9 (1942): 336–40.

—— *Secondary Worlds*. The T. S. Eliot Memorial Lectures Delivered at Eliot College in the University of Kent at Canterbury, October 1967. London: Faber, 1968.

—— *Selected Poems*. Ed. Edward Mendelson. New York: Vintage, 1979.

—— "Squares and Oblongs." *Poets at Work*. Ed. Charles D. Abbott. New York: Harcourt, 1948. 163–81.

Auden, W. H. and Christopher Isherwood. *Plays and Other Dramatic Writings, 1928–1938*. Princeton: Princeton UP, 1988. *The Complete Works of W. H. Auden*. Ed. Edward Mendelson. 3 vols. to date. 1988– .

Babuscio, Jack. "Camp and the Gay Sensibility." *Gays and Film*. Ed. Richard Dyer. New York: Zoetrope, 1984. 40–57.

Banville, John. *The Untouchable*. New York: Knopf, 1997.

Beach, Joseph Warren. *The Making of the Auden Canon*. Minneapolis: U of Minnesota P, 1957.

Beaver, Harold. "Homosexual Signs: In Memory of Roland Barthes." *Critical Inquiry* 8 (1981): 99–119.

Bennett, Paula. "The Pea That Duty Locks: Lesbian and Feminist-Heterosexual Readings of Emily Dickinson's Poetry." *Lesbian Texts and Contexts: Radical Revisions*. Ed. Karla Jay and Joanne Glasgow. New York: New York UP, 1990. 104–25.

Bersani, Leo. *Homos.* Cambridge MA: Harvard UP, 1995.

— "Is the Rectum a Grave?" *AIDS: Cultural Analysis, Cultural Activism.* Ed. Douglas Crimp. Cambridge MA: MIT P, 1988. 197—222.

Blair, John G. *The Poetic Art of W. H. Auden.* Princeton: Princeton UP, 1965.

Bloomfield, B. C. *W. H. Auden, A Bibliography: The Early Years Through 1955.* Charlottesville: UP of Virginia, 1964.

— "W. H. Auden's First Book." *Library* 5th ser. 22 (1967): 152–54.

Boly, John R. *Reading Auden: The Returns of Caliban.* Ithaca: Cornell UP, 1991.

— "W. H. Auden's *The Orators:* Portraits of the Artist in the Thirties." *Twentieth-Century Literature* 27 (1981): 247–61.

Britten, Benjamin. *Letters from a Life: The Selected Letters and Diaries of Benjamin Britten, 1913–1976.* Ed. Donald Mitchell and Philip Reed. 2 vols. to date. Berkeley: U of California P, 1991– .

Bryant, Marsha. *Auden and Documentary in the 1930s.* Charlottesville: UP of Virginia, 1997.

Buber, Martin. *I and Thou.* Trans. Ronald Gregor Smith. 2d ed. New York: Scribner, 1958.

Buell, Frederick. *W. H. Auden as a Social Poet.* Ithaca: Cornell UP, 1973.

Lord Byron. *The Complete Poetical Works.* Ed. Jerome J. McGann. 7 vols. Oxford: Clarendon, 1980–93.

— *Selected Poetry and Prose of Byron.* Ed. W. H. Auden. New York: Signet, 1966.

Callan, Edward. *Auden: A Carnival of Intellect.* New York: Oxford UP, 1983.

Campbell, Roy. *Flowering Rifle: A Poem from the Battlefield of Spain.* London: Longmans, 1939.

Carpenter, Humphrey. *W. H. Auden: A Biography.* Boston: Houghton, 1981.

— *Benjamin Britten: A Biography.* New York: Scribner, 1992.

Caserio, Robert. "Auden's New Citizenship." *Raritan* 17 (1997): 90–103.

Cecil, Robert. *A Divided Life: A Personal Portrait of the Spy Donald Maclean.* New York: Morrow, 1988.

Chamberlin, J. Edward and Sander L. Gilman, ed. *Degeneration: The Dark Side of Progress.* New York: Columbia UP, 1985.

Clark, Thekla. *Wystan and Chester: A Personal Memoir of W. H. Auden and Chester Kallman.* Intro. James Fenton. New York: Columbia UP, 1997.

Collecott, Diana. "What is not said: a study in textual inversion." *Sexual Sameness: Textual Differences in Lesbian and Gay Writing.* Ed. Joseph Bristow. London: Routledge, 1992. 91–110.

Connolly, Cyril. *Enemies of Promise and Other Essays: An Autobiography of Ideas.* New York: Anchor, 1960.

Craft, Christopher. "Alias Bunbury: Desire and Termination in *The Importance of Being Earnest.*" *Representations* 31 (1990): 19–46.

Craft, Robert. *Stravinsky: Chronicle of a Friendship, 1948–1971.* New York: Knopf, 1972.

Crompton, Louis. *Byron and Greek Love: Homophobia in Nineteenth-Century England.* Berkeley: U of California P, 1985.

Cunningham, Valentine. *British Writers of the Thirties.* Oxford: Clarendon, 1988.

David, Hugh. *On Queer Street: A Social History of British Homosexuality 1895–1995.* London: Harper, 1997.

de Lauretis, Teresa. "Queer Theory: Lesbian and Gay Sexualities." *differences* 3 (1991): iii–xviii.

De Mott, Benjamin. *Supergrow: Essays and Reports on Imagination in America.* New York: Dutton, 1969.

Dollimore, Jonathan. *Sexual Dissidence: Augustine to Wilde, Freud to Foucault.* Oxford: Clarendon, 1991.

Dowling, Linda. "Ruskin's Pied Beauty and the Constitution of a 'Homosexual' Code." *Victorian Newsletter* 75 (1989): 1–8.

Ellmann, Richard. *Yeats: The Man and the Masks.* New York: Morrow, 1948.

Farnan, Dorothy J. *Auden In Love.* New York: Simon, 1984.

Fenton, James. "Auden's Enchantment." *The New York Review of Books* 13 April 2000: 62–66.

—— "Auden's Shakespeare." *The New York Review of Books* 23 Mar. 2000: 24–28.

Firchow, Peter. "Private Faces in Public Places: Auden's *The Orators.*" *PMLA* 92 (1977): 253–72.

Foucault, Michel. *The History of Sexuality.* Trans. Robert Hurley. 3 vols. New York: Vintage, 1990.

Four Weddings and a Funeral. Dir. Mike Newell. Perf. Hugh Grant, Andie MacDowell, Kristin Scott Thomas. PolyGram and Channel Four. 1993.

Freccero, John. "The Fig Tree and the Laurel: Petrarch's Poetics." *Literary Theory/Renaissance Texts.* Ed. Patricia Parker and David Quint. Baltimore: Johns Hopkins UP, 1986. 20–32.

Freud, Sigmund. *Standard Edition of the Complete Psychological Works of Sigmund Freud.* Trans. James Strachey. 24 vols. London: Hogarth, 1957.

Fuller, John. *W. H. Auden: A Commentary.* Princeton: Princeton UP, 1998.

Gardiner, Margaret. "Auden: A Memoir." *New Review* 3.28 (1976): 9–19.

Gide, André. *If It Die. . . .* Trans. Dorothy Bussy. London: Secker, 1951.

Gilman, Sander L. *Disease and Representation: Images of Illness from Madness to AIDS.* Ithaca: Cornell UP, 1988.

Gooch, Brad. *City Poet: The Life and Times of Frank O'Hara.* New York: Knopf, 1993.

Gorky, Maxim. *On Literature.* Seattle: U of Washington P, 1973.

Greenberg, David F. *The Construction of Homosexuality.* Chicago: U of Chicago P, 1988.

Griffin, Howard. *Conversations with Auden*. San Francisco: Grey Fox, 1981.

Groddeck, Georg. *The Book of the It*. Trans. V.M.E. Collins. 1923. New York: International UP, 1976.

Haffenden, John, ed. *Auden: The Critical Heritage*. London: Routledge, 1983.

Heard, Gerald. *The Social Substance of Religion: An Essay on the Evolution of Religion*. New York: Harcourt, 1931.

Hecht, Anthony. *The Hidden Law: The Poetry of W. H. Auden*. Cambridge MA: Harvard UP, 1993.

Hocquenghem, Guy. *Homosexual Desire*. Trans. Daniella Dangoor. Durham NC: Duke UP, 1978.

Hollander, John. *Reflections on Espionage: The Question of Cupcake*. New York: Atheneum, 1976.

Housman, A. E. *A Shropshire Lad*. New York: Bodley Head, 1906.

Hynes, Samuel. *The Auden Generation: Literature and Politics in England in the 1930s*. Princeton: Princeton UP, 1976.

—— *A War Imagined: The First World War and English Culture*. New York: Atheneum, 1991.

Isherwood, Christopher. *Berlin Stories: The Last of Mr. Norris, Berlin Diary*. 1935, 1939. New York: New Directions, 1963.

—— *Christopher and His Kind: 1929–1939*. New York: Farrar, 1976.

—— *Lions and Shadows: An Education in the Twenties*. 1938. New York: New Directions, 1977.

—— "Some Notes on Auden's Early Verse." 1937. *Exhumations*. New York: Simon, 1966. 17–22.

Isherwood, Christopher and Edward Upward. *The Mortmere Stories*. London: Enitharmon, 1994.

Jacobs, Alan. *What Became of Wystan: Change and Continuity in Auden's Poetry*. Fayetteville: U of Arkansas P, 1998.

Jagose, Annamarie. *Queer Theory: An Introduction*. New York: New York UP, 1996.

James, Clive. "Auden's Achievement." *Commentary* 56.6 (1973): 53–58.

Jarrell, Randall. "Changes in Attitude and Rhetoric in Auden's Poetry." *The Third Book of Criticism*. New York: Noonday, 1971. 115–50.

—— "Freud to Paul: Stages in Auden's Ideology." *The Third Book of Criticism*. New York: Noonday, 1971. 153–87.

Jenkins, Nicholas. "Auden and Lenin?" *W. H. Auden Society Newsletter* 10–11 (1993): 13–14.

Johnson, Richard. *Man's Place: An Essay on Auden*. Ithaca: Cornell UP, 1973.

Kettle, Michael. *Salome's Last Veil: The Libel Case of the Century*. London: Granada, 1977.

Koestenbaum, Wayne. *Double Talk: The Erotics of Male Literary Collaboration*. London: Routledge, 1989.

Lane, Christopher. *The Burdens of Intimacy: Psychoanalysis & Victorian Masculinity.* Chicago: U of Chicago P, 1999.

Lane, Homer. *Talks to Parents and Teachers.* Intro. A. S. Neill. 1928. New York: Schocken, 1969.

Lanham, Richard. *The Motives of Eloquence: Literature and Rhetoric in the Renaissance.* New Haven: Yale UP, 1976.

Lawrence, D. H. *Fantasia of the Unconscious.* 1922. New York: Boni, 1930.

Layard, John. "Malekula: Flying Tricksters, Ghosts, Gods, and Epileptics." *Journal of the Royal Anthropological Institute of Great Britain and Ireland* 60 (1930): 501–24.

—— "Shamanism: An Analysis Based on Comparison with the Flying Tricksters of Malekula." *Journal of the Royal Anthropological Institute of Great Britain and Ireland* 60 (1930): 526–50.

Lehmann, John. *In My Own Time.* Boston: Little, 1969.

MacDiarmid, Hugh. *Three Hymns to Lenin.* Edinburgh: Castle Wynd, 1957.

Mackinnon, Lachlan. *Eliot, Auden, Lowell: Aspects of the Baudelairean Inheritance.* London: Macmillan, 1983.

McGann, Jerome J. *The Beauty of Inflections: Literary Investigations in Historical Method and Study.* Oxford: Clarendon, 1988.

—— "Byron and the Anonymous Lyric." *Byron Journal* 20 (1992): 27–45.

—— "Hero With a Thousand Faces: The Rhetoric of Byronism." *Studies in Romanticism* 31 (1992): 295–313.

Mendelson, Edward. *Early Auden.* New York: Vintage, 1981.

—— *Later Auden.* New York: Farrar, 1999.

Miller, D. A. *Bringing Out Roland Barthes.* Berkeley: U of California P, 1992.

Mitchell, Donald. *Britten and Auden in the Thirties: The Year 1936.* The T. S. Eliot Memorial Lectures delivered at the University of Kent at Canterbury in November 1979. Seattle: U of Washington P, 1981.

Mizejewski, Linda. *Divine Decadence: Fascism, Female Spectacle, and the Makings of Sally Bowles.* Princeton: Princeton UP, 1992.

Moon, Michael. *Disseminating Whitman.* Cambridge MA: Harvard UP, 1991.

Morris, John. "Sex, Subversion and Spying." *Times Higher Education Supplement* 3 February 1984: 15.

Morton, Donald, ed. *The Material Queer: A LesBiGay Cultural Studies Reader.* Boulder: Westview, 1996.

—— "The Politics of Queer Theory in the (Post)Modern Moment. *Genders* 17 (1993): 121–50.

Mosse, George L. *Nationalism and Sexuality: Respectability and Abnormal Sexuality in Modern Europe.* New York: Fertig, 1985.

Newton, Esther. *Cherry Grove, Fire Island: Sixty Years in America's First Gay and Lesbian Town.* Boston: Beacon, 1993.

Norse, Harold. *Memoirs of a Bastard Angel.* New York: Morrow, 1989.

Nunokawa, Jeff. " 'All the Sad Young Men': AIDS and the Work of Mourning." *Yale Journal of Criticism* 4 (1991): 1–12.

—— "*In Memoriam* and the Extinction of the Homosexual." *ELH* 58 (1991): 427–38.

O'Neill, Michael and Gareth Reeves. *Auden, MacNeice, Spender: The Thirties Poetry.* London: Macmillan, 1992.

Orwell, George. *Inside the Whale and Other Essays.* Harmondsworth: Penguin, 1962.

—— *The Road to Wigan Pier.* 1937. London: Secker, 1959.

Page, Norman. *Auden and Isherwood: The Berlin Years.* New York: St. Martin's, 1998.

Patrick, Julian. "Going Round versus Going Straight to Meaning: The Puzzles of Auden's 'Our Bias.' " *Lyric Poetry: Beyond New Criticism.* Ed. Chaviva Hošek and Patricia Parker. Ithaca: Cornell UP, 1985. 281–97.

Perloff, Marjorie. *The Poetics of Indeterminacy: Rimbaud to Cage.* Princeton: Princeton UP, 1981.

Pike, James A., ed. *Modern Canterbury Pilgrims and Why They Chose the Episcopal Church.* New York: Morehouse-Gorham, 1956.

Replogle, Justin. *Auden's Poetry.* Seattle: U of Washington P, 1969.

Rieff, Philip. *The Triumph of the Therapeutic: Uses of Faith After Freud.* New York: Harper, 1966.

Rimbaud, Arthur. *Complete Works, Selected Letters.* Trans. Wallace Fowlie. Chicago: U of Chicago P, 1966.

Roberts, Michael, ed. *New Country: Prose and Poetry by the Authors of "New Signatures".* London: Hogarth, 1933.

Rollings, Hyder Edward, ed. *A New Variorum Edition of Shakespeare: The Sonnets.* 2 vols. Philadelphia: Lippincott, 1944.

Roof, Judith. *A Lure of Knowledge: Lesbian Sexuality and Theory.* Between Men—Between Women. New York: Columbia UP, 1991.

Rougemont, Denis de. *Love in the Western World.* Trans. Montgomery Belgion. New York: Doubleday, 1957.

Sedgwick, Eve Kosofsky. *Epistemology of the Closet.* Berkeley: U of California P, 1990.

—— ed. *Novel Gazing: Queer Readings in Fiction.* Durham NC: Duke UP, 1997.

Shakespeare, William. *Shakespeare's Sonnets.* Ed. Stephen Booth. New Haven: Yale UP, 1977.

Shoptaw, John. *On the Outside Looking In: John Ashbery's Poetry.* Cambridge MA: Harvard UP, 1994.

Sinfield, Alan. *Cultural Politics—Queer Reading.* New Cultural Studies. Philadelphia: U of Pennsylvania P, 1994.

—— *Literature, Politics, and Culture in Postwar Britain.* Berkeley: U of California P, 1989.

Sinfield, Alan. *The Wilde Century*. Between Men—Between Women. New York: Columbia UP, 1994.

Smith, Bruce R. *Homosexual Desire in Shakespeare's England: A Cultural Poetics*. Chicago: U of Chicago P, 1991.

Smith, Martha Nell. *Rowing in Eden: Rereading Emily Dickinson*. Austin: U of Texas P, 1992.

Smith, Stan. *Inviolable Voice: History and Twentieth-Century Poetry*. Dublin: Gill and MacMillan, 1982.

—— "Loyalty and Interest: Auden, Modernism, and the Politics of Pedagogy." *Textual Practice* 4 (1990): 54–72.

—— *W. H. Auden*. Rereading Literature. Oxford: Blackwell, 1985.

Sontag, Susan. *Against Interpretation*. New York: Farrar, 1966.

Southworth, James. *Sowing the Spring: Studies in British Poets from Hopkins to MacNeice*. Oxford: Blackwell, 1940.

Spears, Monroe K. *The Poetry of W. H. Auden: The Disenchanted Island*. New York: Oxford UP, 1963.

Spender, Stephen. *The Temple*. London: Faber, 1988.

—— ed. *W. H. Auden: A Tribute*. London: Weidenfeld, 1975.

—— *World Within World*. New York: Harcourt, 1951.

Spiegelman, Willard. *The Didactic Muse: Scenes of Instruction in Contemporary American Poetry*. Princeton: Princeton UP, 1989.

Stallybrass, Peter. "Editing as Cultural Formation: The Sexing of Shakespeare's Sonnets." *Modern Language Quarterly* 54 (1993): 91–103.

Stambolian, George and Elaine Marks, ed. *Homosexualities and French Literature*. Ithaca: Cornell UP, 1979.

Stimpson, Catherine. "Mind, Body, and Gertrude Stein." *Critical Inquiry* 3 (1977): 489–506.

—— "The Somagrams of Gertrude Stein." *Poetics Today* 6 (1985): 67–80.

Stockinger, Jacob. "Homotextuality: A Proposal." *The Gay Academic*. Ed. Louie Crew. Palm Springs: ETC, 1978. 135–51.

Sulloway, F. J. *Freud: Biologist of the Mind*. London: Deutsch, 1979.

Szladits, Lola L. "Foreword." *W. H. Auden 1907–1973*. Ed. Edward Mendelson. New York: New York Public Library, 1976. N. pag.

Tennyson, Alfred. *Tennyson's Poetry*. Ed. Robert W. Hill, Jr. New York: Norton, 1971.

Tiddy, R.J.G. *The Mummers' Play*. Oxford: Clarendon, 1923.

Tillich, Paul. *The Interpretation of History*. Trans. N. A. Rasetzki and Elsa L. Talmey. New York: Scribner, 1936.

Tolley, A. T. *The Poetry of the Thirties*. London: Gollancz, 1975.

—— "The Printing of Auden's *Poems* (1928) and Spender's *Nine Experiments*." *Library* 5th ser. 22 (1967): 149–50.

Upward, Edward. *The Railway Accident and Other Stories*. Harmondsworth: Penguin, 1972.

Wasley, Aidan. "Auden and Poetic Inheritance." *Raritan* 19 (1999): 128–57.

Weeks, Jeffrey. *Sex, Politics and Society: The Regulation of Sexuality Since 1800*. 2d ed. London: Longman, 1981.

Wilde, Oscar. *The Artist as Critic*. Ed. Richard Ellmann. Chicago: U of Chicago P, 1969.

Woods, Gregory. *Articulate Flesh: Male Homo-Eroticism and Modern Poetry*. New Haven: Yale UP, 1987.

Yingling, Thomas E. *Hart Crane and the Homosexual Text: New Thresholds, New Anatomies*. Chicago: U of Chicago P, 1990.

INDEX OF AUDEN'S POEM TITLES
AND FIRST LINES

Poem titles are enclosed in quotes. Long poem titles are *italicized*. Three poems, "Control of the passes," "Letter to Lord Byron," and *The Orators,* are analyzed separately in the index of subjects. Auden's prose works and works by other authors are also located in the index of subjects.

INDEX OF SUBJECTS

This index contains an analysis of subjects, Auden's prose works, and works by other authors. Auden's poetry is located in the index of poem titles and first lines.

COPYRIGHT ACKNOWLEDGMENTS

BETWEEN MEN ~ BETWEEN WOMEN

LESBIAN AND GAY STUDIES

LILLIAN FADERMAN AND LARRY GROSS, EDITORS

Richard D. Mohr, *Gays/Justice: A Study of Ethics, Society, and Law*

Gary David Comstock, *Violence Against Lesbians and Gay Men*

Kath Weston, *Families We Choose: Lesbians, Gays, Kinship*

Lillian Faderman, *Odd Girls and Twilight Lovers: A History of Lesbian Life in
Twentieth-Century America*

Judith Roof, *A Lure of Knowledge: Lesbian Sexuality and Theory*

John Clum, *Acting Gay: Male Homosexuality in Modern Drama*

Allen Ellenzweig, *The Homoerotic Photograph: Male Images from
Durieu/Delacroix to Mapplethorpe*

Sally Munt, editor, *New Lesbian Criticism: Literary and Cultural Readings*

Timothy F. Murphy and Suzanne Poirier, editors, *Writing AIDS: Gay
Literature, Language, and Analysis*

Linda D. Garnets and Douglas C. Kimmel, editors, *Psychological Perspectives on
Lesbian and Gay Male Experiences*

Laura Doan, editor, *The Lesbian Postmodern*

Noreen O'Connor and Joanna Ryan, *Wild Desires and Mistaken Identities:
Lesbianism and Psychoanalysis*

Alan Sinfield, *The Wilde Century: Effeminacy, Oscar Wilde, and the Queer
Moment*

Claudia Card, *Lesbian Choices*

Carter Wilson, *Hidden in the Blood: A Personal Investigation of AIDS in the
Yucatán*

Alan Bray, *Homosexuality in Renaissance England*

Joseph Carrier, *De Los Otros: Intimacy and Homosexuality Among Mexican Men*

Joseph Bristow, *Effeminate England: Homoerotic Writing After 1885*

Corinne E. Blackmer and Patricia Juliana Smith, editors, *En Travesti: Women,
Gender Subversion, Opera*

Don Paulson with Roger Simpson, *An Evening at The Garden of Allah: A Gay
Cabaret in Seattle*

Claudia Schoppmann, *Days of Masquerade: Life Stories of Lesbians During the
Third Reich*

Chris Straayer, *Deviant Eyes, Deviant Bodies: Sexual Re-Orientation in Film and
Video*

Edward Alwood, *Straight News: Gays, Lesbians, and the News Media*

Thomas Waugh, *Hard to Imagine: Gay Male Eroticism in Photography and Film
from Their Beginnings to Stonewall*

Judith Roof, *Come As You Are: Sexuality and Narrative*

Terry Castle, *Noel Coward and Radclyffe Hall: Kindred Spirits*

Kath Weston, *Render Me, Gender Me: Lesbians Talk Sex, Class, Color, Nation, Studmuffins . . .*

Ruth Vanita, *Sappho and the Virgin Mary: Same-Sex Love and the English Literary Imagination*

renée c. hoogland, *Lesbian Configurations*

Beverly Burch, *Other Women: Lesbian Experience and Psychoanalytic Theory of Women*

Jane McIntosh Snyder, *Lesbian Desire in the Lyrics of Sappho*

Rebecca Alpert, *Like Bread on the Seder Plate: Jewish Lesbians and the Transformation of Tradition*

Emma Donoghue, editor, *Poems Between Women: Four Centuries of Love, Romantic Friendship, and Desire*

James T. Sears and Walter L. Williams, editors, *Overcoming Heterosexism and Homophobia: Strategies That Work*

Patricia Juliana Smith, *Lesbian Panic: Homoeroticism in Modern British Women's Fiction*

Dwayne C. Turner, *Risky Sex: Gay Men and HIV Prevention*

Timothy F. Murphy, *Gay Science: The Ethics of Sexual Orientation Research*

Cameron McFarlane, *The Sodomite in Fiction and Satire, 1660–1750*

Lynda Hart, *Between the Body and the Flesh: Performing Sadomasochism*

Byrne R. S. Fone, editor, *The Columbia Anthology of Gay Literature: Readings from Western Antiquity to the Present Day*

Ellen Lewin, *Recognizing Ourselves: Ceremonies of Lesbian and Gay Commitment*

Ruthann Robson, *Sappho Goes to Law School: Fragments in Lesbian Legal Theory*

Jacquelyn Zita, *Body Talk: Philosophical Reflections on Sex and Gender*

Evelyn Blackwood and Saskia Wieringa, *Female Desires: Same-Sex Relations and Transgender Practices Across Cultures*

William L. Leap, ed., *Public Sex/Gay Space*

Larry Gross and James D. Woods, eds., *The Columbia Reader on Lesbians and Gay Men in Media, Society, and Politics*

Marilee Lindemann, *Willa Cather: Queering America*

George E. Haggerty, *Men in Love: Masculinity and Sexuality in the Eighteenth Century*

Andrew Elfenbein, *Romantic Genius: The Prehistory of a Homosexual Role*

Gilbert Herdt and Bruce Koff, *Something to Tell You: The Road Families Travel When a Child Is Gay*

Richard Canning, *Gay Fiction Speaks: Conversations with Gay Novelists*

Laura Doan, *Fashioning Sapphism: The Origins of a Modern English Lesbian Culture*